Sarah Orne Jewett

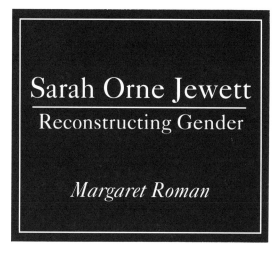

Sarah Orne Jewett
Reconstructing Gender

Margaret Roman

The University of Alabama Press
Tuscaloosa and London

∞

The paper on which this book is printed meets the minimum requirements of
American National Standard for Information Science-Permanence of Paper for
Printed Library Materials, ANSI Z39.48-1984.

Library of Congress Cataloging-in-Publication Data

Roman, Margaret, 1949–
    Sarah Orne Jewett : reconstructing gender / Margaret Roman.
       p.   cm.
    Includes bibliographical references and index.
    ISBN 0-8173-0533-5
    1. Jewett, Sarah Orne,   1849–1909—Criticism and interpretation.
2. Sex role in literature.   3. Women in literature.   I. Title.
PS2133.R6   1992
813'.4—dc20   90-20598
                                                      CIP

British Library Cataloguing-in-Publication Data available

To my mother,
Margaret Blisko Roman,
who has always spoken to me
from her heart,
and in memory of
my father,
Steven Roman,
who loved words and taught me
how to sing them

Contents

CONTENTS

Preface

In her fiction, Sarah Orne Jewett consciously collapses gender dichotomies. She, in effect, dissolves the binary oppositions of gender, of the polarities termed woman and man. Sometimes the discontent with this polarity is a peripheral fragment that exists as a quiet backdrop to a Jewett story, barely noticeable; often it erupts as the central issue. In all cases, there is a movement within the text to break from rigid gendered thinking.

While Jewett preferred rural values to those of the industrial system, there is more at issue here than her nostalgia for a country way of life that was fast disappearing. I see this condemnation of the industrial rise in Jewett as a cry against the separate spheres for women and men emphasized during her Victorian time period. Carroll Smith-Rosenberg defines "The True Woman and the Common Man" as

> twin mythic constructs of the emerging male middle class, [which] assured that their newly constructed social and economic arrangements were in fact timeless, rooted in the biology of man's competitive and woman's nurturant natures. They simultaneously rationalized and symbolized the fragmentation of old unities: the radical separation of home and work, of private and public, of producer and capitalist. They embodied identifiable norms of legitimate bourgeois behavior. ("Writing History," 40)

In truth, Jewett's fiction seems to have common underpinnings with Marxism. Her condemnation of her characters' acquisitiveness is often linked with the rise of industrialism. Jewett's "The Gray Mills of Farley," in fact, reads like a socialist tract. And it would be quite feasible for Jewett to have linked rigid gender roles with capitalism. Early on, Frederich Engels delineated the relationship between the two. Capitalism shifted the importance of use value to surplus value. With the accumulation of wealth as the determining factor, man's position became increasingly more important than woman's. Man took command of the home, and woman was reduced to the position of servitude (50). Engels maintained:

> The first class opposition that appears in history coincides with the development of the antagonism between man and woman in monogamous marriage, and the first class oppression coincides with that of the female sex by the male. . . . the husband is obliged to earn a living and support his family, and that in itself gives him a position of supremacy. . . . Within the family he is the bourgeois and the wife represents the proletariat. (58, 65–66)

Gender dichotomies were concretized into man as superior and woman as inferior. The so-called male and female dimensions became the stereotypical associations with which we are still struggling today. These prescriptions suggest that man is culture and woman is nature. Man is active, goal-oriented, competitive, rational, uncontrolled, and powerful. Woman is passive, relational, cooperative, emotional, controlled by men, and powerless.

Jewett endeavors to rewrite that script. Her characters, both women and men, often deflate these dichotomies, and where they cannot, Jewett shows them as malformed beings who disintegrate in the concretized roles they have assumed. There is a choice. Simone de Beauvoir's axiom comes to mind when one thinks of the quests of Jewett's protagonists: "One is not born, but rather becomes, a woman" (301). Judith Butler describes de Beauvoir's view of gender as "an incessant project, a daily act of reconstruction and interpretation. . . . Oppression is not a self-contained system that either confronts individuals as a theoretical object or generates them as cultural pawns. It is a dialectical force that requires individual participation on a large scale in order to maintain its malignant life" (131–32). Jewett empowers many of her characters to make responsible choices for gender construction.

Jewett creates a woman's imaginative universe. She turns the tables and subverts the male-dominated form. A female mode bursts in upon the male fixed social structure, which is decaying rapidly. What women have thought, felt, and experienced about themselves, as well as the patriarchal system, regulates the Jewett text. The dominant group no longer controls society's maxims or the structure of the fictional narrative. Whether men or women, if they subscribe to patriarchal norms, they become the inept, the distorted, the maimed. In the process of this reversal, gender differentiation as a social construct loses its power.

Nearly everything Jewett wrote embodies the pattern of breaking free from patriarchal society with its dual norms for men and for women in order that a person of any sex might grow freely. I have tried to show the pervasiveness of this theme by incorporating a discussion of Jewett's whole body of writing rather than restricting this study only to close readings of the texts that have received widespread attention from feminist critics—*Deephaven, A Country Doctor, The Country of the Pointed Firs*, and "A White Heron." It is also not within the scope of this text to discuss Jewett's strong women at length, which has been done and done well; these women are discussed only in terms of rigid gender roles. Except for some minor stories, I have included mention of most of the stories in the nineteen volumes Jewett published during her lifetime, as well as a dozen from *The Un-collected Stories* edited by Richard Cary.

Incorporated in this study are pieces never discussed at length before, from a feminist perspective or otherwise, including the essay "The Confession of a House-Breaker," the short stories "Jim's Little Woman" and "Mr. Bruce," and Jewett's volumes of stories for children. From a feminist perspective, except for Dr. Leslie of *A Country Doctor*, almost no attention has been paid to Jewett's men or to her married couples. While mention has been made of the false value system of Miss Chauncey and Miss Brandon of *Deephaven*, a thorough discussion of all of Jewett's elderly aristocratic women is intrinsic to the present study. The concept of the fairy godmother is a new one, and an evaluation of Jewett's attitude toward romance in her works is also an unexplored line of thought. It is also necessary to further analyze what it is about the nature of Jewett's women that endows them with such strength of character. While the feminist focus has been on the characters' nurturing powers, powers that sustain relational living, it represents only one side of the image. The vibrant, life-supporting women in Jewett have also developed their so-called male dimensions. They are aggressive, goal-oriented individuals. They are leaders, forthright in their opinions, who stimulate people to make constructive changes.

This book begins with a discussion of Jewett's natural setting. Jewett preferred the country, the natural domain, for her characters since this environment exhibited the fewest forms of control. Here is the absence of formal institutions with their rules and regulations. The gender roles assigned by society are a destructive force that can obliterate the person who is not a strong individual.

The next section centers on those characters who temporarily escape from society and its demands for rigid gender behavior. Jewett allows her characters time to germinate. "Childhood Escapades" contains Jewett's plea for "organic" growth for children. "Adolescent Retreat" is Jewett's description of the troubled limbo of young women trying to choose a non-conforming pattern. Finally, in "Fairy Godmothers," Jewett displays her own escapist fantasy in wishing powerful women could swoop down to help and nurture other women in turmoil.

Yet some people are incapable of perceiving the need to escape. In part two, characters are portrayed as subsumed into the sexually divisive society. While feminist criticism tends to focus more on the vigorous, emotionally ripe women in Jewett, of whom there is a delightful overabundance, it is equally important to note how often Jewett appears saddened by the sight of malformed human beings, products of the system. One colleague of mine asked me what Jewett did with her anger, how she could be so compassionate and reconciliatory all of the time. I think this section provides an answer to these questions. These products of the patriarchal system include the "Paralyzed men" as well as the "Aristocratic Women" and those other women who participate in "The Standard Marriage." All of these shadowy figures lead a dismal existence following the prescribed roles that thwart them. It is essential to include a separate chapter entitled "Romance," for Jewett was well aware of the many women who are unable to feel fulfilled unless they have aligned themselves with men. They damn themselves to a shell-like coexistence with men whom they have accepted, even lauded, as superior. Individual growth comes to a halt. In addressing the subject of romance, Jewett also attempts to warn the young women who have not yet made this deadening error.

In the third, and largest, part of this book,"Breaking Free," Jewett provides alternatives for a sick, sexually divided society. "Sexual Transformation" contains a discussion of Jewett's experiments with reversing the roles of her characters, but this stance is not viable, for it still manifests sexually exclusive behavior. Nevertheless, her core group of robust, nurturing

women in "Women Unrestrained" embodies both traditional
male and female characteristics. Her "Redeemed Men" are also
integrated, but to a lesser degree. Jewett's male figures are generally not as fully developed as characters; but then, Jewett
wrote best what she knew best—women's lives. Jewett also demonstrates that men and women can live together in a "Postponed
Marriage," where women's biological roles can be set aside and
the couple can relate on a level of greater equanimity and reciprocity, even to the point of a periodic interchange of gender
behavior or roles. The need for a rejoining of the male and
female dichotomy in humans is symbolically addressed in Jewett's story "A White Heron." Sylvia must be a part of the "vast"
world approached from her nurturing perspective. Finally, in
the last chapter, "Beyond Gender: *The Country of the Pointed
Firs*, Jewett examines the reverse situation. Unlike Sylvia, the
narrator of *Pointed Firs* has become too much like the vast world,
forgetting her nurturing center; so she must return to relearn
relational living. Yet the narrator cannot remain in Dunnet
Landing. Jewett's point is crystalline. Patriarchal society has the
power to obliterate the nurturing, female dimension, which it
does not value, but separation from this society can be equally
destructive to the human personality. The narrator must pursue
her goal of writer in the "awesome world," but now she will
bring news of the forgotten female dimension to a society sickly
divided, bent on egoistic destruction.

Sandra Gilbert has suggested that "though the pressures and
oppressions of gender may be as invisible as air, they are also as
inescapable as air, and, like the weight of air, they impercep-
tibly shape the forms and motions of our lives" (33). Jewett appears to have been acutely aware of the insidious effects of
gender expectations. In her fiction, she dispels the myths and
provides her characters the freedom to take wing.

Acknowledgments

Many have helped me to write this work. At Drew University, Arthur Jones introduced me to Sarah Orne Jewett in a seminar on American realism. I am most grateful to Merrill Skaggs, who guided my research and provided invaluable advice, criticism, and support. I am also indebted to the other two members of my dissertation committee, Janet Fishburn and Janet Burstein, for their time and assistance. Robert Ready, in a seminar on British Victorian prose writers, provided important information on and insight into the period, while Barry Qualls of Rutgers University introduced me to Ruskin's "Of Queens' Gardens" and raised some key questions about women writers during the Victorian era. At the College of Saint Elizabeth, the English Department offered me tremendous support. In particular, Laura Winters's perceptive comments and editorial skills were invaluable during the final stages of this book.

I would like to thank the Society for the Preservation of New England Antiquities for permission to reproduce the cover photograph. I would also like to thank Colby College Library for allowing me to consult and to quote from their Sarah Orne Jewett Collection. Letters from Jewett to Anna L. Dawes are found in the Manuscript Division of the Library of Congress. Especially, I would like to thank Houghton Library at Harvard

University for permission to consult their fine Jewett Collection and to quote from manuscripts as well as letters by Theophilus Parsons.

I am particularly grateful to The University of Alabama Press. The director, Malcolm M. MacDonald, lent me interest and encouragement for this project throughout the selection process. From Nicole Mitchell, acquisitions editor, I was given support and valuable criticism. Ellen Stein, assistant editor, shared her expertise with me, and Trinket Shaw, my copy editor, was most thorough and helpful.

My greatest source of sustenance was, in true Jewett fashion, the loving nurturance of friendship. At the Academy of Saint Aloysius in New Jersey, the faculty and students were unflaggingly encouraging and interested for the duration of the researching and writing of this book. I wish I could name all of them individually. Sister Marie Henry and Maria Malais assisted me in my research. Debbi Greh taught me word processing. At the College of Saint Elizabeth, I received a great deal of support for this project during its final stages from administration and faculty alike. Rosemary Marra from Central Duplicating was particularly helpful. My colleagues from Drew University, Marion Alcaro and Sondra Fishinger, offered me consistently good advice and support. A host of friends and family members sustained me with generous responses of interest, patience, and concern. In particular, I am grateful to my son, Keith Roman-Snellgrove, for the love he has brought to me. And to my husband, Paul Snellgrove, my special thanks—for his enthusiasm, insight, clarity, aid, and perspective.

Sarah Orne Jewett

Introduction

Jewett's "Housebreaker" versus Ruskin's "Queens": Liberation from the Victorian Home and Garden

Sarah Orne Jewett was a Victorian woman, subject to the socialization process of her time. Yet she repudiated the belief of her era that women could occupy only a narrow, separate sphere. In her life and work, Jewett rejected the Victorian concept of "the angel in the house," a term coined from Coventry Patmore's poem of the same title, which has come to mean a vaporous upholder of spiritual values and familial bliss within the confines of the home. John Ruskin enlarged upon this definition in his 1865 essay "Of Queens' Gardens," which Walter E. Houghton assessed as "the most important single document . . . for the characteristic idealization of love, woman, and home in Victorian thought" (343). Basically, woman's work to Ruskin entailed providing a haven of moral and spiritual values away from the money-hungry commercial world. In order to accomplish the task, woman had to be protected from any contact with that outside world so she could remain untainted. Her sphere was "a place apart, a walled garden, in which certain virtues too easily crushed by modern life could be preserved, and certain desires of the heart too much thwarted be fulfilled" (Houghton, 343).

Yet unrestricted by patriarchal fences, Jewett's women characters break out of the Victorian home and garden. True, Jewett regrets the passing of the Puritan grandmothers' gardens, which for her signified the passing of rural life. In "From a Mournful Villager," she thinks sorrowfully of the impending extinction of the front yards and the kind of New England village character and civilization with which they were connected (*CB*, 116). Yet Jewett's yearning reflects her fear of the imminent destruction of country life by industrial progress. It does not signify her belief that woman's position in society should remain unaltered. In fact, later in this same essay, Jewett clarifies her support of woman's advancement from the symbolic, attenuated garden into the wider world in exhilarating tones:

> The disappearance of many of the village front yards may come to be typical of the altered position of woman, and mark a stronghold on her way from the much talked-of slavery and subjection to a coveted equality. She used to be shut off from the wide acres of the farm, and had no voice in the world's politics; she must stay in the house, or only hold sway out of doors in this prim corner of the land where she was queen. No wonder that women clung to their rights in their flower-gardens then, and no wonder that they have grown a little careless of them now, and that lawn mowers find so ready a sale. The whole world is their front yard nowadays! (121)

It is no accident that Jewett made reference to queens in the preceding paragraph about gardens. She was familiar with John Ruskin's 1865 essay "Of Queens' Gardens" and quoted from it in her own "Miss Sydney's Flowers." Although the quote is a flowery passage typically depicting woman as administering angel, Jewett is applying the words to Miss Sydney, isolated by her own choice in a shell-like existence devoid of human warmth. It in no way implies that Jewett agreed with Ruskin's definition of woman's place. She has called that definition into question in "From a Mournful Villager," published after "Miss Sydney's Flowers," and she would subsequently refute it throughout her work. Jewett refused to present woman as elemental nature—a simple, virtually mindless embodiment of fecund Mother Earth, who existed to bear fruit for others to consume.

While Ruskin in his garden appears to glorify woman's place and power by disclaiming the idea that "woman . . . is not to guide, nor even to think for herself" (84), he succeeds in promoting the constriction of every facet of a woman's development. And he disguises this reduction by presenting his argument in an appealing flowery, lush language akin to the Victorian garden itself. Woman and the garden are one, and their job is the same—"order, comfort, and loveliness" (99). Ruskin uses this metaphor to advance the three major points of his essay: woman's particular sphere and her power therein, her education for this role, and her duty to the state. In each section, Ruskin equates woman with the natural world, which exists only to give service to man.

In part one of "Of Queens' Gardens," Ruskin states that woman's power is a "*guiding*, not a determining function" that consists primarily of "praise" (86). Although man is "*always* hardened" (87) by his experience in the world, he is "the doer, the creator, the discoverer, the defender" (86). Meanwhile, man protects woman in her confined status in "his" home from all danger (and experience). Ruskin declares, "This is the true nature of home—it is the place of Peace; the shelter, not only from all injury, but from all terror, doubt, and division" (87). Woman is " the rock in a weary land, and light as of the Pharos in the stormy sea. . . . And wherever a true wife comes, this home is always round her. The stars only may be over her head; the glow-worm in the night-cold grass may be the only fire at her foot: but home is yet wherever she is . . ." (87).

Next Ruskin outlines the type of education a girl should have in order to prepare for her duty. While advocating a serious, similar program of study, he makes it quite clear that the boy must learn his subjects thoroughly, but a girl needs to learn "only so far as may enable her to sympathise in her husband's pleasures, and those of his best friends" (92). In the process of procuring this education, Ruskin pictures the young woman as the proverbial flower, as well as the young, innocent animal. The girl has been "set loose in the library" like "a fawn in the field" (94). Ruskin may say: "She grows as a flower does,—she will wither without sun; she will decay in her sheath, as the narcissus does, if you do not give her air enough" (94); yet, the library has been purged of any injurious selections, and the only narcissistic activity that will be allowed the young woman is to provide a reflection of man to himself.

For his final point, Ruskin asseverates a broadening of woman's horizons from mere "housewife" to "queen," but the text is the same. It is delightful to see her "go out in the morning into her garden to play with the fringes of its guarded flowers, and lift their heads when they are drooping, with her happy smile upon her face, and no cloud upon her brow, because there is a little wall around her place of peace" (103), but she must do the same for all the needy, not just her family. Ruskin makes it clear that "there is not a war in the world, no, nor an injustice, but . . . women are answerable for it . . ." (101). Shifting his point of view, Ruskin appeals directly to woman's conscience:

> flowers only flourish rightly in the garden of some one who loves them. I know you would like that to be true. You would think it a pleasant magic if you could flush your flowers into brighter bloom by a kind look upon them: nay, more, if your look had the power, not only to cheer, but to guard them—if you could bid the black blight turn away, and the knotted caterpillar spare—if you could bid the dew fall upon them in the drought, and say to the south wind, in frost—"Come, thou south, and breathe upon my garden, that the spices may flow out." This you would think a great thing? And do you think it not a greater thing, that all this (and how much more than this!) you *can* do, for fairer flowers than these—flowers that could bless you for having blessed them, and will love you for having loved them. . . . (103–4)

Ultimately, Ruskin, spokesperson for Victorian society, has restricted woman under the pretense of a glorified profession. The world is reduced to an opulent garden of self-sacrifice and service. Woman's loveliness, like the evanescent loveliness of a flower, can embrace and support others' lives, but not her own. She is frozen in perfection, a part of the landscape—a landscape at the beck and call of men, to be used, conquered, and, consequently, destroyed.

Just as Ruskin's "Of Queens' Gardens" typifies ideas regarding the position of woman in the Victorian period, Sarah Orne Jewett's "Confession of a House-Breaker," published in 1884 in the volume *The Mate of the Daylight, and Friends Ashore*, decodes and shatters that myth. Looking below the level of the text, which appears to be a delightful account of awakening before dawn and leaving the house to witness daybreak, Jewett, consciously or subconsciously, presents a dramatized account of woman breaking out of the confines of the Victorian home and its garden. The result is a new awareness discovered with wild abandon on a natural landscape, which is equally unconventional as it pertains to woman, for it contains various levels of experience, and it defies Ruskin's definition of woman and nature, which limits existence to the transference of "order, comfort, and loveliness" (Ruskin, 99).

At the beginning of the essay, the Jewett narrator speaks of going to watch the sunrise in terms of committing a crime: "This confession differs from that of most criminals who are classed under the same head; for whereas house-breakers usually break into houses, I broke out" (*MD*, 234). It is a task she must complete quickly before she is caught and forced to remain: "I dressed myself hurriedly, and took my boots in my hand, and prepared to escape. It was no easy matter, for I belong to a household of light sleepers, who are quick to hear an untimely footfall. I stole carefully by the open doors and down the stairs, . . . and I hardly took a long breath until I found myself out in the garden" (235).

The description of the unfolding of the journey gives its purpose considerable weight. It will be a journey of momentous awareness. Unable to sleep, the narrator is drawn to "a tinge of light" (234) outside of her window. She becomes "possessed by a desire to go out-of-doors . . . and to see the world before the sun himself did" (234). Her movement takes on the significance of a religious experience, with birds singing matins and she herself "at best an unpunctual worshiper at this service" (234).

Since no metamorphosis is untroubled, shadows, bats, and ghosts also populate the scene. Although the narrator does not directly identify with the ghosts, an analogy is implied, for they, too, are "flitting, . . . trying to keep out of sight" (237). While the narrator may be associated at this point with the vaporous "angel in the house," her garden is atypical. Though it at first appears to be a standard Victorian garden—pretty and lush with its fragrant petunias, geraniums, and mignonette, its "odorus" honeysuckle, and its perfumed roses—the narrator leaves the presence of the waning moon, and the roses shun her. The narrator explains, "They appeared to be sound asleep yet, and turned their faces away after I had touched them" (236). Both the moon and the rose are common metaphors for woman loved or in love. No longer can the narrator associate with these symbols, which will serve ultimately to confine her as the caretaker of the home. Nor will the roses acknowledge her presence, for they represent women still unconscious, satisfied to exist as sweet-smelling ornaments.

Suddenly it is morning, not a prim, perfect day, but a realistic chronicling of uneasy change. Greeting the dawn is a peewee, a "sad-song" bird, who "began a prelude somewhat despairingly and without enthusiasm" (237). But his message is balanced by a joyful robin, who serves to encourage the narrator on her new path. She comments: "It must have been the dawn of a long-looked for day with him, at any rate, he was so glad to have it come at last" (238). Additional assistance comes in the unlikely form of a "sober-minded" toad. Again, the luxuriant, flowery nature usually aligned with woman has no place on this natural plain. More than one critic has commented that if Sylvia, protector of nature in "A White Heron," were given her choice between a toad and a prince, she would choose the toad. A similar situation exists in this piece as well, for the toad here commiserates with the position of the narrator in society: "He was a philosopher, that fellow; he sat and thought about it, and made his theories about me and about the uncertainty of temporal things. I dare say he comes out every morning, and looks up at the bench, and considers his ambitions and the adverse powers that thwart them, in common with many of his fellow-creatures" (238). Heeding this candid revelation, the narrator leaves the land of shadows behind, and all becomes clear as "the color of the world grew brighter and brighter." She perceives that "the outline of the trees, and of some distant fields even, became distinct; yet it was a strange, almost uncanny light,—it was more like looking through clear water,—and I still expected something out of the ordinary to happen" (239).

What subsequently transpires leaves the narrator with a mixed feeling of joy and anxiety. Amid a type of psychic experience, not uncommon in Jewett among people who care for one another, the narrator becomes conscious that one of her friends is also awake, "and an understanding between [them] sprang up quickly like a flame on the altar to Friendship, in [her] heart" (239).

She welcomes this human support; however, she is also aware that all of her other friends are sleeping. The fearful threat of again dissolving into an unconscious state continues. She maintains that it is not death that is the problem, but a false sleep induced by drugs or the bewildered state of some of the elderly, which is "like a long darkness and drowsiness, from which the enfeebled mind and body cannot rouse themselves until the brightest of all mornings dawns" (240). In other words, it is living a death-in-life, where decisions are made for you and where you are protected and cared for like a child—the defined state of the Victorian woman.

With this recognition, the light grows clearer, and "the veil was lifted again at daybreak" (240). Although the London pride is "most gorgeous to behold, with its brilliant red and its tall, straight stalks" (240), the narrator senses its "soldierly appearance, as if the flower were out early to keep guard" (240–41). Furthermore, the "grand chorus" is over, and the birds have "a crowd of duties" (241) to perform. Rather than yield her present freedom to return to duty now that the sun has fully risen and people will expect proper behavior, the narrator decides to leave the garden for a larger sphere:

> I had a desire to go out farther into the world, and I went some distance up the street, past my neighbors' house; feeling a sense of guilt and secrecy that could hardly be matched. It had been one thing to walk about my own garden. . . . But if any one had suddenly hailed me from a window I should have been inclined to run home as fast as my feet could carry me. In such fashion are we bound to the conventionalities of existences!
>
> But it seemed most wonderful to be awake while everybody slept, and to have the machinery of life apparently set in motion for my benefit alone. (241)

In her travels, the narrator also becomes "very intimate with a poppy" (242), an unlikely sensuous choice for a Victorian woman. Now she can identify with her own passionate nature; she is no longer a shadow or ethereal angel.

Yet she comes to acknowledge that this new awareness of her condition is hers alone: "It was piteous that no one should know that the night was over, and it was day again. It was like the flicker of the lamp at a shrine,—an undying flame that can lighten the darkness neither of death nor of life . . ." (242). All of the signs are negative: a little child is crying as if she'd been sick all night "and the morning brought no relief" (242); the peewee again begins "his plaintive morning song" (243); and finally, the cocks crow. The narrator realizes that "the spell of the dawn was lifted" (243) and she must return home. Although she leaps over the front fence instead of opening the front gate, she checks to make sure she hasn't startled any passersby. The house is dark and hot. After relocking the doors, she steals upstairs to "shut out the dazzling light of the sun" (243) and return to sleep.

At first glance, it appears as if nothing has changed. But upon arising, the narrator remains conscious and different. She has experienced the rejuvenating sleep she had previously described, "the real sleep" that brings "change and restoration and growth to the mind and soul" (240). Her awakening is removed from historical time. She characterizes it as the "daylight that was neither to-morrow's nor yesterday's" (243). In the last line of this sketch, the narrator explains that she is "as much delighted and puzzled with [her] morning ramble as if it had been a dream" (243), for a dream it is—a vision of a reality that Sarah Orne Jewett tenders throughout her canon. Out of the hot, dark house, freed even from the effulgent garden, Jewett's women will be able to occupy a multidimensional realm where they can work out their own lives without imposed restrictions.

When Jewett describes the gardens in her stories, they are suggestive of the natural landscape if the characters connected to them are themselves vigorous and vital. The prim, precise, ornamental Ruskinesque garden usually signifies the presence of the aristocrat who continues to conform to the maxims dictated by society. In Miss Brandon's garden in Deephaven, the scene of a much decayed aristocracy of which Miss Brandon is a part, the flowers actually have manners, for "the lilacs in front and the old pensioner plum trees in the garden are seen exchanging bows and gestures" (*D*, 44). Mrs. Flagg in "The Guests of Mrs. Timms," who cares only for status and material possessions, has pretty, neat plants guarding her house: "the syringa-bushes were tall and green on each side of the stone doorsteps, . . . covered with their lovely white and golden flowers" (*LN*, 262). The converse of this kind of proper garden, a deteriorated one, also carries the same connotation, that of a putrified aristocracy. The Bellamys' garden in "A War Debt" and Miss Chauncey's garden in *Deephaven* fit this description. The Dunport garden in *A Country Doctor* becomes the scene for Anna Prince's desire to propitiate her stultifying existence through her niece: "Miss Prince's was one of the finest old houses which kept its garden behind it, well-defended from the street, for the family's own pleasure" (*CD*, 224). It is gnarled and neglected. Since Nan feels confined in the house with its carefully fastened shutters, she leaves to prune and train the shrubs and vines. Ironically, it appears that Nan has given shape to the garden so her aunt can try to entrap her there, for soon after, Miss Prince has Captain Parish escort Nan into the garden to try to convince her she should marry George Gerry, claim her rightful inheritance, and remain in the Prince home forever barricaded.

Most Jewett gardens are not prim and neat. Instead, they are serviceable and free in their wandering, disheveled, surging, imperfect state, rather like the women who tend them. The young girl working "lustily" in "The White Rose Road" has a mélange of growing plants—"straight rows of turnips and carrots and beets, a little of everything" (*SW*, 261), including a superfluity of blue sage. In "A Bit of Shore Life," Cynthia cultivates "a gorgeous little garden to look at, with its red poppies, and blue larkspur, and yellow marigolds, and old-fashioned sweet, straying things,—all growing together in a tangle . . ." (*OF*, 264). Miss Peck's garden assumes indefinite proportions. From her spot, she can drink in "the glory of the sunsets in the great, unbroken, western sky . . ." (*KF*, 187). Where Mrs. Todd's garden ends and where the landscape begins are indiscernible. Her mystical, magical "curious wild-looking plants" (*CPF*, 5) exist as an extension of the landscape, and Mrs. Todd moves interchangeably between the two sites. Indeed, Miss Powder of "Law Lane" contends that the best garden is the natural plain:

> "Gimme pasture-lands rather 'n the best gardins that grows. If I can have a sweet-briar bush and sweet fern patch and some clumps o' bayberry, you can take all the gardin blooms. Look how folks toils with witch-grass and pusley and gets a starved lot o' poor sprigs, slug-eat, and all dyin' together in their front yards, when they might get better comfort in the first pasture along the road. I guess there's somethin' wild that's never got tutored out o' me. I must ha' be'n made o' somethin' counter to town dust. I never could see why folks wanted to go off an' live out o' sight o' the mountings, an' have everything on a level." (*TN*, 172–73)

In other words, these women are in control, making their own decisions, paving their own routes. For Mrs. Todd, Mrs. Powder, and the coterie of Jewett heroines, the natural panorama is before them. They have gotten through the windows, out of the houses, and hopped over the fences.

An attenuated or panoramic view for Jewett's characters depends on their ability to flee the enclosure. There exists only a narrow view for the woman who remains behind, adhering to the traditional framework. Jewett infuses with genuine sentiment the frequent image of a woman at the window, a spectator whose emotional life has atrophied. Most often it is a woman who has been trapped in a relationship serving a cold, hard, often greedy, sometimes mentally deranged man. This image is repeated twice in "The King of Folly Island" with increasing pathos. Initially, it is the greedy postmaster's wife who is looking toward shore with a "sallow, unhappy countenance" (*KF*, 8).

Later, it is Phebe who can only long for human association by watching her relative's funeral through a spyglass, since her father, after coming to believe he had been slighted by the inhabitants, has vowed never to set foot on St. John's Island again. Eventually, confined to the raw climate of Folly Island, Phebe will die of consumption, as her mother did before her. In "The Landscape Chamber," it is the visiting narrator rather than the oppressed daughter who begins to feel cheerful when she looks out of her bedroom windows, which "stood open to the fading sky and sweet country air" (99). Appalled by the "awful stagnation and hindrance of the processes of spiritual life and growth" (105) generated by the "mysterious tyranny" (105) of the father, the narrator will quickly depart, but the daughter is doomed. Both the mother and the daughter in "A Neighbor's Landmark" will continue to stay with the proud, unbending John Packer, whose motivation to sell his two massive landmark pines occurs at the moment he realizes his wife and daughter believe he would be wrong to do so. Immediately after "he saw the anxious faces of two women at one of the kitchen windows, . . . the blood flew to his pinched face" (*LN*, 247). He turns on his heels to complete the sale.

The situation is somewhat reversed in the story "In Dark New England Days." Here a robber is peering from the outside in to see two sisters discover the treasure left by their recently deceased father. At this point, the sisters have ceased to look out of the window, for they have become as greedy as the father who deprived them of physical comfort and emotional warmth all of their lives. As they have been servants to their father, now they are slaves to his false value system.

Another set of women, glancing at life through their windows, has come to believe in this mode of existence. Madame Jaffrey of "The Village Shop" and Mrs. Graham of *A Country Doctor* both spend their days watching and nodding to the passersby whose days they serve to brighten with a smile. Mrs.

Meeker, also in *A Country Doctor*, has a different motivation for the same practice. A "sentinel" (57) at her window, Mrs. Meeker spends her days garnering information to use to assail the peace of mind and reputation of her neighbors. In a comment passed in *Betty Leicester*, a book she wrote for girls, Jewett gives the impression that this breed of woman constituted quite an extensive group. At one point, Betty remarks: "'All the old ladies are looking out of their windows, just as they were the day I was coming to Tideshead'" (264). Her friend Becky replies that "'their faces were always at just the same pane of glass'" (265).

In only one case is viewing the world from a window related as a positive experience. In *The Country of the Pointed Firs*, Mrs. Blackett offers her seat by the window so the narrator can see from the best view in the house. With one person's concern for another, suddenly the view is a "quiet outlook upon field and sea and sky" from "a place of peace" (54); a constricted view of emotional and spiritual deprivation has suddenly expanded into one that can perceive all of the elements in all directions.

For the many who are trapped behind the windows in the houses, however, Jewett advocates the same choice taken by the narrator in "The Confession of a House-Breaker"—break out. Jewett's heroines are constantly trying to get out-of-doors, and other characters, usually women, frequently disapprove of this attempt. Many of the younger characters fit into this pattern. Betty Leicester declares that "'nothing gets a girl out of a tangle of provocations and bewilderments and regrets like going out into the fields alone'" (120). When Becky decides to form an out-of-doors club, her aunt initially objects. Aunt Barbara tells her: "'In my time . . . girls were expected to know how to sew, and to learn to be good housekeepers'" (175). In "The Girl with the Cannon Dresses," Dulcidora, age ten, is named for her father's schooner, and "all she cared for was out-of-door life" (*U*, 24). Dulcy unhappily admits to her older friend, Ann Channing, that her mother is ashamed of her: "'I don't take to sewing or anything in the house. I wish I'd been a boy, and father does too, but mother says she don't see why we should fret, for she can't see but I'm the same as one in my ways,'"(20). Rebecca of "A Christmas Guest" also functions best outdoors. Similarly, her grandmother disapproves, while her uncle brags that she is as much help to him on the farm as a man (112–13).

Another group of young women who align themselves with nature seem virtually unconcerned with criticism and unwavering in their decisions. In "Where's Nora," the protagonist decides to work out in the good air; she refuses to be imprisoned in a factory (*QT*, 48). Nan Prince begins her stay with Dr. Leslie by reading *Robinson Crusoe*. Barbara Johns in her article, "'Mateless and Appealing': Growing into Spinsterhood in Sarah Orne Jewett," finds that the characters of Sylvy in "A White Heron," Polly Finch in "Farmer Finch," and Nan Prince of *A Country Doctor* speak for Jewett's belief in a productive future for single, young women: "they are able to repudiate the traditional, patriarchal restrictions on women and to resist the domesticating promptings of their mothers or aunts. Their independence is not confined within small houses, but is given flight, like the birds with whom they are frequently compared. Their work outside, not their place at the hearth, gives meaning to their lives" (156–57).

There are also references to older women who are able to live emotionally satisfying lives only after leaving the house. Miss Peck of "Miss Peck's Promotion" feels "too much shut in by this village life" (*KF*, 187) and must return to the country, while Miss Sydney of "Miss Sydney's Flowers" finds contentment only after she "closed the door behind her very carefully, as if she were a mischievous child running away" (*OF*, 165), and enters the community.

In Jewett's travel essays as well, this motif of leaving society behind for the freedom of the woods is prevalent. To get the "real delight" of the journey, Jewett advises in "A Winter Drive" that "it is necessary to go far out from even the villages across the country" (CB, 165). Although Jewett speaks a great deal about gardens in "From a Mournful Villager," she is always riding or walking through wild woods, or escaping into them. Mounting her horse, Sheila, in "An October Ride," she enters woods seldom traveled. In this piece, Jewett registers her annoyance at young boys who throw stones at her and Sheila, presumably because it is so rare to see a woman traveling alone on horseback. Jewett recognizes the unconscious criticism of patriarchal society, which would restrict a woman's movement. Finally, in "River Driftwood," Richard Cary compares Jewett to Mark Twain on the Mississippi. Traveling on the "archetypal river," she "used it as the hub for a discontinuous series of adventures of the eyes and heart" (Introduction to *Deephaven*, 19).

While her characters are sojourning, Jewett also refrains from describing these women in customery flowery terms. They are likened neither to pink rosebuds nor white lilies. Nan, for one, is compared to "untamed wilderness":

> one who had known her well had discovered sooner or later the untamed wilderness which seemed like the tangles which one often sees in field-corners, though a most orderly crop is taking up the best part of the room between the fences. Yet she was hard to find fault with, except by the very short-sighted persons who resented the least departure by others from the code they themselves had been pleased to authorize, and who could not understand that a nature like Nan's must and could make and keep certain laws of its own. (CD, 270)

Sylvia is "a part of the gray shadows and the moving leaves" (TN, 141–42). More specifically, she is compared at one point to a flower with a broken stem. Other unusual, but still complimentary, metaphors compare Polly Finch to a barberry bush and Mrs. Goodsoe to a dried mullein leaf. Jewett herself tells us in

"An October Ride" that she thinks "it is far better to be a stern and respectable mullein than a . . . clematis, that clings . . . and cannot bear wet weather" (*CB*, 106).

Commandeering woman out of the home and expropriating the natural landscape as her domain, comparing her to various aspects of nature on any level, typical or atypical, still involves the risk of equating woman once again to Mother Nature. Annis Pratt in "Women and Nature in Modern Fiction" warns that "there is the possibility that we have come full circle back to the same old set of stereotyped assertions allocating earthiness and personalism to the female and 'transcendence' and abstract thought to the male" (489). Jewett, however, avoids this pitfall. In contemplating her relationship to "untamed nature," Jewett declares: "I am only a part of one great existence which is called nature" (*CB*, 101); she does not mean here to imply that either she or her characters melt into nature. Nature is only the arena. It is alive and growing, free from outside manipulation, as are Jewett characters. Therein lies the sole reason for the comparison.

It is not unusual for Jewett's women to stand out against nature rather than to blend with it. Mrs. Todd looms gigantic as "a huge sibyl," "grand and architectural, like a caryatid," "a large figure of Victory," and "Antigone alone on the Theban plain" (*CPF*, 10, 46, 61, 78). In "A Dunnet Shepherdess," Esther Hight "stood far away in the hill pasture with her great flock, like a figure of Millet's, high against the sky" (*QT*, 121). In analyzing Jewett's art of landscape in *The Country of the Pointed Firs*, Robin Magowan notes that "Jewett admires Millet and his large looming peasant figures who look as if they have risen straight out of the landscapes in which they occupy a frontal position" (239). To recall Jewett's characters is to remember impressive figures who project beyond their own "Theban plains." It is to visualize Sylvy's face as a pale star, almost above the tree itself that she has climbed, searching for the white heron in the morning sky; it is to observe Miss Peck, alone, working in her garden on the hilltop, massive against the horizon. Even Mrs. Goodsoe, who is periodically lost to view as she bobs up and down among the junipers, doesn't become part of the landscape; rather, she pulls up the land with her as she walks—using it in her herbal medicine as she has done all her life.

Jewett's characters, primarily women, who live fruitful lives, do so because they exist independently of the Victorian society that attempts to enclose them. The degree that the characters are able to free themselves from existing institutions and their given roles—economic, religious, and, especially, marital—equals the degree to which they divorce themselves from decay. Jewett also entertains the feasibility of this experience for men who can do the equivalent. But it is the women characters' relationship to windows and gardens that offers a clue to their prospective independence.

I
Escape and Denial

ewett appears to write her own account of the developmental stages in the aging process. Growth should occur naturally, coming full circle from childhood through adolescence and adulthood to a maturity that embraces childhood's open vitality once again. Characters may travel from a wish-fulfillment realm of the fantastic, which frees them from all restrictions, from all society, like Emerson's definition of boyhood—free "as a lord to do or say aught to conciliate one, . . . the healthy attitude of human nature"—to a reality of a wholesome community of people freed from static gender roles. Jewett perfects her vision in *The Country of the Pointed Firs*, but her characters represent various stages of this developmental process throughout her writings. Some attain maturity, while others remain trapped in the roles they assumed during adolescence. Yet, once in a while, Jewett simply allows a character to escape joyfully for a breath of fresh air from all tedium and necessity.

This section concerns itself with such pauses. Jewett provides a psychological playground for her characters where they can remove themselves for a while and simply exist unimpeded. For Jewett's aggressive children, it is a believable situation; for her adolescents, it is a fearful longing; and for her adults, it is simply a land of make-believe, a necessary space where they can dream of release.

1

Childhood Escapades

No one represents Jewett's concept of an ideal, free childhood better than Jewett herself. She first lived the life she willed to her young female characters. She did not participate in the typical girlhood activities that are scheduled to foster ladylike behavior. In his biography, Frost called Jewett "rebellious" as a young child (37). She loved to run beyond the picket fence across the fields, unmindful of discipline and reluctant to return (4–5). Always running and jumping, she was recalled by one playmate as the sort to step in a puddle if there was one (12). Harriet Spofford remembers Jewett dashing with the other children to mount the logging wagon from the woods and then riding into the town over the encrusted snow (*Friends*, 24). Coasting, skating, snowshoeing, fishing, rowing, diving, riding—Jewett loved sports and retained that enthusiasm all her life (Frost, 79). She was also fascinated by what would be classified then and now as boys' hobbies. Sarah collected white mice, woodchucks, crows, pigeons, and turtles (10). Not squeamish, she saw fit to display her bug collection by impaling the insects with pins to a door. At one point, she gathered a heap of mussel shells, which she had forgotten until the grownups sadly noted the odor of the decay (110).

Rigid and formal, her paternal grandmother, and doubtless other well-bred aristocratic women as well, found Sarah's conduct deplorable. In "From a Mournful Villager," Jewett herself mentions:

> My grandmother was a proud and solemn woman, and she hated my mischief, and rightly thought my elder sister a much better child than I. I used to be afraid of her when I was in the house, but I shook off even her authority and forgot I was under anybody's rule when I was out of doors. I was first cousin to a caterpillar if they called me to come in, and I was own sister to a giddy-minded bobolink when I ran away across the fields, as I used to do very often. (*CB*, 134)

Sarah's worst offense, however, seems to be the oft-cited instance of her snapping off the bud, stemless, with its first hint of color, from a prized rosebush. Jewett never forgot the chilled response of her grandmother at the sight:

> I snapped it off at once, for I had heard so many times that it was hard to make roses bloom; and I ran in through the hall and up the stairs, where I met my grandmother on the square landing. She sat down in the window-seat, and I showed her proudly what was crumpled in my warm little fist. I can see it now!—it had no stem at all and for many days afterward I was bowed down with a sense of my guilt and shame, for I was made to understand it was an awful thing to have blighted and broken a treasured flower like that. (137)

Jewett, nevertheless, provided the perfect model for her young heroines. To play sports with a boy's enthusiasm and to adopt a boy's interests was to choose freedom over enclosure. Enthusiastic boys were forgiven their indiscretions in favor of the growth that must not be thwarted. They had been traditionally encouraged not only to wonder, but also to turn that wonder into discovery, regardless of the cost in grime and bruises. Jewett was a born writer; wonder was her essence. She would not be enclosed by rules and regulations. And her nipped rosebud can be interpreted on a symbolic level, for even at an early age, Jewett valued life's essence more than any decorative purposes it might serve. She couldn't divine the ornamental value of a rose any more than she could divine the ornamental value of a passive, mannerly woman-child quietly embellishing the interior of a building.

One may puzzle then over the didacticism so prevalent in her children's stories. Despite her unhampered attitude as a child, Jewett seems to praise in her children's stories the very values she downplayed. She urges her female readers to be neat and clean and obedient. Richard Cary expresses the established critical view of Jewett's stories for children: "Immediately prominent is her flair for finger-wagging moralization. Fondly but firmly, like the maiden aunt she was, she advocates through illustrative episodes the standard virtues of honesty, respect, industry, prudence, charity, self-reliance, decorum, and humility. She tells no rattling tales. . . . Little girls are incipient mothers and housekeepers with rampant maternal instincts" (*Jewett*, 155).

Perhaps Jewett steadily moralizes because she herself has mirrored the behavior of these unruly children. Jewett echoes the platitudes she has always heard because she continues to feel the "guilt and shame" concomitant with snapping off the rosebud and other rebellious acts, a pain resulting not from the acts themselves, but from the alienation to the adult world her unacceptable behavior produced. Yet Jewett subconsciously subverts these morals. Looking beyond the pat final lessons of her stories, the reader is able to decode a vital, adventurous world inhabited by female children who fake the act of swallowing the lessons they are being taught. Counter-instructions and warnings keep intruding into these saccharine messages. Although Jewett in 1878, the year she wrote the children's volume *Play Days*, still wishes for acceptance and would like to make life a bit easier for the little girls she addresses through her stories, her own nature will not allow her wholeheartedly to endorse passive patterns for young ladies so that they can exist placidly alongside adults.

Vibrant, rambling, and frequently rebellious girls figure in *Play Days*. Barbara in "Beyond the Toll Gate" is "always interested in everything new and strange" (201). In "The Desert Islanders," after the children read *The Swiss Family Robinson*, Polly germinates the plan to go and live for a while on Spring Island. "Half-Done Polly" is a remarkable dreamer who diverts the family at breakfast with astonishing adventures from the previous night, while Nelly of "The Best China Saucer" exhibits a reproachful fascination with her unsavory, dirty neighbor, Jane. Except for Barbara, none of the heroines initially does as she is told.

By the end of the story, each child appears tamed as well as somewhat diminished. All of the conclusions seem quite predictable, lauding correct, safe, and obedient behavior; yet each registers a subtle, unsettling note. Even in the case of Barbara, who has always been neat and cheerful, there is a hint that she has lost something in the course of her journey. Although the story ends with the moral that "it costs something to go through [the gate] to get to the untold surprises, Barbara could not help growing sorry; it had been better to think all those treasures were there and not to go through the gate, than it was to be here and find everything so much like what she had seen before" (209). If Barbara continues in her patterns, her adventures will be no more than she is—neat, clean, and predictable. Barbara nevertheless realizes that being "good" does not unequivocally result in what she desires, "new and strange" experiences. Each time Barbara's mother insists that Barbara will be happy wherever she is if she's "always a good girl" (213), Barbara immediately contradicts her by saying "it is a great deal pleasanter living in the new house than it ever was in the city" (213).

Barbara's story ends on a note of possibility; the other girls are not so lucky. Their enthusiasm is subdued and thwarted. In "The Desert Islanders," mosquitoes attack the children, noises alarm them, and, finally, an upcoming storm results in their having to be rescued. The children have been so terrorized carrying out Polly's plan to sneak over to Spring Island to spend the night that "nobody had the heart to scold the miserable and penitent little Desert Islanders" (104). "Half-Done Polly" is finally brought into submission when her imaginative dreams, which generally provide her with astonishing experiences, turn into a nightmare. Her irrepressible sphere has been invaded by adult reprisals in a world where tasks are left unfinished. Formerly, Polly tried to do too many things, but now she will calm down and methodically work at finishing one task before she moves on to another. Nelly of "The Best China Saucer" also conforms to her mother's wish that she avoid associating with dirty, vulgar Jane after Jane's brother breaks the creamer and saucer of the treasured tea set. She, too, experiences a nightmare of the saucer's funeral, which forces her to confess Jane's visit to her mother.

The initiation process is complete. Only Barbara escapes the terror and nightmare of adult conditioning that the others who refused to be either clean or good must suffer. Defrauded of their animated approach to life, these children must settle for confined, conditioned behavior. Jewett appears to give her stamp of approval. Yet Jewett could hardly have openly told these girls to be on their guard and to rebel in the face of adult restraint. Instead, in these and other stories from *Play Days*, she subconsciously provides her readers with clues and counter-instructions primarily in her disparaging remarks about dolls and in her use of naturalistic detail.

While Jewett appeared to like dolls and featured them regularly in her children's stories and in several poems, she seems aware of the limitations a doll-like existence would have for women. In playing with dolls, young girls practice adult behavior. The dolls are the women these girls will become if they

continue to listen to adult women's advice. Jewett's ambivalence
surfaces in the manner in which dolls function within her texts.
It is a pathetic picture of dolls concerned with appearances,
masking their suffering and powerlessness at any cost. Nelly's
friend Alice Russell has dolls who "thought a good deal of dress"
(73), and Nelly must hurry to dress her own dolls appropriately
for the visit. Polly in "The Desert Islanders" notes that "the
dolls sat around the house looking very happy, but then they
always did that, even if one left them out in their best clothes in
the rain" (94). True martyrs emerge in Jewett's 1868 poem "The
Baby-House Famine," where the dolls are literally starving, yet
they remain dutifully downstairs "dressed for callers." They are
"very hungry, but they sat there smiling." The image of the sick,
powerless doll is repeated. In the unpublished poem "The Old
Doll," Rosa sits in the attic with dusty curls and her nose bitten
off by a mouse. The speaker muses, "I wonder why you sit alone
in the garret thrown away" (MS Am 1743.24 (3), Houghton Library, Harvard University). Nelly's pale and sickly doll, Miss
Amelia, spends most of her time in "one of the rooms in the
baby-house [which] was kept dark" (77). When Nelly finally
brings her outside, Miss Amelia is so bundled up to keep the
cold air from reaching her, she can barely move or breathe. Another constricted picture appears in "Half-Done Polly": "The
dolls were left in the hot sun until they were nearly baked to
death, and their clothes and faces were faded. And the one who
had fallen out of the carriage was terribly frightened by the bugs
that wandered over her. She was lying with her dear face just
over an ant-hill, but Miss Polly forgot all her dolls and hurried
away to her flower-bed" (109). Jewett's tone suggests her sympathies are with Polly, for the dolls are laughably and justifiably
victims. The only doll who is not vacuous and inept is Miss
Elizabeth Adora, who also appears in this story. In Polly's nightmare, it is Miss Adora who uncharacteristically suggests that
she and Polly pursue entertainment by going to watch some boys

"half-drown a few very nice Maltese kittens" (117). Evidently, Miss Adora's confined status has resulted in a deep-seated hostility, which, in all likelihood, duplicates Polly's.

Below the surface, Jewett, too, appears to be seething. It may be her suppressed hostility that is being expressed toward her grandmother, perhaps even her own mother, who tried to entrap her within the confines of prescribed feminine gentility. For an author who has been frequently cited as unable to present the seamier side of life, Jewett in *Play Days* presents an inordinate number of naturalistic details. It is doubtful that there are an equal number in the entire rest of her canon, for Jewett's depiction of rural poverty is generally realistic rather than naturalistic. Her portrayal is also characteristically imbued with sympathy. In *Play Days*, the pictures are graphic, grim, and unfeeling.

Miss Adora is not the only one to suggest drowning kittens. There are three more references in this thin volume to killing kittens, the ultimate domestic pet. The mother in "The Kitten's Ghost" gives the gardener's boy twenty-five cents along with "a bag of proper size," telling him "to catch Kiesie and drown her" (136). Kiesie has too much "daring and mischief" to be a house cat, and her final transgression is to break some dishes. Although Kiesie is able to escape from the bag, she steals so much meat from the storehouse one morning that she dies in a fit that afternoon. In "The Yellow Kitten," the cat's death is far more grotesque. While it isn't unusual in children's literature for inanimate objects to come to life, the thread spools in this story are vicious and vindictive. The yellow kitten of the title doesn't play with spools since he once knew of a kitten who abused spools and died "a most shocking death," for "one morning he was found dead in the hall with a little spool . . . in his throat. The family supposed he had swallowed it accidentally, but the cats knew better" (174). The worst account of a cat's death is told in "The Shipwrecked Buttons" by the blue and gold button: "The boy ran down an alley, and helped two others, worse looking than he was, to hang a poor, thin old cat they had caught in the street" (165). The moral seems to be that if you are a domestic animal, being too playful or being caught by boys can result in death.

The more graphic examples of naturalistic detail can be seen in the two stories "Woodchucks" and "The Best China Saucer." In the first story, Nelly and her brother, sent by their father, go off with their dog Tiger to kill the woodchucks who will destroy the crops. A gruesome scene follows: "Joe takes the club he had brought and killed him with two good blows. Tiger ran away yelping, but soon came back; and when he found his enemy was dead he barked triumphantly, wagged his tail, and proceeded to shake the creature until nothing was left but a forlorn bunch of brown fur, torn and bloody and covered with dirt" (127). Perhaps this scene demonstrates Jewett's inner animosity toward the import of her comment at the beginning of the story: "By and by Nelly's work will be nearly all in-doors and Joe's nearly all out-of-doors, but now it is very pleasant for them to work and play together" (119). Jewett doesn't advise Nelly to fight enclosure, so she gives her a picture of what it's like to have the life's blood shaken out of her.

Jewett's most subversive message, however, appears in "The Best China Saucer," wherein she constructs a perfectly despicable child who is preferable to all the other pallid, well-behaved girls. Jewett makes Jane far more interesting than boring, squeamish Nelly, even though Nelly is the penitent heroine. By drawing Jane as such a lively, independent individual, Jewett subconsciously demonstrates her favoritism for "unfeminine" behavior. Belligerent Jane breaks all the rules. Her anger is imminent in her every action and in every word she speaks. She abandons all female qualifications as outlined by society. Instead of playing with dolls, she undresses Nelly's sick doll Agatha, who has been left in her care, and steals her petticoat. Neither is Jane maternal with the baby brother who has been left in her charge. She complains to Nelly: "'I have to lug him everywhere. Long as he couldn't talk I wasn't bothered with him, for if worst came to worst, I used to tie him to the lilac-bush and clear out, and only be sure to get back in time to unhitch him before mother came; now he goes and tells everything . . .'" (76).

For the gentility and compassion generally considered a woman's province, Jane manifests a void. Defiance and impenitence mark her most outrageous act—stringing a live fly necklace. Just before Nelly notices Jane's jewelry, she has been mentally excusing her for swearing and throwing stones and other evil habits, attributing them to bad company. (Actually, Nelly is warming up to Jane because she is friendly and quiet for a change.) Then Nelly is quite horrified:

> Nelly saw for the first time a most shocking and heathenish decoration. "Oh, Jane!" she cried, "what have you been doing to those poor flies, you horrid girl?"
>
> "Want me to string you some?" said [Jane] with a grin. "I did every bit of this this morning, before I came over. I'll bring you one that will go round your neck twice, to-morrow, if you will give me two cents."
>
> It was a necklace of flies, on a long piece of white thread, to which the needle was still hanging. Oh! those dozens of poor flies. Some were dead, but others faintly buzzed.
>
> "Jane Simmons," said Nelly, "you can eat that pudding, and then you go right straight home, and I never will play with you any more. How could you be so awful. . . ."
>
> "I was going pretty soon, any way," said Jane. "I guess there are flies enough left; you needn't make such a fuss. They let them stick on papers and die, in your house. You're an awful little 'fraid cat. Who wants to play with you any way?" (79)

So Nelly comes to believe her mother, who had told her she did not want her playing with Jane, who was naughty and would teach Nelly bad words, bad manners, and disobedience. Jewett, however, has tried to warn Nelly, for she begins her story with the injunction: "Mind your mother,—unless, of course, you are perfectly sure she is a foolish and unwise woman, and that you are always the most sensible of the two" (71). Nelly has opted for a vacuous existence.

As Jewett moves from stories for children, primarily those contained in the volume *Play Days*, her real voice emerges and saccharine lessons virtually disappear. It is not merely evidence of a more mature writing technique but, rather, a more mature vision. Jewett states her convictions outright in an array of healthy female children instead of reacting below the surface of the text to the existing platitudes. She presents an entire troupe of young women who make it clear they do not want to spend their lives doing so-called woman's work. As an alternative, they select men's work. Prissy, a forerunner in the children's story "The Water Dolly," begs to go with her father and brother to fetch kelp. Her agreeable father replies: "'I'm afraid you aren't going to turn out much of a housekeeper!'" (*PD*, 11). Katy of "The Hiltons' Holiday" is a "real little farmer" who doesn't care about boys or marriage. The heroine of "Farmer Finch" would rather be a boy who works on the farm, and she does. Rebecca in "A Christmas Guest" works outside along with her uncle. In "Tom's Husband," Mary's father says she should have been a boy. Likewise, Dulcidora and her father in "The Girl with the Cannon Dresses" both wish she were a boy. In each of these cases, the girl is supported in her choice by a male figure, usually her father. Generally, as well, there is a mother figure who opposes the work as an unnatural preference.

Jewett's paradigmatic girl-heroine, however, is Nan Prince of *A Country Doctor*. It is no coincidence Jewett designated this book her personal favorite, for it strongly parallels her own childhood, and it includes all the values she esteems for young girls. The relationship between Nan and her mentor, Dr. Leslie, also closely mirrors the relationship Jewett had with her own father, to whom this volume is dedicated. Like Jewett, Nan also longs for escape; for her, "there was nothing better than being out of doors, and the apple trees seemed most familiar and friendly, though she pitied them for being placed so near each other" (49). Jewett's counterpart also displays a deficit of ladylike behavior. Aggressive, unruly, forceful, yet captivated by all that is around her, Nan can be found falling from an apple tree while refusing to let go of a squirrel she has caught, tumbling into the river chasing a family of ducks, and fixing a turkey's broken leg.

Enclosure is anathema. Nan loathes school, and one teacher refuses to have her there, for at recess she lures the students out into the pasture, where it takes half an hour to coax them back. Nan's grandmother also misunderstands and disapproves of Nan's atypical behavior and interests. Restless and dissatisfied, Nan is discontented with household duties and needlework, and in several instances, probably as Jewett herself had done, voices the desire to be a boy.

Yet just as Dr. Jewett aided Sarah, Dr. Leslie champions Nan. Dr. Leslie comments: "'She's a bright child, and not over strong. I don't believe in keeping young folks shut up in the school house all summer long.'" (60). Finally, Nan's grandmother confesses she can't handle her because "'she's made o' different stuff'" (71), and Dr. Leslie assumes the responsibility for her care. Dr. Jewett, as well, assumed the role of educator for Sarah, whom he rescued from the school building in order to take her traveling so she could learn all there was to know of the countryside, his patients, his best-loved books, and, ultimately, his values and beliefs.

When Jewett has her narrator comment that "it is very hard to be constantly reminded that one is a child, as if it were a crime against society" (52), Jewett is speaking for herself, Nan, and all her free children who must actively stand against a society that begins to inculcate female stereotyping from a very early age. It may be a premature offering for some, an ideal dream for others, but for Jewett and Nan Prince it is reality. Nan grows naturally like a plant, "not having been clipped back or forced in any unnatural direction. If ever a human being were untrammeled and left alone to see what will come of it, it is this child" (102). For all children, Jewett speaks in terms of "organic" possibility.

2

Adolescent Retreat

Out of childhood, Nan Prince is transfigured into an atypically free adolescent. Her trauma is minimal; her path is set. In fact, the chapter describing Nan's decision to become a doctor and her entrance into medical school is entitled "A Straight Course." Jewett's own decision to become a writer was equally apparent and secure. At times, Jewett's course could only be chosen by ignoring or escaping from the demands placed upon her by school, church, and home. Whether Jewett acted subversively or impulsively, she was able to retreat from the expectations society placed upon women. Jewett, like Nan, was able to carry her childhood freedom with her into adolescence and beyond.

As an adult, Jewett's frequent, unabashed references to herself as a child are well known. Frequently, she refers to her activities as playing and to her friends and relatives as playmates. To Horace Scudder, she wrote, "I'm not a bit grown up if I am twenty, and I like my children's books just as well as I ever did, and I read them just the same" (Matthiessen, 35). When she was forty-eight, Sarah Jewett told Annie Fields, "This is my birthday and I am always nine years old" (Fields, 125). Both Richard Cary (*Jewett*, 19) and Eugene Hillhouse Pool (503–9) view this tendency as an emotionally regressive desire to remain a child. Pool erroneously stipulates. "It is the passionless, or rather passion-spent province of her father and the elderly person with which she is truly, and only, at home" (506). Jewett did write that she felt the last generation, where her grandfathers, granduncles, and grandaunts were her best playmates, was the one to which she really belonged. Nevertheless, this feeling does not have to be interpreted as either passionless or regressive, for as a child, Jewett was able to associate with adults without having to assume adult roles. As a child, she received better treatment than she would have had as a woman in Victorian society. If she didn't have to grow up, she didn't have to accept the norms. (Interestingly enough, the age of nine that Jewett cites as her maximum is the age that signals the end of childhood, for the beginning of early adolescence, with its hormonal changes and prepubertal spurt in growth, occurs in most girls between ten and eleven [Lidz, 312–13].) Jewett was not cowering in fear; she simply cloaked herself in the raiment of childhood and defied the world to command her differently. She would do as she pleased; she would be who she was. Jewett was filled with passion—for Annie Fields, for her friends and relatives, for her work. In the afterword to her edition of Jewett's letters, Fields wrote that Sarah "never put her dolls away but her plans were large and sometimes startling to others" (252–53).

Nevertheless, growing up and out of childhood was not as easy for Jewett as it first appears. Consciously or unconsciously, and quite probably on both levels, Jewett was capable of subterfuge. She created mechanisms to evade the inculcation of woman's expected behavior. Although Jewett's lifelong bouts with rheumatism and arthritis have been well documented by her biographers, the severity of her illness as it applies to her frequent absence from school must be questioned. School, or any of society's institutions for that matter, teach the so-called normal behavior patterns for girls and boys. It is altogether possible that Jewett used her infirmity as a ready excuse for missing school. With her father as a coconspirator, Jewett could skip school to travel the country byways as her father's companion, under the premise that she needed fresh air and light. During the winter session of 1864, when Jewett was fifteen, the school records cite her as thirty-six times present, with twelve times absent and five times tardy (although she lived only five minutes from school) (Frost, 20).

It is doubtful that Jewett, an avid, capable sportswoman, suffered with the intensity that she and her father reported. Fresh air and vigorous exercise may help build a physical resistance to rheumatic spells, but they cannot change a frail, sickly individual into a robust anatomical wonder. There are numerous biographical references to Jewett's constant solitary excursions— hiking, boating, and horseback riding over the countryside. The distances were long. Jewett thought nothing of riding nine miles to York (Frost, 30) or of traveling seventeen miles to visit her friend Celia Thaxter (Thaxter, 156). Jewett loved the "exhilaration in a sea ride" (Cary, *Letters*, 169) and, on one occasion, jumped boat and ran to shore instead of being carried (Frost, 124–25). At the age of twenty-eight, Jewett impulsively went coasting on her childhood sled, the "Flying Tiger," alongside a small neighbor (Frost, 48–49). The following year, she wrote to Anna Dawes, telling her of a prolonged absence she had had from home and of her fear she would have to break her horse, Sheila, in again: "But I am luckily very strong and Sheila knows I mean to be captain" (Hollis, 130).

While Jewett's use of illness is somewhat different from the rash of invalidism occurring among nineteenth-century women, it does have similarities to this phenomenon as well. Lorna Duffin contends that "illness may have been used by women as way of escaping from the tedious chores and equally tedious social events which comprised the greater part of their lives. This was a view about which they of necessity had to keep silent as long as their situation remained unchanged" (Delamont and Duffin, 51). Duffin goes on to quote Florence Nightingale, who wrote in her autobiographical book *Cassandra*: "Bodily incapacity is the only apology valid. . . . In the conventional society, which men have made for women, . . . they *must* act the farce of hypocrisy" (51). While Jewett assuredly did not live the constricted life of Nightingale and other nineteenth-century aristocratic women, she did seem to feel the need to escape situations that would impede her development. She appears to have made good use of her illness.

Another of Jewett's evasionary tactics can be detected in her attitude toward institutionalized religion, second only to school in maintaining male/female stereotypes. Her biographer John Frost states that Jewett was not a natural churchgoer. In an undated letter to Annie Fields, Jewett remarked that she had been to church, for she hadn't been "preached *at* [emphasis mine]" for some months (Fields, 54). In her 1869 diary, Jewett complained of the boredom and stupidity of certain sermons, and as her mind began to wander, she would look across the aisle to occupy her time by making faces at her friends (Donovan, *Jewett*, 5), or she would let her thoughts travel to imaginary hillsides and other company (Frost, 88). Frequently, she would create stories to be later written down (88). In December 1888, Jewett wrote to Fields that a dreadful sermon led to the conception of a first-rate story to be written shortly after Christmas (Fields, 38). Josephine Donovan notes that "like many nineteenth-century women, [Jewett] found certain aspects of the establishment religions unappealing, especially any remnants of Calvinism with its harsh doctrine of damnation. In several of her works she rejects this fire-and-brimstone, patriarchal religion in favor of a more compassionate, humanistic creed" (*Jewett*, 17). Jewett retreated from another area of negative influence. When she attended services, it was frequently in body only. More often, like her characters, she preferred to read the Bible by her bed, in the privacy of her home, where she could foster her faith rather than convert to patriarchal demands.

Of course, although school and church have profound sway over developing youth, the main source of influence for any child is the home. Though Jewett's father nurtured and upheld his daughter's need for unrestricted development, there seems to be evidence by virtue of the very lack of documentation that Jewett's mother did not encourage Sarah in the same vein. It is quite likely that Mrs. Jewett, while she was not the complaining, severe despot Sarah's paternal grandmother was, did try to foster ladylike behavior and womanly duties in her daughter, who wanted very little to do with either. It would be quite normal for her to try to teach these values, for these were the values she upheld by her own behavior. Esther Forbes gives us Sarah's sister Mary's description of their mother: she was "a typical New England lady," "a gentlewoman with lovely manners" (73). Margaret Thorp maintains Sarah's mother had the New England gift called "faculty," for whatever she did, she did well. Yet Thorp's list of Mrs. Jewett's accomplishments appears traditional and slight indeed compared to the ambitions of her daughter Sarah: "her cakes were always light, her biscuits delicately browned, her rooms well swept and garnished with flowers from her own garden" (13).

Once again Sarah slips away from the issue. While she cared for her mother tremendously, she could not use her for a model, so she deleted her from the text. Richard Cary notes: "In contrast to the many epistolary and literary tributes Miss Jewett paid her father, she said remarkably little about her mother outside of citing her illnesses and death" (*Letters*, 21). Indeed, Sarah says little of mothers in her stories as well. The notable exception comes at the end of her writing career in the figure of Mrs. Blackett. But, as indicated at the beginning of this division, there exists a group of mothers on the periphery of the narratives who call their daughters away from boys' activities and back into the home, and often, the children in Jewett do not have mothers or do not have mothers who are visible. Sarah Way

Sherman views Jewett's unpublished manuscript "The Christmas Ghosts" as a "renewed, strengthened intimacy with her mother's memory, even her mother's spirit" (55). But Sherman acknowledges that this reintegration can take place "only after the mother is safely dead" for "to identify with the mother is to accept the mother's role and, with it, subordination to the male, restriction to the domestic sphere, and finally, reproduction without control" (187).

Ultimately, Jewett avoided contact either physically or emotionally with people who would persuade her to deviate from her untrammeled development in order to substitute a traditionally female sphere—one of safe, passive, unstimulating devotion to others. With all those who held sway over her in school, at church, and at home who were inclined to give her negative information, Jewett retreated. She ran free, and if she couldn't, she capitalized on her sickness or just simply closed her ears and heart.

Jewett was willful, but it was not easy to be so in the face of such authority. On 1 September, 1879, Jewett wrote to Anna Dawes: "It is a puzzle sometimes to me—but I grow more certain that I cannot write so much as I do and do everything that other girls do beside" (Hollis, 134–35). In Jewett's diary, Donovan notes that she speaks of "loneliness," of "unaccountable melancholy," and of feeling "restless and unhappy" (*Jewett*, 21). Jewett had marvelous coping mechanisms, but she suffered since her personal expectations were not society's. She would have liked to escape. She does so temporarily through her literature. In *Deephaven*, Jewett explores the desire to retreat, to prolong adolescence in order to evade the undesirable, limited role assigned to women. In *Deephaven*, there is a glimpse of Jewett's pain and longing.

In 1877, the year Sarah Jewett published her first book, *Deephaven*, she was twenty-eight. The characters of her book, Helen Denis and Kate Lancaster, are both twenty-four. Jewett chron-

icled her "restless and unhappy" emotions in her diary entry of
17 July 1872, when she herself was twenty-three, and she wrote
of her "loneliness" and "unaccountable melancholy" in 1874 at
the age of twenty-five. In 1872 and 1874, and even with the
publication of her first book, Jewett might have been sure of her
desires, but she did not know whether she would succeed as a
writer. Having rejected marriage as an option, Jewett, in her
twenties, faced a crisis. If she did not marry as was expected,
and if she was not successful in her chosen career as she
wished, what options were left? How could she fit into society
without any label—prescribed or unusual for a woman? In
Deephaven, therefore, Jewett mirrors her own upset in the
characters of Helen and Kate. Helen and Kate are also unlikely
candidates for marriage, and at twenty-four, not much time is
left to deliberate (indeed, the subject is never discussed between
them), for soon society will affix its own label of "spinster" and
relegate them to the care of their respective family domiciles.
Helen and Kate attempt a retreat; they wish to stop time in a
place where time itself appears to have stopped. While they are
there, Kate and Helen examine all the roles that can be assumed, but every option contains some element of suffering,
decay, insanity, or death. Robert Horn sees in *Deephaven* "some
of the most devastating portrayals of isolation, frustration, self-
delusion, human dry-rot, and at times, indomitability in all of
Jewett's fiction" (284). *Deephaven* contains Jewett's hunger to
find a fulfilling niche in society and her accompanying realiza-
tion at that age that there is to be no relief for her angst and
isolation. It is to be a journey that will offer no plausible solution
to the perplexity. Yet it will be an opportunity to turn from the
existing structure, to move toward self-acceptance, and to take a
brief, though tenuous, glimpse of more fruitful possibilities.

As the story opens, Helen sets the tone of anxious confusion:
"It happened that the morning when this story begins I had
waked up feeling sorry, and as if something dreadful were going

to happen. . . . To this day I have never known any explanation of that depression of my spirits, and I hope that the good luck which followed will help some reader to lose fear, and to smile at such shadows if any chance to come" (37). Although Helen tries to salve her fears, the reality exists that the trip does not serve to alleviate her depression. Disconnected and totally alone (both girls are parentless: Kate's parents are in England; Helen's father is also traveling and her mother is deceased), they embark upon a journey that will provide no external solutions. Helen and Kate may bounce along and gloss over the deprivation of the people they meet, but the disconcerting details that Helen records shows that the effect on her is not lost. Lingering in childhood, possessing an eternally pleasant and carefree disposition toward all the people they meet regardless of the horrors those people live, cannot be perpetuated, as Helen desperately desires: "It might be dull in Deephaven for two young ladies who were fond of gay society and dependent upon excitement, I suppose; but for two little girls who were fond of each other and could play in the boats, and dig and build houses in the sea sand, and gather shells, and carry their dolls wherever they went, what could be pleasanter?" (38).

Kate, in turn, sings to Helen: "'Will ye step aboard, my dearest, / For the high seas lie before us?'" (39). Kate and Helen will not be able to maintain this stance of two children on their way into an adventurous fairy tale. Shortly, doubt will descend, and Helen will admit that "sometimes in Deephaven we were between six and seven years old, but at other times we have felt irreparably grown-up, and as if we carried a crushing weight of care and duty" (54). Although Helen says on the train: "'I do not mind riding backward in the least'" (41), the truth is, she has no progressive step to take. She and Kate are going to stay in the home of Kate's dead Aunt Katherine who, "kept everything just as it used to be in her mother's day" (41), and that is the only foreseeable role open to these young aristocratic women at the

moment. As they comprehend the "care and duty" of this position, their pretty trip will become as sour as the oranges they
share with Mrs. Kew on the train. Tossing the sour fruit out the
window serves as a symbolic gesture for Helen's and Kate's ultimate rejection of the sobering revelations to come: "after the
first mouthful we looked at each other in dismay. 'Lemons with
oranges' clothes on, aren't they?' said [Mrs. Kew], as Kate threw
hers out of the window, and mine went after it for company"
(41).

In the following two chapters, "The Brandon House and the
Lighthouse" and "My Lady Brandon and the Widow Jim," Helen
and Kate are introduced to the two definitions afforded women,
both explained in terms of a woman's relationship to a man—
single or married. Neither is presented as desirable. Presumably, Lady Brandon was in the economic situation to decline
marriage, whereas Mrs. Kew and Widow Jim, being from the
lower classes, would have had to align themselves with men to
facilitate survival. The girls conclude from a packet of letters
that the reason Miss Brandon chose not to marry was because
her lover had probably been lost at sea. Instead, Miss Brandon
took care of the Brandon House, the only other choice she had.
Jewett discloses the emotional waste of this shut-in existence.
Not until Miss Brandon is ill does it "occur to [Kate] that she
had a spark of tenderness or sentiment," and now Kate remembers a song with a "sweet wild cadence" that Miss Brandon frequently played when she had been particularly "quiet all day
and rather sad" (60).

But the house is everywhere reminiscent of death, as is most
of Deephaven. Helen and Kate enter funereal rooms. In one of
the front rooms, they stand in dread of the dismal atmosphere; it
contains a lounge where many of the Brandon relatives have lain
dead. Overlooked by hostile portraits, the best parlor has something about it "which suggested an invisible funeral" (46), while
in their favorite room, the west parlor, a great coffin stands in

the foreground of the two last tiles of the fireplace. In retrospect, Helen recalls telling ghost stories in this room, where the young women stayed up all night nearly scared out of their wits. Miss Brandon, in fact, led a ghostly existence in life. Her only power, in the words of Mrs. Kew, was "a power of china" (48), and the girls are "convinced that the lives of her grandmothers must have been spent in giving tea parties" (48). There are ten sets of cups, quanitities of stray ones, and a collection of pitchers. It is no surprise to learn that later in life Miss Brandon's "mind failed her" (58). The picture in the front room of Joan of Arc "tied with an unnecessarily strong rope to a very stout stake" (45) is a symbol for Miss Brandon, who has been tied and martyred to another patriarchal cause. Helen and Kate seem to respond to the cadences of imprisonment in the house, for they rescue from the parlor a projection of themselves in the sole portrait of a young girl "who seemed solitary and forlorn among the rest in the room" (47). While they might be living in a state of limbo, Kate and Helen are instinctually clear-sighted about which option is not for them. With further exposure to "Deephaven Society," a subsequent chapter, in the forms of Miss Honora Carew and Miss Lorimer, living versions of Miss Brandon, Helen ends the chapter with the words: "When the moon is very bright and other people grow sentimental, we only remember that it is a fine night to catch hake" (77). The aristocratic woman's life cannot be glazed over by the romantic light of the moon, for her mean, base existence is reflected in the image of this common codfish, *Merluccious vulgaris*. Helen and Kate will not be able to romanticize this veneered mode of existence.

The view of married life the girls ascertain is no less degrading. Mrs. Kew's arrangement is the most favorable, for at least she and her husband have compromised. Raised in the hills of Vermont, Mrs. Kew cannot abide her husband's continual voyages upon the sea, so they have agreed to live in and keep the Deephaven lighthouse, though "it is lonesome in winter" (42) and Mrs. Kew will always miss the up-country. This dreary existence is inconsequential compared to the horror the Widow Jim has undergone. She recalls her marriage in terms of war: "She did not seem to mind talking about the troubles of her married life any more than a soldier minds telling the story of his campaigns, and dwells with pride on the worst battle of all" (63). Warning Helen and Kate, she says: "'Don't you run no risks, you're better off as you be, dears'" (63). According to her neighbor Mrs. Dockum, the Widow Jim's husband was shiftless and drunk. The culminating insult took place one morning after the Widow Jim had sliced cucumbers, one of her husband's favorites, for his breakfast. Mistaking the "sperrit" bottle for the vinegar, he repaid her thoughtfulness by hurling the stone vessel at her and adding a permanent dent to her forehead. Although the girls are shocked, Mrs. Dockum explains that the Widow Jim excused his behavior as accidental. With this self-effacing attitude, it is no wonder Widow Jim Patton does not even have a female first name in the text. She is lucky to have weathered the experience with her husband, never mind develop an identity of her own.

Marriage as a battleground is a subsequently repeated theme. Old Dinnett, the sailor, drinks to Helen's and Kate's health: "'Bless your pretty hearts! . . . May ye be happy, and live long, and get good husbands, and if they ain't good to you may they die from you!'" (84). Captain Lant's wife forces him to become a farmer, giving him "no peace of mind" (80) until he agrees to stop sailing for good. When the sun shows itself through the rain, Captain Scudder says it is a sign that "'the Devil is whipping his wife'" (121). Marriage is debilitating. Captain Sand's daughter, who has always been robust enough to go out on the sea with her father, has had "slim health" (122) since her wedding.

Helen and Kate leave the town with its negligible options to attend "The Circus at Denby." This scene serves as an ironic

comment on all that has gone before, for this circus symbolizes
the discomposed life of the masses versus the enthusiastic, vital
vision Helen and Kate desire. Again, Helen records only dissolution at the circus, which should offer by its very nature a fantastic adventure. Helen notices shabby performers who "looked
as if they never had a good time in their lives" (104). The animals are equally listless. One great elephant has a "look of general discouragement . . . as if he were miserably conscious of a
misspent life" (102).

Death is proximate. Literally, Mr. Craper, who is taking his
gloomy children to the circus, is looking "ghastly pale, and as if
he were far gone in consumption" (101). A conversation ensues
between two farmers who are discussing the preferential size of
an animal to be slaughtered. The one is telling the other "with a
great confusion of pronouns, about a big pig which had lately
been killed" (103). In truth, the lives of people and animals are
quite interchangeable in this community. The next person
Helen and Kate meet is the Kentucky Giantess. Seeing her
makes the young women "ashamed of [them]selves for being
there" (106), for the giantess is woman totally degraded. Jut like
the pig, she is valued for her tonnage. She tells Helen, Kate, and
Mrs. Kew, an acquaintance from her youth: "'I believe I'd
rather die than grow any bigger. I do lose heart sometimes . . .'"
(107). The giantess Marilly, who, according to Mrs. Kew, was
"'real ambitious'" (108) as a girl, has been reduced to this state
by her father's drinking, which used up every cent they had and
eventually killed him. Marilly has never recovered. She declares:
"'I began to grow worse and worse, till I couldn't do nothing to
earn a dollar, and everybody was a-coming to see me, till at last I
used to ask 'em ten cents a piece, and I scratched along somehow till this man came round and heard of me, and he offered
me my keep and good pay to go along with him'" (106–7).

It is certain that Helen and Kate will never have to embrace
the life of the giantess, since their aristocratic status removes

them from any economic danger. However, the incident with Marilly foreshadows and emphasizes in a grotesque fashion their own predicament. In the final section of this "circus" chapter, Helen and Kate discover that they are not exceptions: men control and they remain excluded and invisible. On a damp, rainy evening, they attend a lecture entitled "The Elements of Manhood," given by a speaker who, even though he is insensitive and blind, dictates the answers and possesses the power. Helen apprises the situation:

> You would have thought the man was addressing an enthusiastic Young Men's Christian Association. He exhorted with fervor upon our duties as citizens and voters, and told us a great deal about George Washington and Benjamin Franklin, whom he urged us to choose as our examples. He waited for applause after each of his outbursts of eloquence, and presently went on again, in no wise disconcerted at the silence. . . . If the lecture had been upon any other subject it would not have been so hard for Kate and me to keep sober faces; but it was directed entirely toward young men, and there was not a young man there. (110)

As women of the nineteenth-century, Helen and Kate could neither vote nor hold office. They could never emulate the qualities of Washington and Franklin, for it was not woman's place to be political, inventive, or experimental. For the first time in *Deephaven*, Kate and Helen actually admit seeing the ludicrousness and duplicity around them. For the first time, they acknowledge that there is a difference between the adventurous, unencumbered life they would like to lead and the limited, restricted situation that society offers.

Until this moment, the young women's experience has been, in the words of Ann Romines, "an adventure in retreat" (206). In "In *Deephaven*: Skirmishes near the Swamp," Romines goes on to say that Kate, in particular, "is adept at fending off social conventions which she finds meaningless, at evading dead ritual. . . . but both are well-schooled in protective conventions, and . . . receptive to Deephaven life when it intrigues or amuses or charms, but always ready (gracefully) to withdraw a chaste cheek from a too-intrusive touch" (206). Degradation is everywhere present; Helen has recorded it, but she and Kate have resisted the knowledge. Moving chronologically through their experience, Helen's perceptions contradict the realities. At the lighthouse, she speaks of "entertaining discoveries" (50) with no show of sympathy for Mrs. Kew's lonely mode of living. After inspecting the Brandon House, Helen remains ignorant of Miss Brandon's situation and, instead, extols her contributions: "it seems to me that it is a great privilege to have an elderly person in one's neighborhood, in town or country, who is proud and conservative, and who lives in stately fashion; who is intolerant of sham and useless novelties, and clings to the old ways of living and behaving as if it were part of her religion" (55). The Carews' superficiality is also interpreted in terms of "the most charming manners and good breeding" (76).

At times, Helen's and Kate's desire to avoid contact with pain and suffering makes them appear hollow and uncaring. When they attend church services where the members obviously appear as decrepit relics, Helen and Kate find them "delightfully old-fashioned" (71). They reserve the members' quaint words and expressions and provincial behavior to "[use] afterward to the great amusement of [their] friends" (73). Later, they observe the destitute fishermen as "agreeable company" (78), "interesting" (84), and "childish in their wonder" (85). As Danny is telling the story of his emotionally vacant, orphaned existence, even Helen is "shocked" by Kate's "irrelevant" question: " 'Do you believe codfish swallow stones before a storm?' " (91). Still, at the "Circus at Denby," Helen amuses herself by putting peanuts on a woman's hat brim and watching them fall off as the woman moves her head. This is hardly "the best fun in the world" (105) she describes, but it does prevent her from absorbing the atrocities around her. Yet seeing the Kentucky Giantess and hearing about "The Elements of Manhood" have sobered Helen and Kate, at least for the time being. Remaining totally ignorant has become impossible.

During this vulnerable stage, Jewett offers two possibilities for relief, two alternatives to the scenes Helen and Kate have witnessed. In the next chapter, "Cunner-Fishing," the interior is substituted for the exterior. Genuine communication that involves emotional connection to other human beings, a necessary quality singularly missing from Deephaven, is disclosed through the use of psychic powers. Captain Sands, a well-liked man with a reputation for being "peculiar, and somewhat visionary" (93), is the medium. Fascinated, Helen and Kate listen to his supernatural accounts. A typical occurrence in Jewett's stories, "The Foreigner" being the most notable example, is for vital information to be disclosed as a storm is commencing. Captain Sands declares that he had not seen the storm coming. He attributes their safe return to shore to his wife: "'I know as well as I want to that my wife . . . impressed it on my mind. Our house sets high, and she watches the sky and is al'ays a-worrying when I go out fishing for fear something's going to happen to me, 'specially sense I've got to be along in years'" (121). Over the many years that they have been together, Captain and Mrs. Sands have developed such strong emotional ties that they often know exactly what each other is thinking. Here where gender roles are not depicted as rigid, genuine heart-to-heart exchanges can occur. Sands remarks, "'My wife and me will be sitting there to home and there won't be no word between us for an hour, and then of a sudden we'll speak up about the same thing'" (123). Captain Sands has even more extraordinary tales to tell of contact made over time and distance between loved ones involved in life and death situations. He has discovered that there's a faculty people hold that they don't understand: "'We've got some way of sending our thought like a bullet goes out of a gun and it hits. We don't know nothing except what we see. And some folks is scared, and some more thinks it is all nonsense and laughs. But there's something we haven't got the hang of'" (124). Jewett, at this point, appears to be advising Helen and Kate to go into the interior rather than to try to find a place in the society that exists. It would be a fruitful endeavor compared to the stultifying behavior that they have seen.

In the subsequent chapter, "Mrs. Bonny," Helen and Kate discover a woman, the only woman living on her own to date with a well-developed interior. Josephine Donovan affirms that "she is an original, uncontaminated by the civilized world. . . . Mrs. Bonny is an archetypal Jewett figure, the single woman who is in tune with nature and who has an extensive knowledge of herbal and natural lore. While presented in a somewhat comic vein here, she prefigures Jewett's monumental women, particularly Almira Todd of *The Country of the Pointed Firs*" (*Jewett*, 39). She lives entirely on her own terms. Rather than subscribe to society's order, Mrs. Bonny totally contradicts the structure by having no order at all. Her outfit consists of men's boots, a man's coat cut to jacket length, some short skirts, several aprons, and a nightcap on her head. Her kitchen is occupied by a flock of hens and a turkey. When she opens the cabinet to get a glass for Helen and Kate, several things fall out, including "bunches of dried herbs, a tin horn, a lump of tallow in a broken plate, a newspaper, and an old boot, with a number of turkey wings tied together, several bottles, and a steel trap, and finally, such a tumbler!" (138). The tumbler itself contains old buttons, squash seeds, and a lump of beeswax Mrs. Bonny had lost. By the time Mrs. Bonny wipes out the glass with her apron, the girls are no longer thirsty. Helen and Kate, nonetheless, are captivated by Mrs. Bonny—her knowledge and her person—for "there was something so wild and unconventional about Mrs. Bonny that it was like taking an afternoon walk with a good-natured Indian" (139).

Yet they love in her what they cannot embrace. Just as they cannot drink out of her tumbler, they cannot at this point abandon all that they have ever known and become primitivistic. Neither can they rely solely on emotional and spiritual ties to give their lives meaning, which seems to be what Jewett is suggesting below the surface of the psychic phenomenon that she details in "Cunner-Fishing." While Helen and Kate cannot seem to find a place for themselves in the society that exists, they do not have the emotional interior yet to create something substantially different from the situations that prevail for women. Instead, they continue to deny all that they see in order to play in a vacuum that cannot endure. Since they reject these alternatives, and since there are no other possibilities with which to replace them, Helen and Kate must return to the existent decay that Deephaven represents. The next two chapters, "In Shadow" and "Miss Chauncey," are somber and horrifying. Even Helen and Kate cannot gloss over the corrosion and blight. In "In Shadow," they reflect on poverty and death. In "Miss Chauncey," they move from a literal death of someone unrelated to them to an example of the death-in-life that awaits them in their female aristocratic status. Before their visit to Miss Chauncey, Kate says, "'We shall certainly meet a ghost'" (151). Miss Chauncey is the replica of what Miss Brandon had become before her death—insane.

In the final chapter of the book, "Last Days in Deephaven," Helen and Kate have reached a stalemate. Unable to go either forward or backward, they want to withdraw even further after these traumatic revelations. The horrors they have beheld symbolize Jewett's own angst at this age. Kate proposes they "copy the Ladies of Llangollen, and remove [them]selves from society and its distractions" (160). These two women, Lady Eleanor Butler and Miss Sarah Ponsonby, were a couple who lived in seclusion in the Welsh countryside for much of their lives at the end of the eighteenth and beginning of the nineteenth century

(Donovan, *Jewett*, 32–33). Donovan interprets this penchant as "a desire not to have to conform to the role demands that 'adulthood' required in Victorian America" (33). Romines refers to these demands as "crippling sexual dualism" (219). Still, Jewett does offer a necessary condition for growth—a deep haven. Helen and Kate, and probably Jewett herself, have been able to stand motionless for a moment to evaluate the most restricted and the least restricted alternatives. Helen and Kate have been shown the possibility of rejecting society's superficial, constricting structure in order to create a life based on a sound, emotional interior. In time, their own incipient friendship may provide a substantial support on which to build this interior. At present, Helen is infatuated with Kate, just as Donovan and others have told us Jewett was infatuated with Kate Birckhead, after whom Helen's friend is modeled. They share few of their fears, if, indeed, they are aware of them.

In Jewett's haven, she provides a sign for future progress. On three occasions, Helen mentions looking outward to the stars. At the beginning of the book, Helen and Kate are rowing at twilight, watching their respective stars, when Helen avers: "'I used long ago to be sure of one thing,—that, however far away heaven might be, it could not be out of sight of the stars'" (53). Helen seems to utter a belief in an earth-bound happiness. Later, at the end of "Cunner-Fishing," Helen and Kate can see the stars from the window as they discuss the myth of Demeter and Persephone. Kate recounts her favorite part: "'I always thought that part of the story beautiful where Demeter throws off her disguise and is no longer an old woman, and the great house is filled with brightness like lightning, and she rushes out through the halls with her yellow hair waving over her shoulders, and the people would give anything to bring her back again, and to undo their mistake'" (130). Kate tells Helen she is always finding a new meaning in the myth: "'I was just thinking that it may be that we all have given to us more or less of another nature as the child had whom Demeter wished to make like the gods. I believe old Captain Sands is right, and we have these instincts which defy all our wisdom and for which we never frame any laws'" (130). In her study, *Sarah Orne Jewett, an American Persephone*, Sarah Way Sherman feels that "Kate and Helen begin to sense a 'personality' speaking through the landscape around them. But they do not see its soul in another person. Their goddess lives only in detached, intellectual interpretations of ancient myths, not incarnated in present flesh" (118). Yet inherent in Kate's description of her favorite part of the myth, and also in her belief that instincts can defy the laws, is the aspiration to free herself from Victorian patriarchal control. Helen's words on the last page of *Deephaven* echo Kate's ardor. Helen envisions returning to Deephaven one day, looking at the changes altered by time, walking along the beach at sunset; and finally, she states, "when we looked up there would be a star" (166). Jewett's 1874 diary ends on a curiously similar note:

> I know this is true of me and at times I drift into an unaccountable melancholy. I am morbid and dreary with self analyzing—with a dread of the future and remorse for real and imagined mistakes in the past. But a little thing blows away all this fog like a fresh wind and I am fearless and happy—strong with the free strength of an untamed creature—and the sunshine of the world comes to me from a clear blue sky and warms me through and through. So my days go—shadow and sun—shadow and sun. And the evening and the morning are the first day and the second—and will better last. But it is only in the dark that I see the stars— (1874 diary, MS Am 1743.1 (341), Houghton Library, Harvard University)

In the 1890s Jewett, upon rereading *Deephaven*, commented: "I felt as if I had come to be the writer's grandmother. I liked it better than I expected. It is the girlishness that gives it value. . . . It is curious to find how certain conditions under which I wrote it are already outgrown" (Cary, "Jewett to Dresel," 38). Jewett and her characters have retreated for the moment, but merely to regroup and then to move out against the ties that bind.

3

Fairy Godmothers

To counteract women's lack of power in society, Jewett employs one fanciful method to exercise a type of wish-fulfillment in the appearance of the figure of the fairy godmother. Within an arena of positive escapism, Jewett endows women with total control. In evaluating Jewett's story "A White Heron," several have commented upon its fairy-tale quality. Given the choice between the heron and the hunter for her prince, critics aver, Sylvia would have chosen the bird. "A White Heron" is not the only story with elements of the fairy tale. In an appreciable number of others, Jewett replaces the prominent position occupied by the prince with the fairy godmother. Nan Prince of *A Country Doctor* envisions her long lost aunt in this role: "It seemed possible to Nan that any day a carriage drawn by a pair of prancing horses might be seen turning up the land, and that a lovely lady might alight and claim her as her only niece. . . . the dreams of her had been growing longer and more charming, until she seemed fit for a queen, and her unseen house a palace" (66). No longer does the fairy godmother of the Cinderella tale merely aid the young woman in adhering to a heterosexual dream; she now occupies center stage to provide opportunities for relief from stressful outside limitations. The kindly, compassionate, and powerful fairy godmother becomes woman's queen and savior.

In Jewett's stories for girls, the fairy godmother makes her appearance as a warm, reassuring mother figure. Lady Mary Danesly of *Betty Leicester's English Xmas* suggests the perfect mother in a child's dream fantasy. Prior to the invitation to visit Lady Mary with her father over the holidays, Betty, whose mother is deceased, declares her feelings: "We all know how perfectly delightful it is to love some one so much that we keep dreaming of her a little all the time, and what happiness it gives when the least thing one has to do with her is a perfectly, golden joy" (9). Immediately following Betty's arrival, Lady Mary mirrors the magical vision of the fairy godmother, who calmly and smilingly responds to the girl child, wrapping her in an emotional cloak of love, understanding, and safety: "Suddenly Lady Mary felt the warmth of Betty's love for her and her speechless happiness as she had not felt it before, and she stopped, looking so tall and charming, and put her two arms round Betty, and hugged her to her heart" (18). As Betty is thinking how good and kind Lady Mary is to come and meet a young stranger who might feel lonely, Lady Mary "wistfully" tells Betty how having her there is "'almost like having a girl of my own'" (20). During Betty's stay, she and Lady Mary often exchange hugs, kisses, and affectionate glances. Amid a palatial setting in the English countryside, with snow frosting the earth, the culminating event of Betty's stay is her organization of a colorful, shimmering Christmas pageant to surprise Lady Mary and bring joy to her guests. Lady Mary is, of course, quite pleased with Betty's endeavor, and the final scene of the book finds Lady Mary with her arm around Betty and Betty with her head resting on Lady Mary's shoulder as they gaze at the falling snow and listen to the Christmas bells chime from Danesly church. "When Lady Mary kissed Betty again, there was a tear on her cheek," and before she returns to her guests, they stand there a moment longer "loving to be together" (68). Betty has been healed emotionally, for she has been given the warm, accepting mother she has needed. Although the volume ends on the didactic note of the importance of giving, the reader espies not only the perfect mother figure, perhaps a reflection of Jewett's own yearning for a mother who would warmly approve of her, but also the ideal woman. Lady Mary Danesly is the ruler of her domain. She has the economic freedom and the autonomy to exert power as well as to dispense the life-giving qualities of compassion and of nurturance.

In "Nancy's Doll," a story from the volume *Play Days*, the fairy godmother figure is more impersonal and magical. She arrives, and as quick as the wave of a magic wand, the storm, physical as well as emotional, is quelled. Nancy, a poor orphan who lives with her grandmother, wishes for two things—a doll and a sister. While the portrayal of a nineteenth-century woman of the leisure class performing social work is historically accurate, the advent of Miss Helen's arrival is much larger than life. Nancy sees "such a pretty carriage stop at the end of the court, and a young lady opened the door and came out" (61). Nancy's friend Nora, who works for Miss Helen, exclaims: "'She's an angel,'" (61), for Miss Helen has been taking care of Nora's sick mother. Now Miss Helen walks into Nancy's life, and presto, Miss Helen produces the doll Nancy has been longing for, as well as a doctor and a cure from the Children's Hospital. In addition, Miss Helen writes a letter that automatically ends a long-standing quarrel between Nancy's grandmother and her sister who lives in the country, thereby providing Nancy an escape from the noisy, dirty city tenement to a happy, healthy life in the country, where she will not be lonely and afraid anymore.

In some of Jewett's better known stories, this pattern of the rich woman, a stranger, appearing out of nowhere to aid another woman in need is repeated. In "The Flight of Betsey Lane," the protagonist, who comes from seafaring stock, has always wanted to see something of the world, but since she now resides at the Byfleet Poor-house, a trip seems impossible. As Betsey is shelling beans one afternoon, the granddaughter of the rich Thornton family, Mrs. Stafford, arrives. Betsey had worked for the family before they moved to London. Although the granddaughter has not seen Betsey since she was a girl, she suddenly pays Betsey a visit and hands her one hundred dollars.

Coincidentally, Mrs. Stafford arrives just in time for Betsey to go to the Philadelphia Centennial. Not only does Betsey's dream come true, but she meets a doctor at the Centennial who is going to come in the summer and do something about removing her friend Peggy's cataracts. In addition, at the close of this delicately beautiful story, it is intimated that Betsey's return to her friends (who presume she is missing because she has drowned herself) will add dimensions to their lives as well when they share in Betsey's adventure: "With this the small elderly company set forth triumphant toward the poor-house, across the wide green field" (*NW*, 218).

In another comical story, "A Late Supper," the fairy god-mother figure, Miss Ashton, does far more than provide Miss Catherine Spring with a long-awaited adventure; she saves her from the hostile industrial system, which cares more for money than it does for people. Miss Spring is ruined financially and will have to leave her home because the railroad has not paid its dividend. She is forced to admit: "'I wish we never had sold our land for the track!'" (*OF*, 95). When Miss Spring borrows from a neighbor some cream for her visitors, she cannot get back home across the tracks because a train has made a stop. Deciding to walk through the train in order to get to the other side, Catherine Spring is taken by surprise as the train begins to move while she is on it. Yet this is where she meets Miss Ashton, "a most kind and refined-looking woman, with gray hair and the sweetest eyes" (96). Eventually, Miss Ashton, who is an invalid, comes with her niece to board with Miss Spring, making it possible for her to retain her home. Miss Spring can also now hire Katy Dunning, the destitute orphan. The matrilineal salvation train has made every stop.

The same scenario can be found closer to home. Frequently, rich women help other women in their own communities who are economically destitute. These incidents are slightly less fantastic though frequently as coincidental. Miss Sydney of "Miss Sydney's Flowers," once she has given up her insular life, finds salvation by aiding the candy stand operator, rheumatic Mrs. Marley, and her lame, deaf sister Polly. Mrs. Marley is too old and ill to be working out-of-doors, and she suspects she and her sister will be in the almshouse before spring. An outstanding molasses bill also needs to be paid. Mrs. Sydney comes to the rescue: "Miss Sydney asked her to go round to the kitchen, and warm herself; and, on finding out more of her new acquaintance's difficulties, she sent her home happy, with money enough to pay the dreaded bill, and a basket of good things which furnished such a supper for herself and sister Polly as they had not seen for a long time. And their fortunes were bettered from that day" (*OF*, 167). This ending sounds remarkably like its fairy-tale counterpart—"and they lived happily ever after."

In *Deephaven*, the gift giving is considerably more in keeping with the friendship existing between Miss Brandon and Mrs. Patton; however, it is still an irregular and quite magnanimous act. Miss Katherine Brandon has named Mrs. Patton in her will:

> "It has put me beyond fear of want," said Mrs. Patton. "I won't deny that I used to think it would go hard with me when I got so old I couldn't earn my living. You see I never laid up but a little, and it's hard for a woman who comes of respectable folks to be a pauper in her last days; but your aunt, Miss Kate, she thought of it too, and I'm sure I'm thankful to be so comfortable, and to stay in my house, which I couldn't have done, like's not." (65)

An essential element of the fairy godmother figure is that she does not give handouts, but rather, she makes it possible for other women to become economically independent, to take care of themselves. Mrs. Patton is grateful for the opportunity: "'I feel better to be able to do for myself than to be beholden'" (65).

Mrs. Trimble in "The Town Poor" will make it possible for the Bray girls to have their home in town back again. Since the sisters could no longer afford to maintain their own home, the selectmen have broken up and sold all of their possessions. Abel James's folks, who have the reputation for being poor spirited and cheap, put in the lowest bid to keep the Bray girls for the town. When Mrs. Trimble and Rebecca Wright come to visit Mandy and Ann, the sisters are in pinched and miserable circumstances. They have no light, no heat, and very little food in the middle of a long and dreary winter. As Cinderella cannot go to the ball because she has no gown, the Bray girls cannot even go to meeting since they have no decent shoes and rubbers. Mrs. Trimble is beside herself with rage. A wealthy woman of influence, Mrs. Trimble will take it upon herself in the morning to impel the selectmen to treat the Bray girls justly. In true fairy godmother fashion, she will restore their home to them, which is fortuitously still vacant. She will force the town into supplying firewood and paying their rent, and she will use her money to provide them with everything else that they need. Rebecca Wright even suggests that they get the doctor to take a look at Mandy's eyes and Ann's arm to see if he can help the Bray girls to get well enough to earn a little something on their own.

In one of Jewett's most poignant stories, "Martha's Lady," Helena Vernon gives Martha much-needed emotional assistance so that she can perform her servant's tasks with ease and skill. Helena, on a visit to her Aunt Harriet Pyne, encounters Martha, the new maidservant, who has so far proved to be "clumsy," "easily confused and prone to blunders" (*QT*, 108). Beautiful Helena, on the other hand, is nearly perfect: "Nobody had ever been so gay, so fascinating, or so kind as Helena, so full of social resource, so simple and undemanding in her friendliness. The light of her young life cast no shadow on either young or old companions, her pretty clothes never seemed to make other girls look dull or out of fashion" (115). In an instant, Helena takes

Martha under her wing, and she is transformed as "Helena showed by a word and a quick touch the right way to do something that had gone wrong and been impossible to understand the night before" (108). Martha is "no longer homesick or hopeless," and her manners have become "perfect" (111). And when Helena pleads Martha's case with her strict and demanding aunt, Martha's life is imbued with purpose: "From that moment, she not only knew what love was like, but she knew love's dear ambitions" (111). Though Helena does not visit again for more than forty years, and though she is unconscious of her impact on Martha's life, Martha thinks of her every day: "To lose out of sight the friend whom one has loved and lived to please is to lose joy out of life. But if love is true, there comes presently a higher joy of pleasing the ideal, that is to say, the perfect friend" (118). And as the years pass, Helena is raised in Martha's heart from enchanting to sacred: "She never thought of trying to make other people pleased with herself; all she lived for was to do the best she could for others, and to conform to an ideal, which grew at last to be like a saint's vision, a heavenly figure painted upon the sky" (118–19).

On some occasions, even a woman of no means can provide the makings of a dream for another woman needier than she. Miss Tempy of "Miss Tempy's Watchers" once gave young Lizzie Trevor sixty dollars to go to see her uncle and to visit Niagara Falls. Lizzie, a splendid scholar, had overworked herself in school and incurred a breakdown as a result. It is not until Miss Tempy dies that Mrs. Crowe hears about her generosity. Mrs. Crowe registers amazement: "'Sixty dollars!' exclaimed Mrs. Crowe. 'Tempy only had ninety dollars a year that came in to her; rest of her livin' she got by helpin' about, with what she raised off this little piece o' ground, sand one side an' clay the other. An' how often I've heard her tell, years ago, that she'd rather see Niagary than any other sight in the world!'" (*TN*, 16).

Miss Tempy, nevertheless, is more a self-sacrificing, extremely compassionate and generous woman than a magical fairy godmother. Jewett's fiction will move in this more realistic direction. Although it is comforting to think that a woman will swoop down out of nowhere and release one of her own kind from emotional and economic deprivation, it does only happen in fairy tales. Jewett constructs a more realistic means of salvation for her characters. Help is not instant or complete, but it is feasible. Miss Tempy is one of these benefactors. Miss Cynthy Dallett and her aunt, both in need, will provide each other with a mutual home. Yet there is psychological validity in Jewett's concept of the fairy godmother. Jewett expresses a belief in women helping women. Unlike the typical fairy godmother who arrives and grants a wish only to disappear, Jewett's figures provide lasting opportunities for women to build lives on their own. It is a type of wish-fulfillment, but one with a basis in reality.

II
No Escape

The Acceptance of Dual Norms

For those characters who accept society's pattern of behavior with its double standards for men and for women, Jewett makes clear there is no room for development. Trapped in the roles assumed during youth, these characters find it impossible to experience release or growth. None are saved. All are physically or emotionally isolated.

In the previous section, a world of possibility was glimpsed—a world where characters could escape or, at least, deny the standards society set. But in the following stories, Jewett shows us the converse. The characters here assume a mindless inculcation of the expected norms. Jewett portrays selfish, callous men who are paralyzed emotionally. She unveils numerous aristocratic women who dutifully become caretakers of empty houses. Finally, Jewett draws a dismal picture of men and women cohabitating in the standard marriage. Stunted in their roles, these miserable couples, though occupying the same space, live separately, unable to communicate.

Jewett shows us the debilitation that results from such alienation. When men and women live in separately defined spheres, they can never really make contact with themselves or others, and they can never become whole.

4

Paralyzed Men

Frequently, Jewett scholars have cited her male characters as malformed human beings. Polar opposites, these men are generally either weak or malicious. Most often, they are flawed precisely because they are proponents of Victorian industrial society, a society that upholds the amassing of material goods as a way of life. Greed and the desire for power have maimed these men to the point where some are barely recognizable as human. In all cases, this egoistic desire to accumulate has stunted the men's emotional growth. Estranged and estranging, they continue with their obsessions either in a lackluster fashion or in a madly driven state.

Pervading Jewett's fiction is the familiar scene of the old sea captains sitting on the rotting wharves, reminiscing about the good old days when shipping was at its peak. Warner Berthoff explains that there were no men or only poorly depicted men in Jewett's writing because all the capable men had gone from New England to the world of progress (149). True, the shipping industry had declined, but Jewett is commenting on more than an economically depressed area of the country. Similarly, she is drawing attention to more than old sea captains who are unable to change with the times and so spend their days living in the past, complaining of a once fruitful existence. Jewett's captains have the same disease as the rest of industrial society. They are men who have defined themselves via marketable commodities. Men should have power, and amassing money provides the key to that might. As long as these captains have been able to flourish monetarily, they have considered themselves enterprising and powerful. In short, they have concentrated only on the exterior without any cultivation of the interior. These sailors are presently unable to live in this rural society, a community that relies mainly on interior qualities now that its means of subsistence is minute. Grandeur here is defined solely according to human stature, not material wealth.

While Jewett's sea captains evoke pathos rather than loathing from the reader, Jewett's condemnation of acquisitiveness is apparent within the cluster of male characters she creates whose hunger for money and/or power makes them no less than odious. It is a scathing attack, devoid of compassion, on these men who have engorged themselves on another's destruction. Like father like son—just as Henry Stroud's father cheated Lydia Dunn's grandfather out of about all he had, Henry has defaulted down South, cheating those with whom he has done business. As "A New Parishioner," Henry continues his hypocritical lifestyle. In an effort to impress his old neighbors while avoiding prosecution in the South, Henry gives liberally to the population, including the donation of a new vestry for the church. Unfortunately, Henry does not have the funds for this venture, so again, people will not be paid, but for the moment, he appears sanctimonious. Misguided values are also apparent in "A Neighbor's Landmark" in the person of Ferris (whose name means "iron" and sounds strikingly like "ferret") as he cons his neighbors out of their valuable woodlands: "Ferris had driven a great many sharp bargains; he had plenty of capital behind him, and had taken advantage of the hard times, and of more than one man's distress, to buy woodland at far less than its value" (*LN*, 254). Ferris disregards all living things, and Jewett, who valued each tree she knew as an individual neighbor, makes an ecological statement about Ferris's behavior: "he always stripped land to the bare skin; if the very huckleberry bushes and ferns had been worth anything to him, he would have taken those, insisting upon all or nothing, and, regardless of the rights of forestry, he left nothing to grow; no sapling-oak or pine stood where his hand had been. The pieces of young growing woodland . . . were sacrificed to his greed of gain" (254–55). In the story "The Failure of David Berry," the betrayal is more personal. Sam Wescott, "an impetuous, thoughtless sort of man" (*NW*, 128), destroys his neighbor David Berry because "he liked to have his own way about things, and was rather fond of his petty grudges" (128). Wescott, who has become impatient for the fifty dollars that Berry owes him, demands immediate payment, thereby inciting a panic on the part of Berry's debtors. Ironically, Wescott had previously coerced Berry into taking the loan because he felt Berry needed to expand his shoe business. With a sentimental flourish, Jewett has Wescott find, after David's ignominious death, a piece of paper pasted on the wall by Berry's shoe bench that reads: "Owe no man anything but to love one another" (135).

Other male characters of this type prey upon destitute women. Mrs. Peet in "Going to Shrewsbury" is concerned with maintaining her pride and independence on the farm she has cultivated for forty-five years. Yet the place falls into the hands of her nephew Isaiah, who reminds the narrator of a fox. Mrs. Peet, like David Berry before her, has concentrated on paying her debts to strangers before settling the small loan she has taken from her nephew. Just as Berry's greedy neighbor Sam Wescott betrays him, Isaiah coaxes Mrs. Peet's husband into signing over the farm to him. Now that Mr. Peet is dead, Isaiah forces Mrs. Peet out of her home.

In another attempt to maintain an independent life on her farm, Mary Ann Robb of "The Night before Thanksgiving," who in her lifetime frequently lent a hand to those less fortunate, also has no more resources. As she daily fears being taken to the poorhouse, her next-door neighbor John Mander waits impatiently to get her farm "like a spider for his poor prey" (*QT*, 226). To further intimidate Mrs. Robb, Mander pretends she still owes him the money that he had advanced to her in her destitution, even after he clears her wood lot to pay himself back. Disrespectful of people and nature, Mander prepares to "plough over the graves in the field corner and fell the great elms" (226). Mander further exacerbates the situation by rebuking Mrs. Robb because she has been "too generous to worthless people in the past" (226) and now she has come to be a charge to others. "In Dark New England Days" also contains a greedy male character, Enoch Holt, who peers into the Knowles girls' home waiting for his chance to steal their dead father's trunk, which holds Captain Knowles's fortune, eventually leaving the two sisters virtually penniless.

"In Dark New England Days" exhibits another factor that comprises the nature of several of these warped men, the love of power as much as, or even more so than, the love of money and material goods; for the Knowles girls are victims of their father as well as of Enoch Holt. Jewett displays the disease that is the result of an acquisitive way of life. To move linearly up the ladder of success precludes a basic egocentricity that is bent on outdoing others. To get, one must control, and for some, the ability to control will outweigh even the hunger for material gain. To enunciate this malady, Jewett creates a group of men, predominantly fathers, who exercise total control over *their* women. Captain Knowles, for instance, lives meagerly while controlling his fortune in a trunk and his daughters in his home. For most of their lives, the daughters have been their father's "dutiful, patient slaves" (*SW*, 226), performing a "thousand requirements and services" (226).

The pathetic element in this story is that the daughters seem to have caught the disease. To repay Holt for stealing their fortune for which they have waited so long, they put a curse, which seems quite effective, on the right hands of the whole Holt family. While it is true, as Elizabeth Ammons has demonstrated in "Jewett's Witches," that this story reflects Jewett's anger over male tyranny (169), the sisters know no peace of mind, "liv[ing] their lives out like wild beasts into a lair" (254). Although Enoch Holt comes to look like "a malicious black insect" in time, "worn and bent . . . enough to have satisfied his bitterest foe" (256), and although Captain Knowles's strokes the last year or two of his life leave him a symbolically "feeble, chair-bound cripple" (222), the women have not escaped the perversion. Obsessed with money rather than overjoyed by their relationship with each other and their freedom from their tyrannous father, they remain trapped in their house with "'a kind of black shadder, a cobweb kind o' a man-shape that followed 'em about the house an' made a third to them'" (254). Now the daughters and their father are one, trapped in a false, grasping value system.

The King of Folly Island contains two stories where fathers entrap their daughters, but here the daughters are not culpable. The father in "The Landscape Chamber" is both parsimonious and tyrannical. The daughter is pathetically sweet, remaining to take care of her father because she has promised her dead mother that she would be patient with him. The narrator, appalled at the waste of human potential, attempts to act as a foil to the father's wishes by requesting he let the daughter go to visit with her for a time. She also insists that he can overcome his miserliness: "'God does not mean that we shall make our lives utterly dismal (110). . . . God meant us to be free and unconquered by any evil power (113). . . . We can climb to our best possibilities and outgrow our worst inheritance'" (114). The father refuses the narrator's offer and insists he is fated by a curse placed upon him by a greedy ancestor. This idea of a curse appears to be an incredible one within the context of the realistic framework of the story, but the idea that the father has maintained a pattern of behavior akin to his aristocratic family, whose main purpose has been to amass wealth, is not. Life has been reduced to so many objects of ownership, of which the daughter is one. The daughter is just another trophy, like the shriveled ear of the father's dead mare pinned to the stable wall. While attempting to leap the yard gate to freedom, the horse caught her foot in a rope and broke her neck. The father would rather see the mare dead than galloping free from his possessive control. So, too, he prefers his daughter to live a restrained existence under his roof as a part of his collection.

Josephine Donovan sees the title story of this volume, "The King of Folly Island," as "Jewett's comment on the patriarchal tyranny of the nuclear family of Victorian America" (*Jewett*, 77). Cary and Garnett have also drawn attention to the ungovernable tyranny of the protagonist, and to be sure, it is impossible to find a male character in Jewett more paralyzed than George Quint. The King of Folly, whose surname resembles "squint," is indeed a person of narrow vision. Since he cannot get along with his neighbors, or rather, since they will not recognize his superiority (at one point in the story, he refers to himself as "number one"), he has chosen to maroon himself on his own island, where no one will dare to disagree with him: "'I could get on with 'em ef 't was anyways wuth while,' responded the island chieftain. 'I did n't see why there was any need o' being badgered and nagged all my days by a pack o' curs like them John's-Islanders. They'd hunt ye to death if ye was anyways their master . . .'" (22). After the isolation kills his wife, George realizes the move was too hard on her, but his ego is so large, he still refuses to move his daughter, who is near death from a combination of consumption and loneliness.

George is indeed the King of Folly, but he is not the only male to have sole rights to this category. Jabez Pennell, the postmaster, gets equal joy from overcharging for goods and services as well as making people wait to get their mail. Then a visitor descends upon the scene. Frankfort, a fort of currency, walled-in by his opulence, is awed by George's intractable personality, which Frankfort views as heroic resolution. Richard Cary perceives the similarity: "Egocentricity, whether it occurs in a trawler or a tycoon, is reprehensible. For Frankfort soon realizes he too is a king of Folly Island. He too has isolated himself from humanity through his obsession to amass as much money as possible" (*Jewett*, 120). Frankfort will remain as unyielding in his misguided direction. Unlike the woman narrator of "The Landscape Chamber," when Frankfort realizes the tragic situation of Phebe, he does nothing to alleviate her plight. While Frankfort advises Phebe to remain on the island so she can avoid "'the great world beyond [which] pushes and fights and wrangles'" (39), he fails to see that she would leave the island to align herself with the people, not the things of the world. His reasoning only helps him to avoid contact with Phebe and her tragedy. Frankfort, who finds it hard to read Phebe's copy of Wordsworth's poems, poems of the natural world, because "business fills [his] mind" (39), will return to mechanical, commercial society. Although Phebe has cared enough about him to send him her (in his eyes) paltry gift of a self-crafted shell house, he will push it into his desk drawer along with his emotional self and, instead, aid the office boy to climb the corporate ladder, totally missing the personal significance of gift giving.

"The Landscape Chamber" and "The King of Folly Island" exhibit extreme instances of male tyranny, but the pattern is repeated in Jewett's characters with varying degrees of severity, yet with similar emotional deficiency. Reverend Dobin's daughters in "The Dulham Ladies" "never accepted the fact that he was a tyrant, and served him humbly and patiently" (*WH*, 197); however, their upbringing has left them eternal, naive children. John Wallis of "A Bit of Shore Life" means well when he forces his mother to come and live with his family in Boston in order to take care of her. Yet Wallis's values are largely materialistic. He has put up glorious stones in the country burying lot for his father and sister. True, he wants his mother to live comfortably, but he also thinks she should "see something" (*OF*, 241) in addition to her rural residence; and he refuses to let her bring any of her poor possessions to his fine home, excluding even the rug she hooked from her dead daughter's rose dress. In reality, John Wallis is wrenching his mother from her closest friends, her most valued possessions—her home. Jewett presents a dismal scene predominated by an anxious, torn elderly woman. John Wallis is blind to her emotions.

This male emotional deprivation can be manifest as well in men who continue to think themselves the superior sex while, in fact, they are totally inept in their daily lives. Blinded to all but their own egos, these men are virtual parasites to their communities, for their so-called contributions are negligible. Leonard Jaffrey of "A Village Shop" is the epitome of unsubstantiality: "Here he was, stranded in the old house with as much energy as a barnacle, . . . the most unproductive man of letters in New England, with no apparent value either social or commercial" (*KF*, 236). Unfortunately, the family fortune has been defunct for some time, and Leonard has achieved his unproductive status as a result of his mother's and sister's sacrifice and suffering. The story has a quasihappy ending, for the town appoints Leonard as the head of the new town library. It appears that even the aura of wealth and status is qualification enough in patriarchal society.

In Jewett, the largest group of ineffectual males are the ministers, culminating in the portrayal of the Reverend Mr. Dimmick in *The Country of the Pointed Firs*. Time and again Jewett pokes fun at the inflated men of God who inspire no one. The very people whose job it is to heal as well as to motivate, in effect, to draw out the very depths of humans, are the ones who are out of touch with any real emotion. The list begins with Mr. Peckham in "A New Parishioner," who is more interested in having a new vestry built as a monument to himself than he is in anything spiritual. Both Mr. Elbury in "Miss Peck's Promotion" and Reverend Dobin in "The Dulham Ladies" preach eloquent sermons with no content. "Never enlightening," Reverend Dobin is "providentially" (WH, 196) prevented from continuing his preaching by a paralyzing stroke in the middle of his career. Unfortunately, this does not stop him completely, for on high church days he "held up his shaking hands when the benediction was pronounced, as if the divine gift were exclusively his own, and the other minister did but say empty words" (197). The parishioners are relieved when he finally dies. When Mr. Elbury's wife dies, he faints two or three times and groans out for Miss Peck's help. She becomes his temporary housekeeper and perceives him closely as "ease-loving, self-absorbed, and self-admiring" (KF, 182), the complete opposite of the nature of his dead wife. Like the superficial Reverend Dobin, Mr. Elbury's discourses are equally "flowery and inconsequent" (183). Jewett also lists one Catholic priest who fails in his calling, Father Pierre of the story "Mère Pochette." Instead of reconciling the two lovers, little Manon and Charles Pictou, Father Pierre indulges in a personal vendetta against Charles and steals his letters to Manon to keep them apart. The narrator comments that "even his holy calling could not lift [him] above the earth and its weaknesses" (327). Yet this is not Father Pierre's only error. His parishioners wish for their previous priest, the benignant Father David. Although Father Pierre tries to do his duty from time to time, his efficacy is minimal, since he believes himself too good for this poor parish, which he refers to as "this hole of a place" (309).

In two of her longer works written back to back, *A Country Doctor* (1884) and *A Marsh Island* (1885), Jewett examines the utterly ironic situation of the man unable to shape his own life, who desires to shape a woman's instead. Based on the premise that to be male is to be superior and in control, both George Gerry and Dick Dale, inept in their own spheres, still possess a deluded sense of superiority, which finds its expression in what can only be termed the Pygmalion complex. Blindly perceiving two strong women as ultimately weaker than they, George and Dick set about shaping these women in their own images.

In *A Country Doctor*, George Gerry has opted for a comfortable law position, where he seems to spend more time thinking by the window of his office than engaged in practicing law. Most of the young men have left the small, flagging city of Dunport for greater opportunities. While Gerry is dissatisfied, the narrator explains that "he had neither enough desire for a more active life, nor so high a purpose that he could disregard whatever opposition lay in his way" (288). George Gerry may be the most prominent young man in Dunport, but there is evidence that he has gotten his position through his association with the aristocratic Miss Prince.

When Nan Prince arrives, he is not only shocked but "uncomfortable" with her decision to become a doctor. Nevertheless, although it is "quite against his conscience" (249), as a man, his impulse is "to rush into the field as Nan's champion" (249), adhering to the stereotype that she can't possibly take care of herself since she is a woman. In fact, when Nan gives evidence of her strength, it literally makes George sick. While out on a picnic, Nan yanks a man's shoulder bone back into its socket. But George "did not like to think of the noise the returning bone had made. He was stout-hearted enough usually; . . . but he felt weak and womanish, and somehow wished it had been he who could play the doctor" (266). To him, Nan is not a doctor; she is merely playing. Yet George cannot ignore the fact that Nan does exert power in this situation, and while "it is in human nature to respect power, . . . all his manliness was at stake and his natural rights would be degraded and lost, if he could not show his power to be greater than her own" (295). Insecure, and obsessed with the superior stance that is due him solely because he is male, George assumes one mental attitude after another in an attempt to find some resolution to his dilemma. He begins by being patronizing. At first he is "amused" by Nan's goals and finds her defense of them "charming" (294), but he ends, threatened and hostile, in a diatribe against women who usurp men's duties. Unfortunately, he has witnessed "good fellow[s]" (294) who have gone straight downhill after marrying women who wouldn't "take the trouble to fit themselves for their indoor business" (295). Since George cares for Nan, he takes it upon himself to show her her "mistake" (295). According to George, Nan, of course, is not responsible for her blunder; it is the fault of Dr. Leslie, Nan's guardian. All a woman like Nan needs is to be "under the guidance of a more sensible director" (294). George will be the new self-appointed superintendent of Nan's life. How best to accomplish this task? He will marry her.

Typically, George does not foresee any opposition to his plan. Even Dr. Leslie should be pleased to see Nan "happily anchored in a home of her own, before he died" (296). Marriage is once again a battlefield on which man, the conqueror, will subdue woman, the weak enemy, so that he can take care of her for her own good:

> all things seemed within his reach in these first days of his enlightenment: it had been like the rising of the sun which showed him a new world of which he was lawful master . . . making himself responsible for her shelter and happiness. . . . She seemed to get on capitally well without him, but after all he could not help being conqueror in so just and inevitable a war . . . with all history and tradition in [his] favor. (298)

Jewett's sarcasm is unveiled. In fact, she seems to be enjoying herself immensely with the character of George Gerry by embodying him with the stereotypical views men hold of women so she can write them down for their absurdity to be plainly seen.

Dick Dale of *A Marsh Island* is from the same mold. His saving grace is that he thinks out loud less often than George, so he is a less offensive and less comical figure.

Like George Gerry, Dick Dale is "unambitious" (9); people who know him laugh at the idea that he will make his mark on the world. Nevertheless, since he is "remarkably free from reproach," "often useful," "always agreeable," and a man, "society valued him and instinctively paid him deference, as if it understood how sincerely he respected himself" (9). As the book begins, Dick, an unsuccessful but wealthy painter, has been abandoned in the country by a local boy who is supposed to return to give him a ride back to the city. Dick, lame from a recent fall from a horse, cannot make his way back on his own. Truly only "a boy on a stolen holiday" (67), Dick will soon reveal during his stay with the rural family the Owens that his lame foot is a symbol of his lame self, a purely egocentric one.

In the Owens' home, Dick wants whatever he fancies. As Dick longs to get into Mrs. Owen's closets to see what treasures are there, he covets Mrs. Owen's antique candlestick, pitcher, East Indian cottons, and her daughter, Doris. Doris is just another manifestation of Dick's grasping materialism. A person of social stature, he feels an inherent right to everything he wishes. While he upbraids himself at one point for his covetousness, he does not change. In particular, he does not change his ideas about Doris. Condescendingly, he likens her to a frightened tree he has painted, to a picture, and to "a garden flower in a field" (20). When he does compare Doris to a person, it is a French peasant.

Doris, however, is self-contained and physically strong. In the face of difficulty, Dick Dale, like his predecessor George Gerry, is inept, becoming ill after a woman takes control of the problem and solves it without him. Dale hastens to help Doris with some unruly horses he believes are beyond her mastery, but he trips and falls "ignominiously" (68) as she brings them under her command. "Disgusted and ashamed of himself" (69), Dick does not cope well with what he considers defeat. Instead of recognizing Doris's capability, he blames his fall on his weak ankle. Further exacerbating the situation for himself, he faints. Interestingly, it is at this time when Doris must physically support Dick the whole walk home that he perceives her as "soulless," "unconscious as a flower," and "utterly commonplace" (72).

George Gerry's solution to the problem of a woman's independence and resolution is also Dick Dale's. Dick will remove Doris from the world of her choice, in this case, the natural world rather than the medical, and put her in his aristocratic realm where he can teach her to be the woman he believes she can be. Dick is convinced that Doris is too superior for her rural setting: "Dick longed to put her in her rightful place, among the books and pictures and silks, among the thoughtful, beauty-loving, and progressive people with whom his own life had been associated" (257). In reality, what Dick truly desires is to dissolve Doris's strength. He has already acknowledged that he feels she is "a garden flower in a field," and he wants to ensure that she is safely taken from the open air to be walled up in his establishment. If he can capture her, he can change her into his ideal woman, for "Nature had made a mistake in putting this soul into so tall and commanding a body; perhaps Doris would have been more at ease in the world if she had been smaller; the sort of woman whom everybody takes care of and pets, if they have a right" (116).

Dick Dale and George Gerry would like to have the right, but Jewett thwarts them. If they choose to remain paralyzed in their view of women as weak objects to be formed by their male standards rather than as independent human beings with hearts and minds of their own, then Dick and George will have to remain alone and emotionally crippled. Nan and Doris make their own choices. Jewett points to a future when women will not consider it a privilege to belong to a man, whether he be rich and handsome or whether he feigns godlikeness in the manner of George Gerry and Dick Dale.

If patriarchal society continues to value aggressive self-indulgence over the building of relationships, Jewett convinces us that these misplaced values can lead only to the alienation of man to man and of man to woman. Paralyzed and stunted emotionally within the industrial system, which sets up money and power as the standards for men, and emotion and bonding as the inferior standards afforded to women, men will remain incomplete and less than humanly developed.

5

Aristocratic Women

As discussed in the first section, the aristocratic, or upper-class, women are removed from the natural landscape. Some of these women are glancing at life through windows; all are enclosed in houses. These are the women who have subscribed to the patriarchal system. As in the case of the paralyzed men, there can also be no human fulfillment among the women who accept and practice the roles these men have chosen for them. Men who value power and aggression do not bestow potent roles to others outside of themselves. The stereotypical characteristics women have been told are theirs may be flattering (good, kind, patient, loving), but they have historically kept women subservient to men's demands. Misses Brandon and Chauncey of *Deephaven* are not isolated instances of crazy aristocratic women, nor are they mere reflections of Kate's and Helen's fear of becoming ladies in the adult world. Jewett presents an entire cast of pathetic aristocratic women characters who have accepted the pattern society has set for them. All are remarkably similar in their beliefs and behavior; in short, all live the same jaundiced lives. While many of these women are contained in Jewett's earlier works, *Deephaven* (1877), *Old Friends and New* (1879), and *A Country Doctor* (1884), they appear on and off throughout Jewett's writings. As late as 1899, in the short story "Martha's Lady," the same type of aristocrat appears in the form of Harriet Pyne. Jewett must have felt continual sorrow for those women leading aborted lives in Victorian homes, women who could not see other options as she did. This second chapter explores what constitutes such a life and why it is so devastating. It is a behind-the-scenes look at Ruskin's idealistic, flowery, majestic picture of "the angel in the house." While Ruskin perceives his view as woman at her best, Jewett shows us the cruel, shriveled reality.

First of all, though these aristocratic women live alone, they define themselves by their relationships to men. They exercise no choice but live on in their fathers', brothers', or husbands' houses, performing the domestic duties prescribed for them. Since these women are wealthy, or carrying on the pretense of wealth after partriarchal fortunes have crumbled, they actually do very little. So they sit; but they do not wait, for nothing ever happens. Most are unmarried but keep the family male surname going on as usual, as best they can, in the family home. Mistress Sydenham insists on returning to the old plantation so that she can "attend to her house" (SW, 25). There are other occupants in Lady Ferry's ancestral home at present, but she is mad (probably driven that way by her aristocratic woman's status) and reappears after a nine years' absence to go directly to her old room in the north gable without a word to anyone. She is incapable of any other behavior. Miss Chauncey dies after a similar return. She becomes ill after trying to return to her uninhabitable family mansion in the middle of a cold, wet winter.

Since Miss Jaffrey and Miss Ball have brothers in residence in their family dwellings, they substitute their brothers for their fathers and do all that they can to serve them instead. In "The Taking of Captain Ball," Ann Ball's life revolves around that of her brother. While he is at sea, she dutifully saves all of his letters and keeps his house. She is sometimes near destitution from sending her money to aid foreign missions, but she saves her brother's money for him because she feels he is too irresponsible to do so for himself. Miss Jaffrey in "A Village Shop" must sacrifice everything for her incapable brother. He, on the other hand, is peaceful, plump (and getting plumper), and pompous, unaware of the family's proximity to beggary and immune to his sister's struggle. But Miss Jaffrey keeps him this way. In fact, she is frequently proud of him, referring to him who sits, reads, and eats as "a man of letters."

Miss Horatia Dane is different in that her life centers on a suitor believed to have been lost at sea many years prior. Although her relationship with him had been brief, she keeps a whale's tooth from him in her room (as Miss Brandon kept the love letters from her shipwrecked suitor), thinks of him often, cries for him at Christmas; in short, he becomes "the romance of her life" (OF, 28). For those few who have married, there is little or no mention of their husbands and little evidence of their ever having existed. Still, Mrs. Fraley proposes marriage as the only viable choice for Nan Prince: "The best service to the public can be done by keeping one's own house in order and one's husband comfortable, and by attending to those social responsibilities which come in our way" (CD, 282).

Due to the thwarted nature of these lives, images of entrapment abound in these stories. Madame Jaffrey and Mrs. Graham, as previously mentioned in the nature section, spend their days longingly looking out at life from their windows. Horatia Dane and Harriet Pyne spend their days closing blinds instead. With regard to Horatia, the narrator comments that "her life had been shut in by safe and orderly surroundings" (OF, 39). Lady Ferry only seems to be able to get out at night when no one can see her outside of her assigned place. Miss Prince admits, "'I'm not in the least free. . . . why I'm tied to this house as if I were the knocker on the front door . . .'" (CD, 204). Mary Hamilton, a young aristocratic woman in *The Tory Lover*, is truly just another object in the domicile where she belongs: "she was part of the splendor of [her brother's] house" (41).

The narrator of "Lady Ferry" muses: "One often hears of the

influence of climate upon character; there is a strong influence of place; and the inanimate things which surround us indoors and out make us follow out in our lives their own silent characteristics" (*OF*, 188). As objects possessed by men in their respective houses, the aristocratic women come to value the same. Life is inanimate; it is defined by articles arranged in neat, orderly patterns. These women make connections more so with things than with people. In the prior discussion of *Deephaven*, Mrs. Kew describes Miss Brandon's strength as "the power of china." This link between a woman and her dishes is repeated. While the Dulham Ladies "clung to their mother's wedding china and other inheritances" with "desperate affection" (*TN*, 32), Madame Jaffrey, Esther's mother, is directly compared to her porcelain. Old now, she exists "like a piece of her own frail china" (*KF*, 229).

Taking good care of these precious possessions is of primary importance. Even after Esther Jaffrey admits that her family has lost its pride and honor (since it has lost its wealth), she is still "careful to follow all her time-honored customs of care taking" (281). The Jaffreys' tea urn (which is about as alive as the Jaffreys) feels secure in its belief that "its owners were capable of starving before their empty plates rather than sell it to a stranger" (252). With Ann Ball, "a princess among housekeepers," it is her new cooking stove that is "the pride of [her] heart" in her home, which resembles a "museum" (*SW*, 161, 162). Miss Prince also lives in more of a museum than a home, for she never parts with furniture for new fads. In fact, she is proud of all of the house's contents; she has schooled her staff well in the care of these items; and, if her "grandmother could return to Dunport from another world, she would hardly believe that she had left her earthly home for a day, it presented so nearly the same appearance" (*CD*, 200). Miss Prince is so busy with keeping her house in order that she barely has time to see her friends, but finally, she has a free evening (202). Nothing much changes. She and Mrs. Fraley, one of her earliest friends, discuss at length "the damage and discomfort inflicted by masons, and the general havoc which follows a small piece of fallen ceiling" (202). Miss Prince's frequent concern with her estranged niece often seems more a question of who will get her house and furnishings when she dies rather than a question of retrieving a lost relationship. Lady Ferry is equally preoccupied with furnishings. Even though she is quite mad, she can perceive that her room is untidy and apologizes to her little visitor, Marcia, for the disorderly contents. Lady Ferry also plans the semantics of her own wake; she arranges the chairs in her room, leaving a space in the middle for the coffin.

When the rules governing proper behavior are examined, they are no less trivial than the rules governing the proper objects to have and the proper care to be given to those articles. The social concerns of the aristocratic women in Jewett pertain to the superficial, to the appearance and not to the substance of life. The women's realm consists of preserving manners and practicing graciousness, all involving the maintenance of aristocratic self-importance. Social customs are Mrs. Fraley's reason for living: "Mrs. Fraley was leaving this world reluctantly; she had been well fitted by nature for social preeminence, and had never been half satisfied with the opportunities provided for the exercise of her powers" (CD, 273). Harriet Pyne is not as enthusiastic about her "sober customs" (QT, 102), but she is just as demanding. Insensitive to her new, young maidservant's pain in her inability to grasp the proper execution of her duties, Miss Pyne displays only annoyance with Martha's clumsy manner. Miss Dane and Mrs. Graham are more tolerant of young women of their own class learning proper social behavior, but they are no less diligent. Horatia Dane downplays her cousin Nelly's vivacious and unfettered manner to concentrate on her practical skill with a needle and her "sensible and economical and busy" (OF, 10) attributes. Nelly is shrewd enough to conceal behavior that would not be approved: "She instinctively avoided all that would shock the grave dignity and old-school ideas of Miss Dane . . ." (10). Since Nan, on the other hand, conceals nothing, Mrs. Graham responds by taking upon herself the responsibility to educate this young lady to fit her social sphere. Interestingly, Mrs. Graham describes society to Dr. Leslie in business terms: "'Society is a sort of close corporation, and we must know its watchwords, and keep an interest in its interests and affairs'" (*CD*, 134). Social behavior merely echoes male business behavior, concentrating on a smooth veneer to hide the competitive nature of the dealings.

Class is everything; guarding the structure is imperative. More and more it becomes clear in these stories that it is not human beings who are important, especially women. "Blood will tell" (221) encapsulates Miss Prince's view of people, and these people of blood must act accordingly. While Harriet Pyne's kind-hearted niece sees fit to invite the maidservant Martha to her wedding, Miss Pyne supersedes this inappropriate invitation and refuses to let Martha attend. In *A Marsh Island*, Mrs. Winchester is even more distraught that her own nephew might step out of his social circles and marry Doris, the farmer's daughter. So, too, there is more than a little consternation among the aristocracy when Esther Jaffrey, in order to keep herself and her brother from starving, abandons her status and begins to run a small notions shop within the grandeur of her grandfather's office where he made his now defunct fortune. Society does make an exception for Esther, however, when it perceives that she is "more friendly and sympathetic than ever" and has "not ceased to be a lady" (*KF*, 242). In addition, Esther's friends primarily blame Mary Destin, who sold her shop's contents to Esther and moved to greater prospects out West: "She ought to have remained in her own lot and place" (239). Esther, too, is class conscious. Even when she has suffered society's censure for not following its rules of behavior, one reason she objects to her brother's getting involved with a country girl is due to the fact that the young woman does not belong to Grafton society.

There is a pathetic aspect to the value systems inculcated by these women. When Miss Chauncey, "proud as Lucifer" (D, 153), displays her aristocratic trappings and uses "long words and ceremonious phrases" (154), the reader pities her for the disparity between the dignity of her words and her actual degraded circumstances. Jewett's censure cannot be missed in two humorously acrid stories that expose the emptiness, the lack of all reason, all warmth, and, ultimately, all human connection in these social patterns. Richard Cary finds Jewett gives uncharacteristic "sly, icy gibes" (Introduction to *Deephaven*, 22) in "The Dulham Ladies," while in "The Guests of Mrs. Timms," she writes her "most intricate and expert social comedy," wherein she "bites with acid sharpness into the encrusted core of social hierarchy and usage" (22). The Dulham Ladies believe it is their responsibility to elevate society, and they feel they will when they arrive back in their small town with false bangs purchased in the city to hide their quickly disappearing hair. Yet with all of their aristocratic pride, they possess only "pathetic dignity" (*TN*, 45) in their outdated fashions and pretentious ways.

In "The Guests of Mrs. Timms," Jewett presents a character, not pathetic, but vituperative. Mrs. Flagg is a mass of superficial trappings. In her there is nothing but hypocrisy below the level of social conventions. With veiled sarcasm, Flagg admonishes her friend, Miss Pickett, for taking the flowers without first asking permission: "'Oh, yes, gather all you want'" (*LN*, 214). Pickett is similarly nondimensional, without the arrogant, cruel streak to be found in Mrs. Flagg: "She was a straight, flat little person, as if, when not in use, she kept herself, silk dress and all, between the leaves of a book" (218). Flagg and Pickett lustily ridicule a woman in their coach who arrives at her destination unknown. Miss Pickett becomes annoyed with the coachman for driving off too quickly, preventing her from enjoying the scene. She, together with her sidekick Mrs. Flagg, relishes the misfortune of another who does not practice the proper social protocol: " 'T was pushin' an acquaintance most too far, wa'n't it?' agreed Miss Pickett. 'There, 't will be somethin' laughable to tell Mis' Timms. I never see anything more divertin' " (227). What Pickett and Flagg don't know is that this scene prefigures their own reception by Mrs. Timms, who far exceeds them in cold, formal politeness. While Pickett and Flagg are interested in impressing people and buttressing their own sense of self-importance with visits to the wealthier Mrs. Timms, Mrs. Timms, a woman of comparable concerns, recognizes her aristocratic stance far outweighs theirs and will have nothing to do with them.

The real irony in the behavior of the women in this story, Flagg, Pickett and Timms, is that they are ardent churchgoers. In fact, Flagg receives her supposed invitation from Mrs. Timms when they meet at a religious conference. While Flagg and Pickett are in Mrs. Timms's dark parlor, she is discussing last Sunday's sermon on "faith and good works" (233); however, it is a sermon she has heard secondhand, for she was too tired from the conference to attend the services. While critics have cited the absence of formal religion in Jewett's works, there is an overabundance of its presence in her stories about aristocratic women. She does not represent here her dominant mode of a nurturing religion fostered by a woman's community. Formal religion is generally just another hallmark of the patriarchal system, wherein women are reinforced in such tenets as "Cleanliness is next to godliness" and "Women, obey your husbands." It seems to serve this purpose in Jewett's stories of upper-class women. The women in these stories belong to an institutionalized religion that fosters neither spiritual growth nor social concern. It is a hollow belief system that mirrors the superficiality of Victorian industrial concerns. The aristocrats who attend the services are as empty as the religion they themselves have devised. When Kate Lancaster and Helen Denis attend church, they notice that "the Deephaven aristocracy came with stately step up the aisle; this was all the chance there was for displaying their unquestioned dignity in public" (71–72). Miss Prince also takes Nan Prince to services for the purpose of showing her off. Miss Chauncey, faithful all her life to going to church and donating as much money as possible considering her circumstances, reads with fervor the biblical passage " 'In my Father's house are many mansions; if it were not so, I would have told you' " (D, 157). Miss Chauncey has translated her value system into religious terminology. She may actually believe that if she leads a good life, she will be given a genuine mansion in heaven to replace the one that has fallen to ruin in Deephaven. Mr. Lorimer, the minister, commends Miss Chauncey after her death. Instead of realizing her spiritual deficit, he finds her "steadfast in her simple faith," "uncomplaining," and consistent with her donations of money to the church.

Other aristocratic women, rather than using religion to their own self-seeking ends, are merely hemmed in by it. For Miss Esther Jaffrey, going to services means listening to her brother Leonard, who once studied for the ministry, quibbling over the text of the sermon with the minister. Miss Pyne, on the other hand, belongs to the old New England of "the most limited interpretation of the word 'evangelical,' and the pettiest indifference to large things" (QT, 103). She prefers formalism to the "outbreak of a desire for larger religious freedom" (103).

Miss Ball, Miss Dane, and Mistress Sydenham are also regular participants in their congregations. The Dulham Ladies' father was a minister, and they continue to be very active in the church after his death. All of these women have been thwarted. Jewett confirms that belonging to institutionalized religion, patriarchal in nature, fosters this condition.

After being indoctrinated in their homes, in their social circles, and in their churches, the aristocratic women become frozen in time amid the mass of rules and regulations. The mad or hallucinating women, Miss Chauncey, Lady Ferry, and the Mistress of Sydenham spend most of their days actually living in the past where they possessed their youth and beauty. Caught up in the whirlwind of the material glory around them, they believed that life had some glamorous purpose. They were blind to the roles afforded them in this affluent society. Miss Chauncey speaks glowingly of her "coming out party." Kate and Helen have been advised by Miss Carew to ask about Miss Chauncey's schooldays, for "'she nearly always spoke of that time . . .'" (D, 155). Elegant and dignified, Mistress Sydenham rides about with "a strange irrelevancy of graciousness" to rule her plantation home, which is no more. Breaking in upon Lady Ferry's reveries, Marcia has to wait a long time for Lady Ferry to answer questions. Lady Ferry is so old, she feels she has been cursed with an "endless life." Yet these three women all lead endless lives in which the scenes never change and the cast of characters never varies and the actions are identical. While the Dulham Ladies are not quite as out of touch with reality as these three women, they, too, hallucinate, but in present surroundings. They are "amazingly slow to suspect that they were not as young as they used to be" (TN, 35). Believing she is as subject as ever to the glances of admiring men, Lucinda Dobin feels "quite coy and embarrassed" (202) by the stare of a plaster of paris head.

Most of these women are not hallucinating but are inept at any change in thought or behavior. In A Country Doctor, Miss Prince, Mrs. Fraley, and, initially, even Nan's friend Mrs. Graham are horrified by Nan's desire to be a doctor, simply because she is a woman. Her immense capability for this profession is never so much as entertained by Miss Prince and Mrs. Fraley. Although Mrs. Graham eventually endorses Nan's choice, she spends more time trying to school her in the ways of society than to encourage her to become a doctor.

Esther Jaffrey is nearly literally frozen because she will not ask for help or make her brother work while they are in pinched circumstances. Yet Esther is somewhat culpable in her poverty-ridden situation, for she maintains as best she can the standards she was taught instead of breaking free from the inane structure: "If she had been the son! she often said to herself with a surging thrill of pride and daring. If she had been the son how she could work and win her way, and not be the least of those who had borne the Jaffrey name unsullied! But she was only a woman, and . . . could not lead public opinion in unfeminine directions; she was not a social reformer but fiercely conservative at heart." (*KF*, 232).

Just as Esther must keep her fantasy about her learned brother, Horatia Dane must keep her fantasy about her lost lover. Both their lives have centered on the revering of these two men. While it would break Esther's heart to see her brother "go into housekeeping" (251), she at least comes to realize he has not been worth her sacrifice. Horatia differs in that she cannot accept the dissolution of the vision she had of her lover. Believing him to have died at sea, she ages quickly once she sees that he is a drunken beggar who has married another woman whom he has also deserted. (He had set sail, ironically, on the *Chevalier*.) Instead of despising him, she faints and later "wondered if she ought to have let him go away, and so have lost sight of him . . ." (*OF*, 39). Miss Dane, "who clung the more fondly to youth as she left it farther behind" (27), can't acknowledge that she has wasted her whole life in mourning a worthless man. This host of aristocratic women all fit the description of Miss Pyne who at thirty-five is "more reluctant than her mother to face an unforeseen occasion, certainly more than her grandmother" (*QT*, 102). The ability to change decreases steadily the more these women practice the codes provided for them. The verdict for Miss Harriet Pyne is the same for all the others: "She had long ago made all her decisions, and settled all necessary questions; her scheme of life was as faultless as the miniature landscape of a Japanese garden, and as easily kept in order. The only important change she would ever be capable of making was the final change to another and a better world; and for that nature itself would gently provide, and her own innocent life" (120).

Not only are Jewett's aristocratic women frozen in time; they have been isolated in the past as well as in the present from real relationships based on human connection. Unlike the army of Jewett's strong, responsive women of clear sight and profound emotion, these aristocrats exist on the fringes of human warmth. Their topics of concern have been so superficial and their lives so programmed that they are pathetically lonely, out of tune with their own needs and those of others. Caged, most of these women are cold and severe. Horatia Dane utters "rare words of approval" (OF, 9–10). Ann Ball is grim and stern, possessing the emotional level of "a chilled lava bed" (SW, 161). A few have been driven out of their minds. Miss Chauncey, Lady Ferry, and Mistress Sydenham are all compared to ghosts. They have lost the power to touch with their bodies, to connect with the human spirit—the ultimate "angels in the house." These aristocratic women have been deprived, most of all, of sustaining friendships with women, the bulwark of Jewett's works.

The visits of one woman to another, which provide the framework for many of Jewett's writings, never result in these stories in any real communication of thoughts and feelings, if the visits occur at all. Pickett and Flagg's friendship survives purely within a social context, and their visit to Mrs. Timms is a total sham. Mrs. Winchester in A Marsh Island is lonely for her nephew's companionship while she is entertaining a houseful of people. Miss Fraley and Miss Prince spend their time together discussing problems of running their respective establishments. Indeed, the narrator records that "even [Miss Prince's] best friends did not know how lonely her life had seemed to her . . ." (CD, 197). Esther Jaffrey is all alone now that her mother has

died. The friends of the Misses Dobin, Ann Ball, and Harriet
Pyne never appear in the text. Although Harriet's cousin Helena
visits her when she is a young girl, Helena doesn't return until
she is an old woman. Horatia Dane is lucky because her young
cousin, Nelly, will visit her often. Yet Horatia never confides the
incessant thought of her lost lover to Nelly. Except for Dr.
Leslie and Nan Prince, Mrs. Graham has few visitors and no
women peers. Mistress Sydenham has only her black servant to
take care of her, while Lady Ferry is so removed from reality, she
barely talks to anyone at all. Her loneliness, however, is apparent when she cries after having been kissed by little Marcia.
The word "lonely," in one form or another, is the singlemost
word repeated contextually to apply to these women.

Jewett does provide a foil to the aristocratic woman in each of
her stories about them. To show the possibility of a fuller life,
another woman appears who displays real emotion, real spirit.
The woman is not necessarily totally unfettered, but she is
basically happy and capable. In three of the stories, a young
aristocratic woman is the foil. This does not necessarily mean
she will succeed where the older aristocrats have failed, but she
at least commands the possibility to live differently. Nan in *A
Country Doctor* acts as a contrast to Mrs. Fraley and Eunice
Fraley, Mrs. Graham, and her aunt, Miss Prince. Nan possesses
"the same strength of will and of determination" (236) as her
aunt, "but Miss Prince seemed to have neither inherited nor
acquired any high aims or any especial and fruitful single-heart-
edness, so her gifts of persistence and self-confidence had
ranked themselves for the defense of a comparatively unimportant and commonplace existence" (236–37). Nan, of course,
uses her qualities to the best advantage in the practice of medicine. Nelly in "A Lost Lover" and Helena in "Martha's Lady"
will marry, unlike their elder cousins, Horatia Dane and Harriet Pyne. Whether their lives turn out qualitatively better is not
indicated by Jewett. Since Nelly and Helena choose to marry

within the present aristocratic structure, it is doubtful they will fare well. In fact, when Helena arrives as an old woman to visit Harriet, she is bent from many sorrows. Marcia, only a child when she met Lady Ferry, is unmarried when she visits Lady Ferry's grave as an adult, but again, what she has done with her own life is not mentioned. At the very least, Jewett shows that women are not naturally "little ladies," they are trained to be so. A free nature can break through the system of roles, if the woman so chooses.

Servants also fare much better than their mistresses. Hetty in "The Dulham Ladies," Melissa in "A Lost Lover," and Martha in "Martha's Lady" all function better than the ones who have had to follow such a strict code of behavior with so few choices. Hetty can see the reality around her. Although she does not have the money of the Misses Dobin, she is no fool. She is the one in control in this story: "Old Hetty Downs, their faithful maid-servant and protector, looked after them in affectionate foreboding. 'Dear sakes, what devil's wiles may be played on them blessed innocents afore they're safe home again?'" (*TN*, 42). Melissa, unlike her mistress Horatia, does not have any romantic notions. She tells Nelly that she wouldn't marry : "'I ain't going to give up a certainty for an uncertainty,—that's what *I* always tell 'em . . .'" (*OF*, 15). At the end of the story the narrator confirms that Melissa will always be the same "with a quaintness and freshness and toughness like a cedar-tree, to the end of her days" (40–41). Martha is not feisty like Hetty or Melissa, but she is tenacious. She loves Harriet Pyne's niece Helena over time and distance. Helena, kind and caring, had taken the time to show Martha how her aunt wanted things done. Helena had believed in Martha. Yet Martha's affection for Helena goes unnoticed by Harriet Pyne, who cannot identify the strength of an emotion she cannot feel.

In "The Guests of Mrs. Timms," the cold, manipulating exteriors of Mrs. Flagg, Mrs. Timms, and, to some extent, Miss

Pickett are contrasted by two sources. Mrs. Beckett is diametrically opposed to Mrs. Timms, for she welcomes hospitably the woman whom she cannot even remember, let alone remember inviting to her home. Indeed, Mrs. Beckett sends for the woman's extra trunk so she can make an extended visit. Miss Pickett and Mrs. Flagg are annoyed and jealous that this woman has done so much better than they. Jewett artfully avoids giving the woman visitor a name, for status is unimportant. Nancy Fell in Mrs. Timms's town affords another counterpoint to the aristocrats. She is of a lower class, but Flagg and Pickett agree to visit her, especially after they have been given nothing to eat at Mrs. Timms's. Nancy is thrilled and serves up quite a feast. Pickett admits that she had not bothered much with Nancy Fell when she lived in her town because Nancy had "lived in a poor part of town, and so been occupied with a different kind of people . . ." (LN, 229).

There is evidence of only two aristocratic women who find more satisfying ways to live their lives. Yet the salvation is incomplete. Esther Jaffrey's decision to run her notions shop, even after her brother has been appointed as the town's head librarian and forbids her to continue, is a minimal victory. Esther has only traded polished silver and flower arrangements for buttons and threads. But her heroism in making a decision on her own that flaunts custom is commendable, as is her refusal to be taken care of by her brother after his appointment. In "Miss Sydney's Flowers," the main character stops looking out of her window and goes outside to help the poor and destitute. While Miss Sydney, who had been selfish and lonely, is now connected to other human beings, she still has no close friendships with her peers. Jewett time and again in her own life and through her writing postulates that each person has a duty that he or she must discharge, but this duty must be self-satisfying as well. Miss Sydney has not really changed her role as an aristocratic woman; she is still too much the sacrificial lamb. The story is a touch too sentimental. Miss Sydney is doing for others, but who is she, and what is she doing for herself? Jewett's strong women have minds and hearts of their own. They have been generous in their estimation of themselves, and that generosity naturally spills over.

None of the aristocratic women Jewett portrays has lived life on her own terms. They have been forced to follow the empty customs that have had as their basis the false value system of status and wealth. Jewett moves from aggregation to communication, from the exterior to the interior, from isolation to bonding. Nan Prince, Jewett's mirror image, has succeeded. Miss Sydney and Miss Jaffrey have made some strides. The rest of these women have been trammeled and subsequently frozen in this diminished state. It will be for other Jewett women to make the break total, an entire host of them.

6

Romance

Sarah Orne Jewett could not write a story about romance, the so-called love story. She had too much integrity. Jewett rejected romance with men for herself, and she wrote of the need for her women characters to act similarly to avoid obliteration. Romance presupposes man's superiority and woman's inferiority. Romance is about power, not love. In attempting to find a definition for *romantic* love (emphasis mine), that which supposedly serves as the basis of heterosexual relationships, Simone de Beauvoir quotes Nietzsche:

> The single word love in fact signifies two different things for man and woman. What woman understands by love is clear enough: it is not only devotion, it is a total gift of body and soul, without reservation, without regard for anything whatever. This unconditional nature of her love is what makes it a *faith*, the only one she has. As for man, if he loves a woman, what he *wants* is that love from her; he is in consequence far from postulating the same sentiment for himself as for woman; if there should be men who also felt that desire for complete abandonment, upon my word, they would not be men. (642)

To participate in romance, therefore, the man must want to possess, and the woman, to be possessed. The man is initially attracted to the woman's beauty and charm, superficial entities to be sure. Yet the most important aspect of her desirability is her capacity to serve him. The man will become her whole life, her raison d'être. This presupposes that woman herself believes she is inferior, for she must define herself through her relationship with the man whom she feels is her superior. Simone de Beauvoir concludes that woman wants to respond to her lover's demands so she can feel necessary, so she can share in his intrinsic worth, something she does not have (650). The result is that "there is no other way out for her than to lose herself, body and soul, in him who is represented to her as the absolute, as the essential" (643).

Simone de Beauvoir goes on to explain that it is a tempting situation for a woman who feels intrinsically dependent, for "she is told that she has only to let herself slide and she will attain paradises of enchantment" (645). She will be protected again as a child. But, in return, she gives devotion, not love, in a dream that is "a dream of annihilation" (646). She has erased herself for someone who will not return this totality of surrender. De Beauvoir quotes Byron: "Man's love is of man's life a thing apart; / 'Tis woman's whole existence" (642). Woman has reduced herself to a cipher for someone whom she is doomed to find out is not that superior, neither God nor essence. She has created a mirage; but reduced to nothing, she is left with no resources to lift herself out of this relationship. The romantic has truly come to mean its dictionary definition—"having no basis in fact: IMAGINARY"; but it has been a deadly experience.

The debilitating aspect of romance for women was not a subject alien to Jewett's literary contemporaries. Isabel Archer, the heroine of Henry James's *The Portrait of a Lady*, becomes a victim of romance, but she is smart enough not to repeat the error. She learns not to trade one possessor for another. Just as her husband, Gilbert Osmond, reveals himself to be cold and controlling, Isabel perceives that Caspar Goodwood would ultimately be caring and controlling. Within the context of this story, the wisdom of the words of Kate Chopin's "The Story of an Hour" becomes apparent. After the death of her husband, Mrs. Mallard suddenly intuits: "There would be no one to live for her during those coming years; she would live for herself. There would be no powerful will bending hers in that blind persistence with which men and women believe they have a right to impose a private will upon a fellow-creature. A kind intention or a cruel intention made the act seem no less a crime as she looked upon it in that brief moment of illumination" (199). Isabel Archer knows the folly of romance. No man can save her and protect her. Only she can do that for herself. To be with Caspar Goodwood would be annihilation. His embrace is described in terms of drowning:

> The world, in truth, had never seemed so large; it seemed to open out, all round her, to take the form of a mighty sea, where she floated in fathomless waters. She had wanted help, and here was help; it had come in a rushing torrent. I know not whether she believed everything that he said; but she believed that to let him take her in his arms would be the next best thing to dying. This belief, for a moment, was a kind of rapture, in which she felt herself sinking and sinking. In the movement she seemed to beat with her feet, in order to catch herself, to feel something to rest on. . . . "Do me the greatest kindness of all," she said, "I beseech you to go away!" (547)

For Goodwood to take over her life would result in a death-in-life, a temptingly peaceful thought, but the antithesis of salvation. To live in antipathy with her husband will at least remove Isabel from his influence. She will not be free, but she will have created a separate space for herself. Isabel will refuse to melt into the person of a man.

Like James and Chopin, Jewett was a realist. There is no

evidence that she seriously entertained the idea of a heterosexual love affair for herself. When John Greenleaf Whittier asked her if she had ever been in love, without reservation she replied no. She explained she was more in need of a wife than a husband (Matthiessen, 72). Jewett seemed incapable of perceiving herself as an inferior in any dimension. No one would take care of her; she could amply give direction to her own life. Jewett had a goal to achieve; serving a man was not on her agenda. Repeatedly, Jewett wrote of the need to stand on one's own feet, the need to reject the romance that reduces woman to a nonentity.

In *A Country Doctor*, Jewett, attempting to ameliorate both sides of the woman's place issue, insisted that Nan was unusual and had a God-given duty to perform; she was not like other women. In the text, Jewett agreed that most women's place was in the home, but that there were exceptions like Nan. However, Jewett could not buy her own script. When she sincerely endeavored to write the neoromantic historical novel, a form that rose with the success of *Lorna Doone* in 1869 and flourished in the 1890s (Cary, *Jewett*, 152), she simply could not. Upon reading *The Tory Lover*, Henry James pleaded with Jewett to abjure the romance: "Go back to the dear Country of the Pointed Firs, *come* back to the palpable present *intimate* that throbs responsive, and that wants, misses, needs you, God knows, and suffers woefully in your absence" (Bishop, 264). In her interior, Jewett must have realized that the romance was neither intimate nor real.

In addition to James's criticism of the lack of content in *The Tory Lover*, many critics have felt that Jewett just could not write traditional plot. Elizabeth Ammons in "Going in Circles: The Female Geography of *Jewett's Country of the Pointed Firs*" explains that Jewett did not usually employ the traditional plot devised by men, because traditional plot reflects a male approach to life, one of linear action or conquest. Jewett writes from a woman's perspective of experience, which is relational rather than competitive. Consequently, Jewett's relational view of living is diametrically opposed to the romantic, another type of conquest between the sexes, another power play in which the man is the master.

In *A Tory Lover*, there is both the romance and the male linear plot. Richard Cary cites the book as the worst Jewett wrote (*Jewett*, 152). While the heroine, Mary Hamilton, possesses the intelligence to think, the athletic ability to be a good horsewoman, and the strength of character to make decisions, all qualities markedly different from the remainder of the women who make slight appearances in the novel, she is also stereotypical. She has "beauty" and "charm" (*TL*, 333). And when she is with her lover, Roger Wallingford, she loses her "usual steadiness," cannot speak, and "tremble[s] with fright and passion" (37). Near the end of her quest, when Mary is about to find the missing Roger, "there was a tumult in her breast, a sense of some great happiness that was very near to her; it was like some magnet that worked upon her very heart itself, and set her whole frame to quivering" (391). A total loss of control is a more apt description of her feelings. A total loss of self is an apt description of the plot. Mary Hamilton has spent most of her time in this book trying to exonerate Roger Wallingford from the charge of treason in America and to free him from captivity in England. Unlike most Jewett stories where women occupy center stage, Mary shares hers with Roger. Much of the novel tells of male conquest of the Americans over the English and of Roger over Mary. Both the Americans and Roger win. The ending of the novel and the language throughout have an uncanny similarity to a Barbara Cartland romance. Again, Mary "could not speak; she was too happy and too thankful. All her own great love and perfect happiness were shining in her face" (404–5). Roger is at no loss for words, and fortunately for him, he, unlike Mary, has a dual purpose in life. Roger expounds: "'I am alive to love you, and to serve my country to my life's end'" (404). "Hand in hand" (405), they rise and step ashore.

"A War Debt"—another romance with a historical framework, the postbellum South—employs even more standard romantic jargon. While Tom Burton, "our hero" (*LN*, 74), is
"read[ing] [the Virginia lady's] unconscious face as if it were a
romance" (73), their eyes meet: "she glanced up suddenly and
held his eyes with hers for one revealing moment. There was no
surprise in the look, but a confession of pathos, a recognition of
sympathy, which made even a stranger feel that he had the in-
most secret of her heart" (74). It is surprising that Tom Burton
feels he is sensitive enough to read a person's heart, since he has
started his evaluation of Miss Bellamy by comparing her to an
unconscious animal: "There was something so high-bred and
elegant in her bearing. . . . The eager talk of the coming races,
of the untried thoroughbreds . . . made more distinct this young
Virginia lady's own look of high breeding . . ." (73). Incidentally,
this Virginia lady is never given a first name and never plays any
part in her fate. Obviously, Burton's attraction for her is sufficient; as a woman, her wishes will automatically coincide with
his. And so the story ends with the usual fairy-tale "happily ever
after" following a valiant rescue: "This was the way that, many
years ago, a Northerner found his love, a poor but noble lady in
the South, and Fortune smiled again upon the ruined house of
Fairford" (96).

While *The Story of the Normans* is more of a history than a
romance, it shares a common basis with both *The Tory Lover* and
"A War Debt." All three stories exhibit one of Jewett's few preju-
dices, her racial bias for the Norman race, the superior race
from which she felt she herself descended. In *The Story of the
Normans*, Jewett occasionally utters statements favoring women
for their intelligence. She tells of Matilda, who ruled "wisely
and ably" (321) during her husband's absence; she recounts how
the men "paid great deference to the instinctive opinions of
women" (326). Nevertheless, in this male script, which sub-
scribes to the conquest of people and their land, Jewett cannot

be herself. Instead, it is far more likely to see a "fair damsel" (160), a wife whose real name is forgotten in favor of her nickname, which means "puppet" or "little doll" (60), women skilled in needlework (116), women who cry as their men go off to adventure (136), and, of course, an "uncomplaining and patient" (145) wife. With the given script, the women characters have no life. Sarah Orne Jewett's writing fails when she reflects society's norms that enslave women. Yet these are the only three pieces in all nineteen of her published volumes that show her attempt at historical fiction. It is also clear that Jewett tries to write them to express her pride in her Norman ancestry.

When Jewett drops the historical framework, the male script, it is impossible for her to write approvingly of romance. As early as *Deephaven*, she shuns the crippling situation. When Kate and Helen find Miss Brandon's little package of love letters tied with "pale," "tired" blue ribbon, Kate says, " 'Yet here's her romance, after all' " (49). The girls set them aside without ever reading them. What they do read instead are the letters tied with black ribbon, suggesting true loss, the letters expressing a mutual, loving relationship between Miss Brandon and her girlhood friend, Dolly. Seven years later, in *A Country Doctor*, Jewett supplies the reason why the young women would not even read the love letters; it is the same fear that Nan has when she becomes involved with George Gerry: "So this was love at last, this fear, this change, this strange relation to another soul. Who could stand now at her right hand and give her grace to hold fast the truth that her soul must ever be her own?" (304).

Jewett underscores the absurdity of such a power play in her May/December romances by entertaining a supercilious and ridiculous portrayal of the older man who chooses a young, pretty girl for his mate so he can shape her soul in his own image. The young girl will adore the older, seemingly wiser man, making him the center of her world. She will be too naive to see the lies lurking below the surface of the romnce. (At least this is the script the male characters would like to write.) Captain Ball, in "The Taking of Captain Ball," is a bit chagrined when his great-niece turns out to be an independent, capable woman of his own age. Although he is much better off with Miss French as she is, Captain Ball "was both surprised and a little ashamed to discover that something in his heart had suffered disappointment in the matter of his great-niece. He had fancied her a pretty girl in a pink dress, who would make some life in the quiet house, and sit and sing at her sewing by the front window, in all her foolish furbelows, as he came up the street" (*SW*, 196).

Miss Peck, of "Miss Peck's Promotion," who has come to help the minister care for his child and his home after his wife dies, is not Mr. Elbury's type either. Instead of choosing for his mate Miss Eliza Peck, a capable woman who sees Mr. Elbury's faults but likes him anyway, Mr. Elbury marries a pretty young incompetent. Upon bringing his new wife home, "he wore a most sentimental expression, and led a young person by the hand" (*KF*, 198). Shocked and indignant, Miss Peck "threw down the sham temple of Cupid which a faithless god called Propinquity had succeeded in rearing" (199), something Mr. Elbury is incapable of doing. Miss Peck can only pity the "empty-faced, tiresomely pretty girl" (200) who has taken on the difficult task of being "the wife of an indolent preacher in a country town" (200).

Nelly Grant in "A Village Shop" appears equally ignorant of what marriage with Leonard Jaffrey will hold. Her father, John Grant, a wealthy farmer, wants his daughter to be elevated to the status of a lady. That is the reason he wants her to live at the Jaffrey house under the tutelage of Esther Jaffrey. Unfortunately, Nelly finds the aristocracy equally appealing in the figure of Leonard Jaffrey. Jewett parodies the traditional love scene. It is spring. The moon is shining on the fragrant pear blossoms. And Leonard Jaffrey is making a fool of himself: "'To my thought there is no flower so sweet as a youthful face,' said

Mr. Leonard Jaffrey. 'You have made a constant spring in our quiet lives.' And Nelly blushed as bright as any rose of the June for which she was waiting" (273). Nelly swallows the romance and marries Leonard, but not before his sister Esther brings the situation into the cold light of realism. While Leonard is spouting aphorisms—"'We are only as old as our hearts are'" (282)—Esther discerns only the voice of a whimpering boy. Too ridiculous to even discuss, Esther's only reply is: "'Be still, Leonard'" (283).

For the women who believe in romance, Jewett laments the waste of their human energy. In "Mère Pochette," old Manon muses, "More than one silly girl had pined away and faded out of this world like the April snow-drifts—for nothing but love's sake . . ." (*KF*, 330). As a young woman, Miss Melinda Ryder of "The Mate of the Daylight" loses her lover at sea a few weeks before they are to be married. She does not pine away, but she might as well have. Miss Ryder has spent her whole lonely life in mourning. During the summer, she periodically visits the grave site, where she feels "a widow indeed" (*MD*, 28). The narrator tells Miss Ryder's pathetic story: "She had never replaced him in her affection; her love and loyalty grew stronger and stronger instead of fading away" (28). Having helped the family pick out the tombstone, Melinda chooses the figure of a mourner beneath a willow tree, with whom she identifies. It is a good choice, for her life has been chiseled shallowly by an outsider. Melinda ironically muses that "it was a matter of great sorrow to her that it would be out of the question for her to be buried at the side of this untenanted grave" (29), for she has figuratively never moved from the spot. That the grave is untenanted makes the romantic illusion complete.

The main storyline in "The Mate of the Daylight" does not have to do with Miss Ryder, but with her niece, Susan, and Susan's lover, Dan. Miss Ryder's story serves as an odd parallel to this story of young love trying to overcome obstacles. Jewett appears to be warning Susan, who will not heed the advice, that it is foolish for women to allow their lives to be spent for men—one dead and one a potential parasite. Although Dan, at the end of the story, has been made the captain of the *Daylight* through a stroke of luck, he would have married Susan even though he had no job. Dan has been disposed to make good use of Susan's father's assets: "Dan would have willingly taken up his residence in the home of Susan's childhood. He meant to settle down into the business and idleness of fishing and coasting, and of doing great things with Captain Joe's savings by and by, when he had the opportunity" (27).

"Marsh Rosemary" demonstrates the aftermath of marrying a good-for-nothing parasite. Miss Ann Floyd has led an emotionally impoverished life caught up in the realm of romantic illusion: "She had waited all her days for this joy of having a lover" (*TN* 111). Her hopes lie in Jerry Lane; her reaction to him is purely adolescent. Jewett alerts us to all the romantic trappings that Ann Floyd has never set aside: "You would think she had done with youth and with love affairs, yet you might as well expect the ancient cherry-tree in the corner of her yard to cease adventuring its white blossoms when the May sun shone!" (104). Miss Floyd speaks to Jerry like "Juliet from her balcony" (105), and Jerry, not in the least drawn into the scenario, finds her romantic trappings comical: "she looked so simple and so frankly sentimental, there was such an incongruous coyness added to her usually straightforward, angular appearance, that his instinctive laughter nearly got the better of him . . ." (110). Jerry Lane is a shiftless opportunist, but Ann Floyd, living in her illusionary world, sees no obstacles. Jerry is much younger than Ann; he has a bad reputation. But love is truly blind, and Ann, at her age and with her values, is desperate. Even after they marry and Jerry does nothing to conceal his nature, one thought of his tender kisses, and Ann forgives all. When he is lost at sea, Ann ages quickly in yearning for his society. On her way to find out if the gossip is true that Jerry is indeed alive and a bigamist, she still has not learned her lesson. In the presence of some unruly boys, she longs for Jerry's protection. The narrator comments: "she forgot why she sought him, and was eager to shelter herself behind the flimsy bulwark of his manhood" (133). Simone de Beauvoir's prophecy has become a reality; Ann Floyd has finally succeeded in "giving her whole self in unselfish, enthusiastic, patient devotion . . ." (133). Unfortunately, Ann has wasted her "hoarded affection" (124) on an "idol [which] had turned to clay" (136). While Jewett's sympathies are with Ann Floyd, whom she compares to the small yet stalwart flower the marsh rosemary, it is equally clear that Jewett is saddened by a woman who has never grown out of her need for romantic love, a woman who has never developed a sense of her own self.

In "The Only Rose," a story much lighter in tone, Mrs. Bickford's lifelong preoccupation with romance emerges as a simple human foible. Having had three husbands, Mrs. Bickford should be very much in touch with the reality of loving. Her second and third husbands were no Prince Charmings who supplied her every emotional need. Bickford left her well off, but he was dull. Wallis was very entertaining, but his ambitious ideas proved impractical. As Mrs. Bickford feels indebted to Bickford, she feels guilty that she never supported Wallis's fantastic inventions. In making three bouquets for her husbands' graves, Mrs. Bickford is stumped as to who should get the only rose. Her obvious preference is her first husband, for it is with him that she identifies "fallin' in love" (LN, 144). They were married young, and he died of a fever shortly after their marriage. The only reason Mrs. Bickford is able to think of Albert as her "true love" (emphasis mine), the one who should get the symbol of love, the rose, is because he faded as quickly as the flower itself. If Albert had lived, Mrs. Bickford would remember his flaws as she does those of Bickford and Wallis. In addition to Albert's sweet voice and handsome face, Mrs. Bickford would dwell on their poverty and Albert's "hasty temper" (145), items she merely skims over now. Neither is Mrs. Bickford a Cinderella. She is portrayed as fussy and complaining. Jewett gently prods in this story, advocating imperfect relationships for imperfect people. Mrs. Bickford has not wasted her life, but her relationships with her second and third husbands could have been better if she had seen them as people rather than as romantic lovers. She would be better off if she could allow the sunlight and flowers into her home, if she could rid herself of "a contracted and assailed feeling out of doors" after "the shade and shelter of the house" (150)—all perhaps symptomatic of her inability to face the truth about men and marriage.

Melinda Ryder, Ann Floyd, and Mrs. Bickford are all older women whose distorted idea of romance has never been able to run its course. They have misspent their energies on an illusion. Jewett also shows the other end of the spectrum. She presents the young women as they make their choices to squander their affections on the men they believe will save them, the very ones they assume they will delight in serving, body and soul. These portrayals seem the cruelest, for they are depictions of strong, caring women who, rather than developing their own powers, subjugate themselves.

In "Jim's Little Woman," Jewett's title smacks of sarcasm. With continual references to Jim's wife's size and childlikeness, Jewett plays on the male concept of woman as inferior, of woman as a child needing to be protected. Jim's wife does not even have a name until nearly ten pages into the story, but it hardly matters. Jim refers to his wife as his "little woman"; others call her "Jim's little woman"; even the narrator addresses her as "the little woman." When Jim first meets Marty (her name), he thinks she is a child until she gets close to him. As they sit talking, he is described as "an erect, great fellow, with the timid-looking little woman like a child by his side" (NW, 72). Marty is so small, she has to climb up on a box to wash her clothes in the sink. Jim seems to delight in her frailty, and in his possession of that frailty: "What a thing to have a good little warm-hearted wife of his own[,] . . . this little bit of a woman, who almost ran, trying to keep up with his great rolling sea strides along the road" (70–71). She even speaks with a "little voice" (71), and their arguments "ended in Marty's stealing into her husband's lap as he sat by the window in his grandfather's old chair" (79).

It is not solely Jim who keeps reinforcing Marty's smallness. She believes in it herself. Marty is an orphan who never thought anyone would love her (73). She is looking to Jim to fulfill her romantic notion, for "somehow Jim was like the moon to her at first" (104). When he is at sea and she is waiting for him, her good omen that he will return is a romantic dream of white clouds and blue sky with Jim on the deck of the boat, the *Dawn of Day*, "holding his head high" (89). All that is missing is the horse and the armor. The sad fact is that Jim is no hero. He is a cheat with the goods on board the boat; he is surly to the point that the other sailors fear him; and he is a drunk. Marty finds it hard to believe that such a strong man cannot master himself. Ironically, Marty has heard vicious stories about Jim, but choosing to ignore them, she desperately replaces them with a romance. Now she is suffering from abuse and poverty.

Jim has promised to change (something he has done before). After one last voyage, he will settle down. He does not return this time, however, and the report is that he has died of fever in a foreign country. Although Marty is quite strong and very capably supports the family while Jim is gone, she never gives up the hope that he will return. She continues to regard him as her hope even though she is functioning much better without him. The story ends with Jim's return. The sky is blue; the clouds are puffy white; and Jim is home. But she has had this dream before. Nothing is going to change. It is just a romantic fantasy. While Marty has been suffering, Jim has been working on a yacht for several months. He has not even cared enough about Marty to write and tell her that he is alive and will not be home for a while; instead, he has paid someone else to write her the letter that never arrived. Jim's father mistreated and left Jim's mother, who is also described as "little" as well as "sad-faced" (67). Jim's mother ended up crying over her reckless, irresponsible son. There has been a history of mistreatment. Now it is Marty's turn. Although this is supposed to be a "happily ever after" ending, Jewett uncovers a jagged edge. On the last page of the story, as Marty is getting ready to go off with Jim and their children on the yacht, the *Dawn of Day* comes into the harbor. Marty, knowing the drunken revelry that takes place on this vessel, decides not to tell Jim his friends have arrived. Jim may be Marty's "hope," but she can never trust him to control himself, to change, to protect and care for her. Jim is not the answer to a woman's dreams.

A Marsh Island relates another tragic story of the heroine, Doris Owen, a much stronger and more independent figure than Marty. Unlike Marty, Doris does not believe in the lie of the romance; it is just that her options seem limited to two— Dick or Dan. *A Marsh Island* is subtler with its bleak proclamation for Doris's future, for at first glance, it appears Doris has made the right choice. The novel establishes a polarity between the city and the country, between Dick Dale and Dan Lester, who represent, respectively, the two different factions. Ostensibly, Doris has done well to choose Dan Lester, whose tie to nature is Doris's own, while Dick Dale's affiliation is with the superficial wealth and status of the aristocracy. It is also wise for Doris to reject Dick's advances, for the first chapter of this section delineates Dick as one who wants to fashion Doris according to his requirements. However, Dan is equally dangerous to Doris's development. He is not as blatant about his intentions as Dick appears in the story, but he is just as male in his desire to master.

Jewett clearly manifests that Doris has no need for a master.

Doris is in control; she is neither hysterical nor parasitic. Time and again Doris is described as "silent," evidence of her well-developed interior: "The changes and events of life had always come to her naturally, as leaves push out of the bare trees in spring and flowers come into bloom. She did not like to speak her gravest and sweetest thoughts, or of her troubles, either; she was self-contained . . ." (127). Doris wants to remain intact. Her insistent reserve indicates that she does not necessarily need to form an alliance with another; in fact, if such an alliance means she will be obligated to let someone else break into this interior life as if it were his own, the alliance will prove fatal to Doris's growth as an individual. She pities the wild animals in the open as if she were one of them: "The least wild creature could hardly find shelter in all the distance; there was no reserve and no secret; the hills were like the telling of some sad, unwelcome news, in their harsh insistence and persistence" (129).

The insistent, persistent unwelcome news comes to Doris in the form of Dan Lester. He is becoming increasingly intent on routing Doris out into the open. Early in the story, as Dan and Doris are traveling in the wagon, he is described in romantic terms—"her cavalier" (46), tucking the lap robe more closely around her. The connotation is to confine, the true meaning of romance as women know it. What bothers Dan is Doris's total lack of interest in their relationship. It is "Doris Owen's lack of self-consciousness and quiet dignity [that] attracted him" (47). It is the conquest that is important to Dan. Doris is not like other girls, he thinks; in other words, she is not interested in him as other girls are. In fact, Doris's only concern for the moment is keeping her eyes on the road to aid in their journey. Dan muses about Doris in terms of control. He feels he can "claim Doris' companionship on the slightest pretext" (46); he feels certain she will someday realize she cannot get along without him; and he is assured that he is in the position to marry a wife whenever he chooses (46–47). Unfortunately, he doesn't seem to afford Doris much leeway in her future. Mr. Owen, Doris's father, reinforces Dan's wish to control Doris. This is the approved course in the male world. Mr. Owen begins by telling Dan he would like nothing better than for Dan to be the new "master" of his farm since his own son Israel is dead. His advice to Dan is as follows: "'Women's a kind of game: you've got to hunt 'em their own track, an' when you've caught 'em they've got to be tamed some. Strange, ain't it?—they most all on 'em calc'late to git married; and yet it goes sort of against their natur', too, and seems hard to come to, for the most part:' and Mr. Owen shook his head solemnly over this difficult question . . ." (92).

This recurrent comparison of the hunted animal to Doris explains her reluctance to marry Dan. Jewett would hardly agree with Mr. Owen that Doris is a typical woman who cannot make up her mind and needs to be tamed by a man, so Jewett must inadvertently be confirming that marriage is not Doris's preference. It is a bad choice that will result in erasure. Doris is uncomfortable in Dan's presence; she keeps trying to get away from him. She experiences "dread" (49), the "fear of impending danger" (101) that Dan will bring up the question of marriage. When Dan exercises what he feels are his property rights by commanding instead of asking Doris to accompany him: "'You and me'll walk up to the house Doris,' he said, decidedly. 'It's a pretty evening'" (103), Doris rebels. She coldly refuses. Later, she thinks: "Dan had no right yet to be master" (120). Yet. So, mastery is a given. Doris cannot deny it. Even though Doris is afraid she will lose Dan, who has moved to town since she snubbed him, she still does not feel comfortable with his lovemaking upon his return. Wanting to escape, she wishes he would stop his entreaties: "The lover's story did not touch her, after all" (197).

With a bruised ego, Dan stomps off again, this time for good, when he learns Doris has been out alone boating with Dick Dale. This is the turning point. Doris, wrestling between "love and pride" (198), decides in favor of love. The narrator of the story, spokesperson for society, cannot be trusted. When Doris refused to be ordered to take a walk, the narrator termed it "unreasonable anger" (103). Now the narrator explains that Doris has "a nature incomplete without its mate, and incapable of reaching its possible successes alone" (175). This is jargon. Doris's self-sufficiency has been manifest throughout the book, whether in her ability to deal with unruly horses or unruly men. Regardless of the narrator's comment, Doris has made the wrong choice. The first indication is that she loses her self-possessed character. Frantic, she crosses the marshes at night to beg Dan to come home. The second indication is that the natural world, with which she is usually in perfect affinity, turns against her to fight this tragic journey of self-denial. Frost has formed; the creek has risen; and the sand dunes appear to recede as she advances, "planted there as a barrier, raised by enchantment" (270). Doris is finally the hunted wild animal out in the open, devoid of secrets: "Where was the sunshiny yesterday, when she had been secure and peaceful, and almost happy, when one compared those hours with these?" (271). Now Doris will be just like the withered fruit of the isolated apple trees amid the sands, "walled-in and condemned to death" (272).

Doris finds Dan. It is all over; he speaks to her "as if she had been a child" (276): " 'Take right hold of my arm. . . . Come, we'd better go home, Doris . . .' " (276). Doris has felt she had to choose between Dan and Dick. It is unfortunate she was unable to see she would have been better off without either of them. Doris has only believed that she had the right to prolong the inevitable. Again, the narrator spouts the usual verbiage: "Dan was part of herself, and closer than she knew to all her pleasure" (247). Yet the last details of the book provide a negative glimpse of the future. There are two references to the enclosure that awaits Doris. At one point, Doris thinks of how "Dan would like to have the house pleasant" (274). In addition, amid aphorisms of love and happiness, Doris steals up to her room for a moment's quiet. Yet while "the sweet warmth of the sun was pouring in at the window[,] some late flies buzzed at the panes, as if they wished to escape and share the freedom of the bright October day" (279). Among the hollow romance lies Doris, possessed. The story ends in winter.

7

The Standard Marriage

In her depiction of the standard marriage, if the reader glances between the lines, Jewett records the tragedy that befalls two people who believe the romantic picture, marry while young, and strain to remain with each other for the rest of their lives. Although they marry early in their adult lives, the partners appear in the stories at various ages; but they have all been together too long. These are the couples who endeavor to adopt society's criteria for men's and women's roles and, sometimes, society's criteria for success—money and status. Both require superficial responses. It is a one-dimensional terrain devoid of nurturing.

Having described marriage as "a battleground" in *Deephaven* to serve as a foreboding of the impending doom, Jewett seems to have turned aside from any explicit discussion of the subject. While Jewett's warnings continue when she is presenting the incipient youthful marriage, if the couple persists in their design, Jewett abandons them at the altar, since she believes they have abandoned any pattern for growth and discovery. The standard marriage never serves as the foreground of Jewett stories; it is always a dismal backdrop. Jewett tends to view the situation as hopeless while it remains intact; it is not even worth discussing. The men and women of the standard marriage may be rigid or weak, hostile or foolish; but all are uniquely dissatisfied and unhappy. In trying to meet the set criteria for behavior, some viciously prey upon each other. Some merely pursue warped value systems. All these married couples display emotional deficiency of some sort. In her unpublished poem "The New Wife," Jewett evinces with sharp clarity her vision of the standard marriage. Traveling by boat, the new wife is being taken from her home amid promises of wonderful prosperity. They will be "man and wife together / King and queen of farmer folk! but she did not heed. / Looking backward over the waste of water," the new wife realizes instead that "love had set the waters wide. Love had made her lonely"; in effect, "love had shut the door" (MS Am 1743.25 (83), Houghton Library, Harvard University).

Mr. and Mrs. Brown seem to have everything but love in "The Two Browns," one of the few stories in which Jewett portrays a young married couple. The light, comic tone of the text mirrors the relationship of the couple. The Browns suffer from both a warped value system and superficial, static gender roles. Communication is virtually nil. When the story opens, it is snowing and Ben Brown is considering staying at home for the day. Instead of being overjoyed at the prospect of being together, Lucy tries to get rid of him because she has counted on thoroughly cleaning the library and Ben will only get in the way. Ben's thought is that "women were such persistent geese" (WH, 211). Ben leads the rather aimless life of the indolent rich. He has become a fourth-generation lawyer because he has been expected to do so. But there are too many of his kind in his community, so he panders to empty offices and lengthy lunches. Yet when he mentions he would have been a good engineer, Lucy is traumatized. She loves the veneer of being married to a fourth-generation lawyer. From sheer boredom, Ben joins with his crafty schoolmate Chelsea to sell an automatic potato planter under an assumed name. Ben tells Lucy nothing. And Lucy does not feel it is her place to ask: "Lucy was one of those delightful women who rarely demand particular explanations and are contented with general assurances. . . . She had a vague desire to know about her husband's business,—it seemed to interest him so much; but she did not like to expose her total ignorance of affairs, and had a theory, besides, that it was better for Ben to shake off his cares when he was home" (230–31). The undertone of these lines is not that Lucy is "delightful," but that she is a lonely, dissatisfied servant. Ben continues in his dishonest second life to the point of discussing a case with a man who wants to employ him to bring charges against his own successful potato planter company. Mr. Grandison feels the company has stolen his invention. Rather than risk his family's reputation, Ben Brown ends the story by extricating himself from the planter company and confessing the whole affair to Lucy. Still, the real import of the situation is unresolved. While the Browns, "the most prosperous young people in the city" (229), are well endowed with "fortune, position, everything that the social heart desired" (229), they only go through the motions of happiness. Ben and Lucy have not discovered that they are living on the periphery of existence. Although Lucy is shocked when she finds out what Ben has been doing, she quickly explains it away: "She knew little about business, but she believed with all her heart in respecting the traditions of one's family. Though, after all, one Brown had kindly made money for the other" (254).

Seeking money and status as the primary goal in a marriage is the surest means to its demise. In "The Luck of the Bogans," one of Jewett's Irish stories, the wife is the one who pushes the husband into leaving their homeland for America, land of opportunity, and then blaming the idea on the husband as he gets more and more enthusiastic and she becomes more lonely for family and friends. Nevertheless, for both it is a case of greed. The story makes clear that the Bogans have been well-to-do on their little farm and on excellent terms with the squire, who is "generous and kindly" (SW, 91). Indeed, the squire cannot seem to determine why they are leaving. Principally, the Bogans want to make a fortune so their son Dan can be a gentleman.

The Bogans' married life is also not a productive one because they impound themselves and their children with stereotypical conduct. When the Bogans are leaving Ireland, the narrator comments on Mrs. Bogan's typical behavior: "Biddy, like many another woman, had set great changes in motion and then longed to escape from their consequences" (87). Surely, the children recognize their mother's squeamishness about accepting responsibility for her actions. In addition, while "Mike was a kind father to his little daughters," he regards Dan as "all his hope" (95). Even when the parish priest advises school attendance for the oldest girl, both Mike and his wife, Bridget, agree she must stay at home to help take care of the little children. Meanwhile, Dan is very bright in school yet very spoiled as well. Since he has been inflated with a huge male ego, he does whatever he pleases, finally ending up stabbed in a drunken brawl. Dan, the "luck of the Bogans," is dead. Hemmed in by materialistic values and rigid sex roles, the Bogans fail in their quest to succeed.

Mrs. Owen is another married woman who desires to leave her productive farm for the money-making urban centers. Mrs. Owen loves her husband, but "when she married him it was with a firm determination to persuade him to sell the farm before many years, and the marsh island was but a stepping stone for her ambition" (25–26). The Owens' relationship is remote, for Mrs. Owen is "secretly grieved and dissatisfied" (26) as a farmer's wife. Mrs. Owen figures as a moody, depressed person concerned with trivialities. Attempting to relive her ambitions through her daughter, Mrs. Owen hopes for a match between Doris and the rich Dick Dale. The narrator comments: "A woman of more quick sympathies and perceptions would never have duped herself so completely" (125). These are the very qualities Jewett heroines possess, but Mrs. Owen has sold her birthright by aligning herself with society's hunger for social rank and opulence. She has no depth of feeling. When Dan Lester suddenly becomes wealthy, fickle Mrs. Owen switches her allegiance to him instead of Dick. Since Dan has always cared for Doris, he is the proverbial bird in the hand to Mrs. Owen.

In "The Failure of David Berry," Mrs. Berry is another spouse who prefers social advancement more than anything else, including her husband's life. David Berry is quite content to earn his living making shoes in his small shop where his friends can drop in and chat during the day. Mrs. Berry has other plans. Determined to have more, she drags her husband to the city, where he can have a bigger shop, more customers, and a better income. Mrs. Berry is continually upgrading their life with finer clothes, better food, grander tea parties, and the like. David gives way, "childishly delighted when she was pleased with herself and him" (NW, 125). In the process of overextending himself for his wife's sake, unforeseen setbacks prevent Berry from paying his bills, and he loses his shop. Mrs. Berry constantly complains of her altered condition. David Berry receives no warmth and care from her, yet when she is ill, he only opens his shop briefly each day in order to remain home to care for her. Beaten and broken, Berry dies ignominiously.

It seems particularly regrettable to Jewett when the woman, drawn into the acquisitive mentality, becomes its primary proponent. In "A Landless Farmer," Serena Nudd dupes her father into signing over his property to her and her husband with the argument that he is no longer capable of taking care of business. This initial scene is only the first of many to display her grasping ways. Serena goes on to word her father's will so that her brother is left out of it, sells her father's beloved desk, which has been in the family for a hundred years, and even eats "with relish" (56) the donuts that the neighbor has sent her father. Marriage has not brought out Aaron Nudd's better traits either. No one likes Serena's husband: "He was a sly-looking, faded-out little man, of no attractions, and a sneaking manner which disgusted the persons he sought most eagerly to please" (57). Fortunately, Parker, the son, returns home, evicts Serena and Aaron, and restores the farm to his father. As Serena Nudd leaves, she "about stripped the house" (90), even to the point of grabbing the meat out of the cellar pork barrel.

The truncated, standard marriage whose sole aim seems to be greed appears again in "Law Lane," a Romeo and Juliet story about feuding families. The Barnets and the Crosbys have spent their lives arguing about who owns a particular two feet of the lane between them. It is such an all-consuming battle that the narrator gibes: "Perhaps this one great interest . . . had taken the place to them of drama and literature and art" (*TN*, 183). As the story unfolds, the Crosbys have finally lost the court case. Whereas the Barnets and the Crosbys had owned the two most prosperous farms in the area, the Barnets have spent all of their savings and the Crosbys have had to mortgage their farm to pay the court costs. Their feuding heritage has left its mark on the families' characters as well; many "Barnets and Crosbys had gone to their graves with bitter hatred and sullen desire for revenge in their hearts" (183). The present Barnet couple seems especially odious. Mr. Barnet is described as "narrow-minded" and "prejudiced," while Mrs. Barnet supersedes him as "a cross-grained, suspicious soul who was a tyrant and terror of discomfort in her own household whenever the course of events ran counter to her preference" (184–85). Mrs. Barnet's disgusting act of "crush[ing] an offending beetle with her brass thimble" tends to symbolize what she and Mr. Barnet have done to all human emotions between themselves and others.

When the external values of society become the concern of the married couple, or one of the partners, these values can become the goal for the marriage at the expense of interior relational development. However, this is not the only danger to the relationship of the married couple. If the couple accepts rigid gender roles, the basis is still that of power. The emphasis has merely shifted from power by virtue of controlling money to power by controlling people, whether the control be exercised within the framework of the couple or with outsiders. Rigid gender roles presume male over female—superior over inferior, strong over weak, possessor over possessed, and, terminally, victor over victim. The following couples are incapable of mutual interchange, of give and take. They have either assumed the roles or buckled under the weight of them. In either case, they are diminished by virtue of their rigidity.

Although Tobias Bascom of "Fair Day" is not disclosed as a tyrant, when it comes time for him to choose his mate, he follows the pattern: "He found it difficult to choose between his favorites among the marriageable girls, a bright young creature who was really too good for him, but penniless, and a weaker damsel who was heiress to the best farm in town. The farm won the day at last . . ." (*SW*, 120). Power is preferable in all directions.

The entire storyline of "Miss Debby's Neighbors" speaks of one continuous power struggle among the male members of the Ashby clan. According to Miss Debby, they are folks who are too proud, who fight almost for the sake of fighting. The women suffer in this atmosphere. The Ashby grandmother, worn out from the constant turmoil, dies from a quick consumption one rainy night in May. Her daughter Marilly, Miss Debby's mother's friend, dies only six months later: "She pined herself to death for her mother, and when she caught the scarlet fever she went as quick as cherry-bloom when it's just ready to fall and a wind strikes it" (*MD*, 194). The men continue their battles as usual.

Like Tobias Bascom, Joseph Ashby marries a woman for her money. Susan Ellen is deficient in most other areas. Miss Debby mentions that Joseph never cared much for this woman, who "was a poor ignorant sort of thing, seven years older than he was . . . and seemed like an overgrown girl of six or eight years old" (196). Yet Joseph's father and brother, jealous of the money Susan Ellen has brought to the marriage, seek to make Joseph's life as miserable as possible. There is a temporary reconciliation among all concerned while Mr. Ashby is ill. Curiously, there is no mention of the father's death except in retrospect. While Jewett gives detailed accounts of the grandmother's and mother's deaths, she skims over the father's, calling attention to the lack of feeling among the men in the story. The father never engendered any close ties with his sons; he fought with them.

Joseph eventually moves to town to work in a machine shop. In a curious reversal for Jewett, a woman appears on the scene as a tyrant embroiled in a power struggle. Brutal John marries "the only living soul he was ever afraid of" (202). Jealous of Joe's success in the machine shop, John's wife finally decides that farming is not productive enough and that they should move to the city, where John can work in the mills. Joseph, at the same time, decides he would like to go back to farming, his first love. While these timely decisions should bring a peaceful settlement to everyone's concerns, they merely exacerbate the most vindictive scene of all. To prevent his brother from living in the farmhouse his father has left him, John tries to drag the house to the city with him as he leaves, resulting in the total destruction of the familial home as well as of his mother's beloved garden. Miss Debby's mother bursts out crying at the scene. For her, Marilly's house symbolizes the friendship between the two women, who could summon each other by looking out of the window over the sweet garden. All sentiment is crushed; all family ties are broken. The warring Ashbys are insensible to the significance of the event. Miss Debby questions where the Ashbys have all gone: "'They'd mistake one place for the other in the next world, for 't would make heaven out o' hell, because they could be disagreeing with somebody . . .'" (209).

Married women cower before argumentative, tyrannical men time and again in Jewett's texts. Mrs. Downs, a minor character in "In Dark New England Days," alters her reaction to the Knowles girls when she encounters her husband on the road home, for "she had formed a pacific habit of suiting her remarks to his point of view, to save an outburst" (*SW*, 223–24). As formerly discussed, the king of Folly Island, the consummate tyrant with everyone, removes his wife and daughter to an isolated island, where they remain silent about their needs to the degree that they die from loneliness as much as from the inclement atmosphere. This scene is similarly repeated in "A Neighbor's Landmark," where the women are isolated under the rule of a tyrant in their own home. Unlike the wife of Folly Island, this wife still lives during the progress of the story, albeit only physically. Jewett admits us to the personal dynamics of such a marital relationship. The marriage has turned sour precisely because John Packer cannot be contradicted even in the most minor areas. True victim, his wife feels it is her fault: "She and John Packer had really loved each other when they were young, and although he had done everything he could since then that might have made her forget, she always remembered instead; she was always ready to blame herself, and to find excuse for him" (*LN*, 250). At present, John Packer is going to sell the two landmark pines for lumber simply because everyone has told him he should not do so. His wife, "the pale little woman" (253) and sacrificial lamb, uncharacteristically tries to stop him by contradicting his decision. John is shocked, for "his wife was never disrespectful, but she sometimes faced every danger to save him from his own foolishness" (253). Of course, John Packer does not listen to her, but, as the reality of what he has done penetrates his thick skull, he saves the trees from the predatory lumberman just in time. It seems, the narrator reveals, that underneath Packer's hard exterior, he really cares about what his neighbors think about him.

The story appears to end on a happy note. The neighbors, pleased that Packer has seen fit to save the landmark pines, throw him a surprise party the following night, Christmas. Staging the party on Christmas Day is the ultimate irony. There is no birth, no change. What Jewett is leaving unsaid is far more important. This destructive marriage will continue on course. The wife will continue to be relieved on the rare occasions John does not enter the house in "surly silence" (249). John will maintain his tyrannical stance by upbraiding his wife for insignificant things, such as leaving the matches around (251), and by burdening her with needless strife. (John never helps his wife by carrying the firewood into the house, and though she has "begged" [269] him to build a shed, since it is so hard to manage the wet wood in stormy weather, he has neglected to do so.) The inanimate trees are reminiscent of a supportive married couple. At the time John Packer decides to save the trees, they seem distressed, cognizant of their fate: "From this point of view they seemed to have taken a step nearer each other, as if each held the other fast with its branches in a desperate alliance" (270). In truth, John feels more for the trees and for the neighbors' opinion of him than for his marriage. He may have saved the lives of the coastal trees, but it is his marriage that will continue in a desperate state on the rocks.

Periodically, the strong versus weak roles are reversed in the marriage. It is still the same representative mold with one essential exception—the women react differently as the more robust of the partners. They do not tyrannize the males but try instead to creatively devise ways to lead useful lives. Some succeed more happily than others.

Abby Martin of "The Queen's Twin" seems the most pitiable of this type of woman. Mrs. Todd recounts the story of Abby's life with her ineffectual husband: "'Mis' Martin's always been in very poor, strugglin' circumstances. She had ambition for her children, though they took right after their father an' had little for themselves; she wa'n't over an' above well married, however kind she may see fit to speak. She's been patient an' hardworkin' all her life, and always high above makin' mean complaints about other folks'" (*QT*, 20). In addition to her hard-working nature, it is Abby Martin's imagination that has helped her to tolerate her lot. Born the same day and hour as the Queen of England, along with other coincidences, has made Abby feel that she and the queen have a special bond that transcends space and time. Through the years, she would discuss her problems with the queen in her mind as she walked through the woods. It has seemed to her the queen understood and told her to be patient for everything would be all right. Now that her family has grown and gone, it is lonely for Abby living in a remote area of the woods where there are few visitors. Still, she has had the queen for company. Mrs. Todd comments positively: "'I expect all this business about the Queen has buoyed her over many a shoal place in life. Yes, you might say that Abby'd been a slave, but there ain't any slave but has some freedom'" (*QT*, 21).

Mrs. Finch of "Farmer Finch," the Widow Bascom of "Fair Day," and Mrs. Trimble of "The Town Poor" are also saddled with inept husbands, but they are able to rise above their husbands' deficiencies. Mrs. Finch has the help of her daughter Polly. On several occasions, Mr. Finch is referred to as a child. Lately, Mary Finch feels that her husband is "somebody to be protected" (*WH*, 49). His farm is in trouble, so he whines, he cries, and, finally, he breaks down totally. While John "had not half so much force as [his wife]" (45), Mary Finch has had to function as "the sunshine and inspiration of the somewhat melancholy house for many years" (46). Luckily, Mary Finch has put her strength and hope into her daughter Polly's upbringing. Polly takes over the farm, succeeding where her father has failed.

When the Widow Bascom's husband dies, he leaves behind "slight proofs of having ever existed at all, except in the stern lines and premature aging of his wife's face" (*SW*, 118). Tobias Bascom was drunken and shiftless while he lived, hindering all his wife's "good judgment and high purpose in life" (117). Mercy Bascom rises to the occasion; "the determined soul would not be baffled by such a damaging partnership" (118). Even when she is left a widow with four children at the age of twenty-eight, she is able to pay off her debts, keep the farm, and raise the children successfully. Only one issue clouds her good record—her long-standing feud with her sister-in-law Ruth. While Mercy cannot really remember how and why she stopped talking to Ruth, the narrator proffers that "the animosity may have had its root in the fact that Ruth helped forward her brother's marriage" (125). But Mercy is not perfect by any means. She has had a reputation for being unamiable with her neighbors. Still the wiser of them have condoned her sharpness because they "understood the power of will that was needed to cope with circumstances that would have crushed a weaker woman" (118). Rid of her torturous husband, Mercy Bascom gains a sense of accomplishment and eventually lets down her defenses to coexist with her daughter-in-law and to reconcile with Ruth.

Mrs. Trimble is the most successful of this combative group. Her story is also one with a far different twist from the rest of these women who have had to deal with weaker spouses—she profoundly misses Mr. Trimble. Mr. Trimble left Mrs. Trimble the farm when he died, but not much ready cash. Unlike her husband, Mrs. Trimble is an excellent businesswoman who has profitably managed her affairs unaided since her husband's death. Warmhearted and generous with her earnings, she is known as "Lady Bountiful" (*SW*, 38) in her community. Money talks, but Mrs. Trimble will use her power selflessly to force the selectmen to remove the Bray sisters from the ranks of the poor and reestablish them in their house in town. Due to Mrs. Trimble's many accomplishments, the townspeople feel "she was better off in the end than if [Mr. Trimble] had lived" (38). Yet Mrs. Trimble thinks otherwise: "She regretted his loss deeply . . . ; it was impossible for her to speak of him, even to intimate friends, without emotion, and nobody had ever hinted that this emotion was insincere" (38).

Herein lies a most important differentiation. The Trimbles

enjoyed an emotionally satisfying, supportive relationship. Mr. Trimble was not a weak man per se; he was simply less accomplished in business than his wife. If only society had been constructed differently, perhaps Mr. Trimble would not have had to assume a position for which he was not suited. If Mrs. Trimble had handled the couple's business affairs from the onset, the Trimbles might have been prosperous while Mr. Trimble still lived.

Jewett provides a clue to the ineffectual husbands. It is not necessarily true that all the good men have traveled to large cities and the West, leaving only the dregs in New England. Perhaps some of these remaining men represent those who could not adjust to male roles and so buckled under the pressure. Some of the townspeople may have perceived them as ciphers. For Mrs. Trimble, it is her husband whom she misses, not his business sense or lack thereof.

Of all the stories about the standard marriage, "The Hiltons' Holiday" is by far the most positive. It almost serves as a model for the others in its display of what can take place if people care about each other in a relationship that manifests the give and take of both parties. The only flaw in the relationship is Mrs. Hilton's discomfiture with the fact that her husband is not in total control all of the time, as a man should be. Roles are sometimes interchanged, but Mrs. Hilton disapproves. Mr. Hilton possesses that enthusiastic childlike wonder to see and hear new things, which Jewett wholeheartedly endorses. Susan Ellen, one of the daughters who is going to town with her father, is even more excited because her father reminds her of a "boy": "Susan Ellen thought that he seemed like a boy at that delightful moment, and felt new sympathy and pleasure at once" (LN, 108). His wife perceives this enthusiasm as unmanly. Mrs. Hilton accuses him of taking his daughters on a trip for selfish reasons: "'I believe you want a good time yourself. You ain't never got over bein' a boy'" (103). She instructs him not to buy "'some kind of a foolish boy's hat'" (110), and as they drive off she speaks aloud, " 'They're nothin' but a pack o' child'n together . . .' " (111).

John Hilton is neither an innocent nor a simpleton. The Hiltons exchange weak and strong positions. Neither is crippled without the other. John may walk on eggshells trying to get his wife to approve of his trip to town with his daughters, a trip he knows she will deem unnecessary. Yet he is glad she is not going with them, for "as much as he usually valued her companionship and approval, he was sure that they should have a better time without her" (108). Mrs. Hilton tells John the wagon needs only one seat. John offers his rejoinder "meekly" (109), suggesting the wagon looks better with both seats, but the two seats remain in the wagon nonetheless. When Mrs. Hilton is heaping one directive after another as they are about to drive off, John "impatiently" calls a halt to the instructions: " 'Yes, yes, hold on!' " (111). John is not simply trying to hold his own with an aggressive wife, for the truth is that he is the one with ambition, an ambition he wants for his daughters, while his wife is content with her lot. The whole import of the trip is so the girls can see a bit of the world.

The fact that John is vulnerable rather than a constant towering pillar of stony strength seems to stand against him in his wife's eyes. John gets excited. John forgets to buy the hoe and seeds while he is in town, one of the chief reasons he has given for the trip in the first place. Yet here is a man who loves his wife and children. He tries to please his wife as best as he can while still retaining his intrinsic character: "Even though she might be completely unconscious of his best ideals, he only loved her and the ideals the more, and bent his energies to satisfying her indefinite expectations" (109). Mrs. Hilton loves her husband as well. The story begins with conversation between them, a conversation that bespeaks a profound knowledge of each other and their differences. And the story ends with the couple contentedly looking over the fields while standing in the shadow of their doorway. The Hiltons balance each other. The Hiltons represent a commingling of ambition and contentment. It seems difficult at times for them to set aside their prescribed roles comfortably, but they do, and they enjoy, as a result, a personally satisfying relationship based on reverence for people.

III
Breaking Free

While Jewett sees the deadening inconsistencies within the patriarchal system for men and for women, she is not one for despair. Although there is far more negativism in Jewett's works than has been noted to date, her conclusions are still overwhelmingly positive. Placing her confidence in the individual, she believes each person, woman or man, can break out of the system that binds. Just as Jewett led an expansive, productive life, so, too, can the average person of either sex who lives according to his or her intrinsic character—the person, that is, who measures life from within rather than from without. In her writings, Jewett attempts to shift society's focus from a grasping power over people to the personal development of each member of society.

On her way to this freedom from confinement, Jewett experiments. Her most primitive depiction is that of role reversal, where the character trades male or female characteristics, choosing the opposite form for the designated one. Jewett's most powerful, and most successful, story of freedom from gender boundaries emerges within her strong and generous community of women. Yet Jewett does not leave the men behind. She represents a core group of redeemed men, many more than have been imagined. Another viable alternative is the marriage postponed until later in life, when, according to Jewett, people's expectations are more realistic and less concerned with rigid gender roles. In "A White Heron," Jewett presents the symbolic possibility for androgyny. Ultimately, in *The Country of the Pointed Firs*, Jewett points neither to a blissful pastoral world nor to an unattainable futuristic one, but to a foreseeable present free from the confines of gender.

8

Sexual Transformation

ith the knowledge that people are entombed in rigid gender roles, Jewett explores the idea of sexual transformation or role reversal. Several critics have noticed this phenomenon in Jewett, mainly Richard Cary, Warner Berthoff, and Josephine Donovan. Cary and Berthoff have seen this theme in a negative vein, as Jewett's depiction of the deterioration of the area in general and of men's masculinity in particular (Cary, *Jewett*, 87, 126; *Appreciation*, 149). Donovan, on the other hand, views the recurrence of the subject as Jewett's movement toward a recognition of the tedium of women's roles and her attempt to allow women a more productive existence ("Woman's Vision," 367). Overwhelmingly, Jewett does not appear to view switching roles as an answer in itself; the change still results in a malformed, one-sided being.

This discussion is limited to the stories wherein specific characters are noticed by others in the story as dressing or acting like the opposite sex. Jewett handles the subject differently for men and for women. The men are depicted in a comical vein, almost as if Jewett acknowledges that it is more of a joke than a reality for a man to want to be like a woman. It is also an exterior change. Literally, the men dress up as women; they are merely changing clothes, trying them on. They are, with the exception of Daniel Gunn in "An Autumn Holiday," not interested in experiencing what it feels like to be a woman, but how it looks. For Israel Owen in *A Marsh Island* and Hallowell in "Hallowell's Pretty Sister," it is just a masquerade executed for the sake of duplicity. During a period of playing pranks, Israel Owen dresses up like the minister's wife in order to fool his family: "Israel looked too much like her, and had just her walk and the way she held her head stepping up the aisle Sunday mornings" (145). Dick Hallowell's prank has more purpose. In order to teach a lesson to his friend Jack Spenser, a ladies' man who has sorely neglected his friends of late for his romantic adventures, Dick arranges for his younger brother, Tom, to dress up as their pretty sister, Alice. Jack is, of course, thoroughly enchanted with Alice, only to find out he has made a fool of himself by lavishing romantic advances on Tom. They all have a good laugh, and the story ends happily with Jack marrying the real Alice. Pretending to be a woman is a good joke. Jewett affirms the fact that no one in "his" right mind would actually want to be a woman.

The account of Daniel Gunn is a different story entirely. Beneath the surface of this seemingly comical tale, Jewett may be offering weighty comments about the necessity to experience both the masculine as well as the feminine modes of existence. Daniel Gunn is not intentionally masquerading. After having sunstroke, Gunn thinks he is his dead sister, Patience. He only semirecovers. During the morning, he is Daniel Gunn, who attends to all the manly jobs on the farm, and after his afternoon nap, he is transformed into his sister. Daniel dons Patience's clothes and sits and knits with a cat in his lap, just as his sister was wont to do. In his delirium, Daniel can learn what life was like for his sister, a diametrically opposite existence to his own. Daniel has been solidly masculine up until this point. Reflecting his last name of "gun," Daniel's occupation has been that of a captain in the militia. His neighbors remember him as being "dreadful precise" (*CB*, 160). Now he must give up his chain of stern command, his life of action, and learn "patience" as he sits every afternoon. Daniel rarely leaves the house. Only once does he go to church, when an exceptional minister is preaching. Aunt Polly, who is telling the story, offers the traditional explanation: "'I s'pose he thought women ought to be stayers at home according to the Scripture'" (157). In time, Daniel manages to attend a meeting of the women's sewing society in his sister's best black silk dress. By the end of the evening, Daniel feels quite at home: "'he kissed 'em all around and asked 'em to meet at his house'" (161). Daniel even learns how it feels to be attracted to a man and have to guess at the man's intentions, waiting for him to make the first move. After the widower Deacon Abel Pinkham comes to visit, Daniel, "in a dreadful knowing way," turns to his Cousin Statiry, who lives with him, and asks, "'Which of us do you consider the deacon come to see?'" (162). Jewett is having great fun, but it is fun with a purpose. Men should experience the passivity, the triviality, as well as the affectionate community of women. The lifestyles of men versus women, of "gun" versus "patience," need to be examined so an ameliorated, healthy version for both can be chosen.

There is nothing humorous in Jewett's stories of sexual transformation for women. Instead of masquerading, women deliberately assume male roles because of an inherent necessity to achieve, an achievement missing in the roles provided for them as women. Mary Wilson, "Tom's Husband," takes over the family mill, and Polly Finch runs her father's farm after her father has given up hope of salvaging it. In "A Stage Tavern," one of Jewett's uncollected stories, Lizzie Harris, recently graduated from Radcliffe, also takes over her father's business, becoming a successful tavern manager.

While Lizzie Harris receives support from her proud father when she decides to run the failing tavern, Mary Wilson's husband merely tolerates her choice to run his failing mill. Actually, Jewett rings the death knell for the endeavor and for the marriage from the very first page. Although Tom and Mary had high hopes for their marriage, when they are finally living together, they find that they "had made themselves slaves to new laws and limitations" (*MD*, 210). Tom and Mary may try to do something distinctively different with their married life, but they will find that convention will win. The initial flaw in the plan has to do with Tom Wilson. Not only is Tom unfit for business; he is unfit for almost anything except coin collecting. After having spent most of his youth as an invalid, Tom has become an "idler" (214) whose only distinct ambition has been to marry Mary Dunn. Mary, on the other hand, is "too independent and self-reliant for a wife" (214). A Jewett prototype, Mary is described in terms similar to the explanation Jewett give Whittier for never having been in love: "she needed a wife herself more than she did a husband" (214). Since Tom has no stamina of his own, he fears Mary's managerial ability. Although he agrees he is the better housekeeper of the two, Tom responds to Mary's decision "indignantly" (220); he fears what people will think of his manhood; and finally, he resents Mary's telling him of her choice rather than "wait[ing] for his formal permission" (223)—all signs of his basic insecurity. But Tom is determined to let her have her way, secretly hoping she is unsuccessful: "If she failed, it might do no harm" (223). When Mary does do well, Tom accepts his reversed role "philosophically" (228), but not emotionally.

In addition to Tom's insecure nature, the nature of his assumed role is also to blame for the failure of his and Mary's new way of life. Jewett explodes the myth that women are essentially trivial, incapable of grasping larger concerns, irrational, and possessive, while men corner the market on the opposite sides of this same coin. Tom, in time, displays all of the supposed feminine traits, while Mary manifests all of the masculine ones. Tom is a victim of narrowness. It is confinement, a lackluster existence that breeds these characteristics and not woman's inherent nature. When Mary brings home guests for dinner without first giving notice to Tom, it is the last straw. Tom mandates Mary to leave her business and winter with him in Europe. It is most likely that there will be some changes when the couple arrives back home, more traditional ones to be sure. In evaluating the story as a whole, Judith Roman explains, "Jewett makes it clear that role *reversal* is not in itself a solution to the role problem. In a successful relationship, both partners must refuse to be limited to *any* single role, whether conventional or not" (128).

The most successful example of role reversal is contained in the story "Farmer Finch," most likely because Polly Finch fends off the idea of procuring a partner. Polly has been romantically interested in Jerry Minton prior to the family crisis precipitated by the bank's failure. Yet in the midst of the crisis, Polly detects in Jerry's sympathy and in his overture to aid her family "an assumption of condescension and patronage on his part" (*WH*, 71). Polly angrily rejects Jerry's offer. Mrs. Finch is worried that her daughter has ruined her chance for marriage to Jerry and warns Polly that " '[a] woman's better to have a home of her own' " (71). Turning red, Polly says, " 'Don't you worry about me. . . . This is my home, and I would n't marry Jerry Minton if he were the President' " (72). Marrying Jerry Minton would only present Polly with a new host of problems that would limit rather than strengthen her. Alone, Polly manages to resurrect the family farm. Having attained a formal education, Polly rejects the one professional path open to her as a woman—that of a teacher. Polly uses her book-learning instead to read "The Agriculturist" and learn the most advanced methods of farming. The point of this story is that it is actually not a story of role reversal so much as it is the account of a determined young woman who has done what she wants to do with her life. Jewett will reject the criteria and eliminate the terms from her vocabulary. Her strong women are not reversing roles; they are being themselves.

9

Women Unrestrained

J ewett recognized the limitations of reversing male and female roles, wherein each would acquire the mannerisms and personality traits usually associated with the other. Isolating and accentuating only certain dimensions of the human person can never result in integrated wholeness and satisfaction for either sex. The active, aggressive male in his outer space, away from the home, physically strong and mechanically adept, will accomplish linear goals. In a calm, collected fashion, examining problems in an abstract manner— theoretically, rationally—man will reach his ends. The antithesis is allotted to woman. She, passive and submissive, in her interior space, physically weak and mechanically deficient, nurtures. Due to the antithetical (and subsequently inferior) characteristics attributed to woman, her job of nurturing takes on a second-class status. Since she is involved in maintaining a relational world, the vehicles she uses to conduct her work—emotion and intuition—are also denigrated. Therefore, the image of man as the hunter, courageous and bold, remains preferable to woman, who is similarly perceived in a historical context, immobilized by pregnancy, child-rearing, and home duties. Jewett knew the self-fulfilling prophecies assigned for biological reasons. She herself never married. Law and custom bequeath authority and property to the man, and to the woman,

almost no opportunity to show her ability in the areas of physical
activity or intellectual creativity. Jewett was aware that these
limitations were the result of the pressures of society and had
nothing to do with sex. Like her character Polly Finch, Jewett
had to disengage herself from the pressures of society in order to
function. Alone, Jewett was able to be herself—whole and
fulfilled. It is a legacy she passes on to her multitude of capable
women characters.

Jewett fitted herself for a goal outside the home. Josephine
Donovan deems it "a peculiar sense of her own destiny" that at
the age of eighteen Jewett was considering that another young
girl of her age might be reading her diary in a hundred years
(*Jewett*, 6). Jewett seemed to know she would not be filling the
prescribed role. To her friend Anna L. Dawes in September of
1879, Jewett wrote: "I grow more certain that I cannot write so
much as I do and do everything that other girls do beside" (Hollis, 134–35). While Jewett invariably maintained that her writing was a God-given duty to be used in the service of others, her
thinking was not, as it might appear at first glance, an ascription
to the traditional womanly role. In 1873, she wrote to the editor
Horace Scudder: "I am glad to have something to do in the world
and something which may prove very helpful and useful if I care
to make it so, which I certainly do" (Cary, *Letters*, 28). But
Jewett was not speaking of a life of total service. Writing requires a total immersion of self. Jewett was neither naive nor
modest about her craft. After attending Harriet Beecher Stowe's
funeral and rereading Stowe's *The Pearl of Orr's Island*, one of
Jewett's earliest influences, Jewett sadly notes the unevenness of
the text in a letter to Annie Fields:

> Alas, that she could n't finish it in the same noble key of sim-
> plicity and harmony; but a poor writer is at the mercy of much
> unconscious opposition. You must throw everything and every-
> body aside at times, but a woman like Mrs. Stowe cannot bring

herself to that cold selfishness of the moment for one's work's sake, and the recompense for her loss is a divine touch here and there in an incomplete piece of work. (Fields, 47)

In the future, Jewett would advise Laura Richards and Willa Cather to give full attention to their craft if they wished to be successful writers. Writing was Jewett's lifeblood. In the 1873 letter to Scudder, written to gain information about copywriting, Jewett remarks: "I am getting quite ambitious and really feel that writing is my work—my business perhaps . . ." (Cary, *Letters*, 27).

And Jewett was aggressive in her "business" dealings. Confident, she accepted suggestions but remained intractable regarding questions of artistic integrity. If she believed a story rejected by magazine editors to be first-rate, she simply included it in her next book. Fortunately, this was the case with "A White Heron," one of Jewett's key stories that has been examined more than any other single story of hers. Jewett also knew what to do with her earnings. While Mary Jewett was responsible for running the family home in South Berwick, Sarah controlled her own income, wisely investing the $75,000 accumulated in her lifetime predominantly in U.S. Steel, the Pennsylvania Railroad Company, Calumet and Hecla, and the U.S. Smelting and Refining Company (Frost, *Jewett*, 124; Cary, *Jewett*, 125).

Yet Jewett did not abandon her matrilineal world for the world of men. Even more important to her was her network of close friends, predominantly women, who provided her with the support she needed in order to write. Jewett maintained relationships with all of the notable women writers of her period, as well as other artists and influential women (Donovan, *Jewett*, 15–16). Richard Cary proposes that while Jewett wrote prolifically, she could have rivaled the output of William Dean Howells had she not spent the morning writing letters to her friends, sometimes as many as thirty at one sitting (*Letters*, 84).

In her introduction to Jewett's letters, Annie Fields maintains that the letters "will show, above all, the portrait of a friend and the power that lies in friendship to sustain the giver as well as the receiver. They are in the easy undress of every-day life, wearing a grace which lies beyond all thought of the larger world" (11–12). In Sarah Orne Jewett's own words to Sarah Wyman Whitman, "the only thing that really helps any of us is love and doing things for love's sake" (130). For Jewett, friendship was almost a religious experience, bringing health to the spirit, imbuing one with the ability to live life. To Sara Norton, Jewett wrote: "There is something transfiguring in the best of friendship. One remembers the story of the transfiguration in the New Testament, and sees over and over in life what the great shining hours can do, and how one goes down from the mountain where they are, into the fret of everyday life again, but strong in remembrance" (126). Jewett believed that even in death a friend's spirit remained as a real presence in her life, for "where imagination stops and consciousness of the unseen begins, who can settle that even to one's self?" ("To Mrs. Fields," 110–11).

Jewett's relationships may be viewed as part of a historical/cultural phenomenon. In her definitive article "The Female World of Love and Ritual: Relations between Women in Nineteenth-Century America," Carroll Smith-Rosenberg explains that it was a common occurrence during at least the late eighteenth and up to the middle of the nineteenth century for women to form strong, highly structured emotional ties with other women, which sometimes included sensual avowals of love (1–2). Smith-Rosenberg attributes the existence of this separate, supportive female world to the rigid gender-role differentiation in the family and society, which led to the emotional segregation of women and men (9). Therefore, women's primary emotional ties—love, sensuality, and perhaps even sexuality—were often with other women rather than with men (27–28) in a female world of shared sensibilities. Jewett's relationships with women were her primary relationships. In her letters, the language she uses mirrors Smith-Rosenberg's examples of a language of sensual love. While in Athens in March of 1900, Jewett wrote to Sarah Wyman Whitman: "And pretty near every waking hour since then I have wished for you at least once. There is nothing for it but to go to the Museum every morning, and to the Acropolis every afternoon" (Fields, 171–72). To Sara Norton, Jewett avows: "I shall not let you go away without a word to say how much I love you" (188). Jewett's most intense relationship with Annie Fields, which lasted for over thirty years, produced letters and poems filled with this mode of interchange. In "The Unpublished Love Poems of Sarah Orne Jewett," Josephine Donovan at long last brings to light poems left unavailable for more than forty years that unveil the depth of Jewett's feeling for Fields. These poems speak of loving, kissing, and holding—of a lifelong relationship of support and comfort.

While Annie Fields was Jewett's senior by fifteen years, she did not function as the protector or caretaker of the relationship. In other words, neither Fields nor Jewett took on a specific male or female role in their association. As early as 1922, Mark De Wolfe Howe in his book *Memories of a Hostess* acknowledged that it was impossible to define either Fields or Jewett as giver or receiver, for both were sustained by their relationship (281). Judith Roman provides a more recent discussion of the nature of their alliance in her article "A Closer Look at the Jewett-Fields Relationship." Roman concludes it was "a complex relationship in which there was an easy exchange of roles that fostered both freedom and security for the two women" (119). Their connection was based on a "reciprocity and lack of fixed roles" (122). Even in their use of childish, loving nicknames there can be seen an interchange of roles within a child/adult or a patient/doctor dynamic (122–27).

Sarah Orne Jewett was both ambitious and nurturing, combining an aggressive, active nature with a strongly emotional one. She could both be cared for and caring, protector and protected. She could function perfectly at ease in the male or female realm; indeed, she drew no definite lines between either in her relationships.

In her writings, Jewett provides a glimpse of a society populated primarily by strong, highly individual, and generally older women. In reality, after most of the capable young men left declining rural New England for greater opportunity in the larger cities and out West, the inhabitants were mainly older women. For Jewett, the setting was a perfect medium. Unmarried, childless, these women characters were unburdened by biological constraints, constraints that would tie them to men and to consequent gender expectations/exploitations. These women characters, removed from the domination of men in their quest for power and material success, could achieve a secure, intimate, and freeing existence.

From her first story in the *Atlantic Monthly*, "Mr. Bruce," published in December of 1869, when she was twenty years old, Jewett stressed the essentiality of a supportive group of women whose tender, compassionate devotion is preferential to assuming the "role" of wife, a shallow masquerade. Within a typical Jewett framework where a visiting narrator tells a story she in turn has heard, it becomes apparent that it is the framework of the story that is paramount; the story itself is fluff. It is a frivolous tale of an aristocratic young woman who pretends she is the servant. The serving girl has been inadvertently called away at the very point when the father brings home unexpected guests, and Kitty Tennant volunteers to "play" the serving girl and attend to the guests during dinner. A trite happily-ever-after ending is achieved a year later when one of the befuddled strangers finds out Kitty's true identity and marries her. Richard Cary, unusually censorious of Jewett's writing, is perfectly within bounds to call the story of Kitty Tennant and Mr. Bruce a "clumsy, unoriginal parlor farce-romance," rife with coincidence and flimsy in characterization (*Jewett*, 91). Cary cannot understand either why Jewett was so proud of this story or why Howells agreed to publish it. Basically, critics have viewed "Mr. Bruce" as one of Jewett's feeble first attempts and nothing more.

Yet this story is not really a story about Kitty and Mr. Bruce, a tale that delineates a trapeze act of deception between the sexes; the bulk of space is given to the women tellers of the tale and their intricate connection to one another. Jewett uses nearly the first five pages to describe the importance of the women to each other, an entire network of interrelationships. Initially, Aunt Mary is disclosing to her niece, Elly, the first time she met Miss Margaret Tennant of Boston. It is a meeting Aunt Mary has long desired, for Miss Tennant is the other intimate girlhood friend of Aunt Mary's friend Anne Langdon. Mary and Margaret immediately become close friends, "taking long walks, and spending the most of [their] time together" (*OF*, 115). In addition to Elly's connection to her aunt, who is connected to Anne Langdon, who is connected to Margaret Tennant, who, in turn, becomes connected to Aunt Mary, who connects both Anne and Margaret with her niece Elly through her story, there is a coterie of women whom Margaret Tennant "matronizes" (116). Aunt Mary relates the popularity of Miss Tennant:

> Then she is such a popular person: it is charming to see the delight her friends have in her. For one thing, all the young ladies of her acquaintance—not to mention her nieces, who seem to bow down and worship her—are her devoted friends; and she often gives them dinners and tea parties, takes them to plays and concerts, matronizes them in the summer . . . and is the repository of all their joys and sorrows. . . . (116)

After Aunt Mary expresses her wish that Elly be part of the "clan" (117), the reader becomes one of the group in front of

Miss Tennant, poised attentively to hear the story of Kitty. By way of introduction, Miss Tennant explains her own important connection to the tale as Kitty's younger sister. Margaret begins by describing a warm encounter rife with personal disclosure, one that is evidently repeated each time Kitty returns home for vacation from Madame Riche's finishing school: "I was sitting with her in her chamber, and she was confiding to me some of the state secrets of her room at school, to my inexpressible delight, for it was my great ambition to be intimate with Kitty . . ." (119).

By way of contrast, the story moves to the story of women in the company of men. It is time for the account of the masquerade. As with Jewett's descriptions of aging aristocratic women preoccupied with propriety, so, too, Mrs. Tennant, Margaret and Kitty's mother, is troubled over a trivial matter of decorum. Hers is a life fraught with the importance of superficial appearances, the ones she was probably taught were her domain when she attended Madame Riche's finishing school. So she approaches her daughters "with her usually cheerful face exceedingly clouded" (119). Although Mrs. Tennant will admit her troubles to the gentlemen and carry on as best as she can, if need be, she finds the better alternative is to accept her daughter's offer to act the part of the maid. She will willingly deceive the guests and lie about her daughter's whereabouts in order to save face.

Kitty, though described by Margaret as beautiful and brilliant, unfortunately displays herself as shallow and condescending. "'Just let me wear one of Ann's white aprons and look stupid, you call me Katherine, and I'll wait on the table as well as she could'" (121), she tells her mother. Kitty goes on to feign a thick Irish brogue and, eventually, displays a total lack of sensitivity by unnecessarily coming into the library after dinner to give her mother the trumped up message that Miss Harriet Wolfe will call for her mother the following afternoon so they can attend a concert. Miss Harriet is presently dead and was deaf while she lived. The masquerade ends in sharp contrast to the beautiful community of women delineated at the beginning of the story.

As Kitty moves outside her father's house to life among men, in general, the distance between her and her mother and sister lengthens as her preoccupation with her relationships with men are more consuming as well as less vital. Her romantic interests are tainted with references to concealment. Kitty is courted by Mr. Davenport, whom she refers to as her "devotedest" (133), yet she acknowledges Davenport possesses "an exceedingly well-developed taste for grief" (133). Kitty believes that "lately his object in life has been to make [her] think he has some dreadful hidden sorrow" (133), which she knows he hasn't. Kitty herself is insincere and keeps Davenport around for sheer entertainment: "'I talk more nonsense to him in an hour than I ever did to any one else in a day. I cannot help 'taking rises' out of him as we used to say at school. But he dances well, and knows every thing apparently; and he is ever so much more entertaining to me than the people who are just like every one else'" (134).

Concealment is also the primary force that seems to bind Kitty to her main love interest, Mr. Bruce. In a series of mishaps, Mr. Bruce becomes more and more convinced that Kitty is a maid posing as a young aristocrat. He is appalled by her deceit. It seems that if one is not a true aristocrat, if one's manners and sophisticated behavior are only the mark of a good teacher and not just good blood, then it is one's duty to at least acknowledge that one is a maid with schooling. Mr. Bruce is a patronizing bore at the very most. Instead of confronting Kitty (who incidentally thinks Mr. Bruce looks familiar but cannot place him as the dinner guest of a year ago), Mr. Bruce believes the worst, turning into "a perfect icicle" (129) in Kitty's presence. Kitty is intrigued. And so the basis for their relationship is comprised of Kitty's attraction to distant frigidity and Mr. Bruce's priggish "contempt" (140) for one whom he believes has superseded her station. After the truth becomes known, the last description of Mr. Bruce given by Kitty in the text is that of "a goose" (141). And so they are married.

This feeble relationship is hardly worth a story. But with another glance at the framework of the tale, it is easy to discern that the real matter at hand is Margaret's loss of her sister, Kitty. The whole account of the haphazard union of Kitty and Mr. Bruce has been read out loud from the letters that Margaret has loyally kept all these years. In addition to conversation, the major means that Margaret has had to foster her "great ambition to be intimate with Kitty" has been through her sister's letters. In the past when Kitty would send letters to Margaret while she was away at Mrs. Walkintwo's boarding school, Margaret would read the "journal letters to a select circle of friends; and they were a green spot in [their] so-considered desert of life" (126). Yet when Margaret starts to receive the letters that speak of Mr. Bruce, she no longer feels the comfort of this "green spot." Realizing Kitty is absorbed with Mr. Bruce, Margaret experiences "a woeful dread of losing her" (131). She attempts to dissuade Kitty from "the foolishness of caring anything for a man who had treated her in so uncourteous a way" (131). Unlike Mr. Davenport or Mr. Bruce, Margaret is the "devotedest." Kitty continues obsessing over Mr. Bruce, forgetting to write to Margaret in the process. When the last batch of letters begins to arrive, Kitty is aware of the trauma she is generating for Margaret: "'My forlorn young sister, are you mourning over the inconstancy of woman in general and your sister Kitty in particular?'" (133). But Kitty is undaunted. She continues without any encouragement: "'I dare say you are making the most awful face, Maggie, but I *will* tell you about him; and why you scold me so I cannot imagine . . .'" (134). In the last missive, Kitty addresses Margaret as "my cross young sister" (137); Kitty has traded loyalties, now holding Margaret cuplable rather than Mr. Bruce. By choosing vapid Mr. Bruce, Kitty has done what is expected of a young lady, but in so doing, she has broken from her sister and the genuine support and understanding offered by the coterie of women in general. While Kitty becomes "Mrs. Bruce," a male name that signals the loss of her birthright, Margaret Tennant remains "Miss," a tenant or possessor of her own personal woman's space.

Miss Tennant avers that Kitty and Mr. Bruce "have always been the happiest couple in the world" (142) for nearly thirty years, but this is simply the pat expression used to describe marriages that last. Perhaps Kitty appears ebullient because she has continued to laugh her way through social faux pas. Perhaps Margaret Tennant, who is transferring the information, has always loved her sister too deeply to acknowledge her flaws. There has been no evidence given to show any vital exchange between Kitty and Mr. Bruce. The lack of intimacy is confirmed by the fact that Kitty never once mentions her husband by his first name; she always refers to him as Mr. Bruce. Role playing can only be a stultifying experience for Mr. and Mrs. Bruce. The only data given for the relationship's existence in addition to the intrigue is Mr. Bruce's attraction to Kitty's beauty and wit and Kitty's attraction to Mr. Bruce's handsome exterior and position of status. The couple is still masquerading, caught in a web of superficial appearances.

The story concludes on a note of real intimacy; it circles back to the women surrounding Miss Tennant, teacher and keeper of joys and sorrows. She has finished the lesson: "'And now,' said Miss Margaret, 'the storm and the story are both over. It's nearly twelve and the fire is low. Suppose we go up stairs'" (142). It is a story of shared experience. It was Jewett's own grandmother who initially shared this story with Sarah. In her diary Jewett wrote: "Was at Grandma's & she told me something I thought would be a good plot for a story so that night I sat up very late over it" (Frost, 42). After two rejections from the *Atlantic*

Monthly, Jewett's grandmother made it possible for Sarah to publish.

The links of this supportive chain extending from Jewett and her grandmother seem endless. Miss Margaret, in the process of telling her tale, has connected Elly to a group of women like herself, as well as to her Aunt Mary and Anne Langdon, and, finally, to Kitty herself. The only one who does not hear the story is Kitty, for she can only give her account through her letters; she is cut off from the other women. Jewett uses the storm as a vehicle for announcing the transferal of vital change and interconnectedness. As in "Miss Tempy's Watchers" and "The Foreigner," when the storm is over, the women are closer and have been transformed. In "Mr. Bruce," when the storm is over, all are closer and intact, except for Kitty, who has been spirited away, a ghostly form present only in her former writing. Marriage is the wrong choice when it is a disruption in women's lives that robs them of their intimacy with each other and with themselves.

Jewett's best portrayals are of older women who have been able to avoid classification altogether. They are mature in the best sense of the word—"full" and "ripe" with all the human person has to offer. They defy the gender boundaries designated in their time period. Jewett subverts the dominant male text by presenting characters who simply do not fit that woman's mold, showing us ways of acting and relating that society ignores or discredits. Independence is the key factor; these women have left the passive, submissive mode in the dust as they have surged forward. Whether taking care of business, as Mrs. Trimble does, or taking leave of everyone to go off alone to visit the Philadelphia Centennial, as Betsey Lane does, the older single woman does not rely on the opinions of others to make her decisions. With a sense of completeness within herself, she often prefers her own company. Miss Lydia Dunn, though she has lived alone many years, "always treated herself as if she were a whole family" (*MD*, 94). In her solitary life, Miss Spring has been "growing more and more contented," for "it is, after all, a great satisfaction to do as one pleases" (*OF*, 81). While Miss Peck's spirits sometimes fail her when the weather is gray and depressing, the remainder of the time she is quite content:

> It is quite a mistake to believe that people who live by themselves find every day a lonely one. Miss Peck and many other solitary persons could assure us that it is very seldom that they feel their lack of companionship. As the habit of living alone becomes more fixed, it becomes confusing to have other people about, and seems more or less bewildering to be interfered with by other people's plans and suggestions. (*KF*, 168)

It is paramount that these women retain their own homes. A frequent episode is that of the older woman who, in the face of great odds, tries to preserve her independent way of living. When faced with sharing her space with her greedy nephew who has stolen her farm, Mrs. Peet is driven to leave: "'twas the only thing *to* do. . . . I wanted to airn my livin'. . . . he didn't give me no chance to stay there without hurtin' my pride and dependin' on him'" (*SW*, 139, 142). In fact, men rarely appear on the scene, even to aid the older single woman with physical labor around her home. Generally, when they do help, they get more than they give. This is the case with young Joel Smith, who offers to do odd jobs for Mrs. Powder as an excuse to eat everything in sight, and for lazy Jonas Phipps, whom Lydia Dunn is trying to teach the value of independent living. Men are unnecessary in this environment.

Unlike Mrs. Peet, who is driven from her home, Miss Spring is rescued by the appearance of two boarders who will provide the money necessary for her to stay afloat. She has refused to ask for help; indeed, "like most elderly women of strong character who live alone, Miss Spring was used to keeping her affairs to herself, and felt a certain pride in being uncommunicative"

(*OF*, 98). Now she can preserve her integrity, for "she knew no other way of living, beside having her own house and her own fashion of doing things" (82).

Even in extreme cases where two of these women compatibly living together would provide additional comfort for the both of them, they are reluctant to form the attachment. In "The Passing of Sister Barsett," Mrs. Crane could provide the financial security that Sarah Ellen Dow needs, and Sarah could be the amiable companion Mrs. Crane desires; yet Mrs. Crane cannot bring herself to suggest they form an alliance. In "Aunt Cynthy Dallett," Aunt Cynthy and her niece's decision to share a home is a perfect solution for Aunt Cynthy, who is getting too old to take care of herself; for Abby Pendexter, who can no longer afford to maintain her home; and for their mutual loneliness. But it is still a decision tinged with regret. It will be a struggle for Aunt Cynthy, who is "a very self-contained person" (*QT*, 197), and for Abby Pendexter, whose "thought of her own little home gave a hard tug at her heart" (220).

Wanting to live alone does not merely preserve a certain way of doing things, but a certain manner of thinking. Time and again these mature solitary figures spew forth a self-reliant, clear-sighted conclusion about a grave situation. Though Miss Peck's heart is being pulled in the direction of the recently widowed minister, she continues to long for her country home, where she knows she belongs. Never once fooled by the mellow tones of the minister's voice, which often impresses others, she finally decides to stop caring for his child and his home the very minute she realizes his affection is insincere. Aware that he has been using her, she quips "disdainfully": "'You can't expect a woman who has property and relations of her own to give up her interests for yours altogether'" (*KF*, 201). On a less personal note, Miss Lydia Dunn will not be duped by the new parishioner, regardless of how low she falls in people's esteem. Everyone else may be enthralled with Mr. Stroud, but Lydia trusts her good instincts. She is concerned because his eyes will not meet hers when he is talking to her, and she cannot help but notice a mean look in his face. Henry Stroud turns out to be a thief and a fraud. Mrs. Goodsoe of "The Courting of Sister Wisby" is an independent thinker on most of the important issues of the day. She rails against the false values of the industrial society, which have been represented as progressive to the greater exclusion of women. Men just do not know what they are talking about. Preachers give vacuous sermons, and doctors, "'book-fools'" (*TN*, 254), give stupid advice. All people care about is "'livin' on wheels'" (255), quickly traveling back and forth to places, accomplishing nothing but homogenization. As an antidote, Mrs. Goodsoe offers the same "'big thoughts then as there is now'" (257), when people "'were n't all just alike, either, same as pine spills'" (255). Within the framework of a woman's culture of holistic herbal medicine, Mrs. Goodsoe advocates taking care of people in their own particular part of the globe.

This is the power these mature single women possess—the power of healing in an overtly sick society. While they are self-sufficient, independent beings who can think rationally and act in a decisive, composed fashion, they continue to embrace a woman's nurturing tradition. When Mrs. Powder avows that "'life means progriss to me, and I can't dwell by the way no more'n sparks can fly downwards'" (*TN*, 159), she is speaking of a healthy progress in which human beings move forward by living the life of their choice commingled with a compassionate connection to others.

The community could not function without these nurturers. Mrs. Trimble is a rare character with her clout in the world of men, the selectmen of her town whom she will force to reinstate the Bray girls in their home. Yet almost without exception, the world of men is not visible in the stories centering around the mature single woman. It is as if it does not exist, or simply that it

is unnecessary in this self-sufficient realm based on an antithetical system to the male monetary system.

The women characters' ability to nurture, to be of service, is
the basis for the *power* they possess within the community. Miss
Peck and Miss Tempy are known and loved for the services they
will render to anyone in need of them. Miss Peck takes care of
her brother's wife and children for six years after his death.
Although there are many people there to aid the minister at the
time of his wife's death, he must have Miss Peck come. Miss
Tempy, too, is often regarded as indispensible: "'None o' the
young folks could get married without her, and the old ones was
disappointed if she wa'n't round when they was down with sickness and had to go. . . . there was nothin' but what she could do
as handy as most'" (*TN*, 24). The largest group of women
characters performing essential services are the herbalists.
Mrs. Powder is frequently "away on one of her visiting tours[,]
nursing some sick person" (*TN*, 198). When Mrs. Crosby is ill,
she prescribes balm of Gilead buds put in new rum, and when
Mrs. Barnet falls, she is summoned to the house. While the
herbal healing skills of Mrs. Goodsoe, who is frequently cited as
a precursor of Mrs. Todd in *The Country of the Pointed Firs*, are
also specifically mentioned, it can be presumed that all of the
women called to the bedside of the sick and dying have had some
knowledge of herbal medicine, a woman's tradition handed down
from one generation to another. This list would then have to
include both Miss Peck and Miss Tempy. In addition, Sarah
Ellen Dow is accustomed to the "rule of the afflicted household," where "her simple nature and uncommon ability found
satisfaction in the exercise of authority" (*NW*, 142). Aunt Polly,
too, in "An Autumn Holiday" is seldom at home, for she is "a
famous nurse . . . often in demand all through that part of the
country" (*CB*, 148).

Miss Peck and Miss Dunn also exert religious power, functioning where ministers fail miserably. Miss Peck supersedes

the mellow yet blathering voice of Mr. Elbury, with "his romantic, ease-loving, self-absorbed, and self-admiring nature" (*KF*, 182), to "unobtrusively, even secretly [lead] the affairs of the parish" (183). It is no secret that Miss Lydia Dunn has more sense and more depth than the materialistic-minded minister who is deceived by Henry Stroud. As good Parson Dunn's granddaughter, Lydia is heralded as the new minister, one with spiritual values and good insight. Jonas Phipps claims, "'Risin' sixty year . . . she's been doing of good works!'" (*MD*, 144). In the past and in the future her neighbors have regarded her as "a person of great consequence and influence, . . . faithful and dutiful to the very utmost" (125).

Besides these new ministers, Miss Powder would make a better lawyer than the ones the Crosbys and Barnets have engaged to end their feud over the ownership of a certain lane. By helping to unite their children in marriage and by tricking Mrs. Barnet into thinking she is dying so she will make peace and expire with a free conscience, Mrs. Powder solves the legal battle that has extended for generations.

These mature, shrewd women characters exercise power divorced from economics. For all the services they render, no fees are collected. Physical problems are not separated from spiritual ones. These characters proffer holistic solutions that have nothing to do with money. In *Communities of Women: An Idea in Fiction*, Nina Auerbach concludes: "The bonds of hospitality and sympathy between women that pervade the isolated landscapes in Jewett's volume are more potent than men's railroad tracks in keeping alive the human world and knitting it together," (10–11).

These women, bonding together, do not project the historical image of the hunter stalking his prey, but, bold and upright in the face of life's challenges, they do embody courage and strength. Yet the emphasis of these self-contained, mature, single women is not on conquering lands and people, but of connecting the same by cultivating health of mind and body in tune with the environment. The result can only be a peace with self and a security with others; in other words, feeling at home amid a supportive group that can enable an individual's growth in all areas of possibility.

The world of these particular stories is a woman's realm. But Jewett is forward-looking. She knows that isolation is not the answer. A segregated society of women would limit their effect on the world at large. Already these rural women, like the women at the beginning of D. H. Lawrence's *The Rainbow*, look out to the world beyond. Lydia Dunn, Eliza Peck, and Abby Harran are all voracious readers. Betsey Lane's life is not complete until her strong desire to see something of the world is sated. After her initial upheaval, Mrs. Peet is content to live in Shrewsbury: "She has been going to concerts and lectures this winter, and insists that Isaiah did her a good turn" (*SW*, 154). Jewett provides a taste of the future. The precursors are Annie Hollis of "A Guest at Home," Nan Prince, and the narrator of *The Country of the Pointed Firs*. These formally educated women will be able to live in both spheres. They can combine careers in the patriarchal world with nurturing. Annie Hollis can help on her country farm and be a painter at the same time. Nan Prince will be a successful doctor in the land of her mother. And the writer will carry the women's realm of the *Pointed Firs* in her heart while she continues to function in male society. The future looks bright.

10

Redeemed Men

ewett did not forget the men. Nor did she only view them as warped, stunted creatures, as critics have upheld. The tone of any Jewett story is devoid of hostility and abhorrence, for it did not seem to be her wish to alienate any faction of humanity. In her intrinsic compassion, Jewett appears incapable of trading misogyny for male-hatred. While her strong women prodigiously fill the landscape of her stories, her redeemed men speckle the horizon. There are many more than appear at first glance, enough of them to make a difference in the way men are perceived. Men, too, can learn to be nurturing; it is a side of their nature as well. It will, however, be a harder task. Women, though assigned a separate sphere from male activity, are nonetheless strong and goal-oriented; they have simply lacked in many cases the opportunity to exercise this dimension. Men, on the other hand, have been under the impression that nurturing is solely the task of the weaker sex. For men to develop their nurturing ability, they will have to reject to some degree that prestigious kingdom of male power conceived as their rightful portion. Jewett can envision men who will be able to develop their long-forgotten female dimension. In her writings, she presents a group of men whose proclivity for the female sphere is emphasized. Her male characters can be emotional, intuitive, and nurturing. They espouse values other than power and money. For some, the learning is excruciating; others seem naturally destined for such cultivation. While Jewett is not as convinced of a balanced development in her male characters as she is in her women characters, she views the men hopefully and tenderly. There exists, Jewett maintains, the potentiality for redemption.

Jewett's optimism was based in reality. Her life was not segregated relationally in the female sphere alone. Richard Cary records that "she established and sustained affable relationships with scores of men" (*Jewett*, 26). In addition to her correspondence of a purely business nature with a long list of editors, she managed to foster personal relationships with men as well. As with women writers, she took the time to encourage and advise male writers such as Andress Floyd and John Thaxter, son of Jewett's close friend, Celia Thaxter. Though neither was successful in his attempt, Jewett sincerely guided each of them (Cary, *Letters*, 52, 68, 69, 118, 119, 120, 123–29, 140, 141). Jewett was equally encouraging and appreciative of the efforts of F. Hopkinson Smith, who became a writer at the age of fifty (*Letters*, 29, 33, 34, 53). On a more personal note, Jewett shared her consoling thoughts with fellow writer George Woodberry on the emotions felt at the completion of a writing project: "The more one has cared to put one's very best into a thing, the surer he is to think that it falls far short of the 'sky he meant.' But it is certain that everything *is* in such work that we have put in. The sense of failure that weighs the artist down is often nothing but a sense of fatigue" (Fields, 223–24).

With several men involved in the field of writing or publishing, the subject of writing was secondary to the friendship Jewett shared with them. In one letter, Jewett addressed Robert Underwood Johnson as "my dear friend" and proceeded to thank him for his book of poems, *The Winter Hour*, which chronicled the joint tour to Italy and Venice taken by Johnson, his wife, Jewett, and Annie Fields. Jewett writes: "I shall be always reading between those dear lines and remembering days that we both remember. . . . I did not need them to recall our friendship: but I put your white flower of a book into the safest place" (Cary, *Jewett*, 79–80). On another occasion, Jewett does not hesitate to tell Johnson how she misses her recently deceased friend Madame Blanc (171). While Jewett describes her relationship with David Douglas, editor of Walter Scott's journal and a volume of his letters, as "a book friendship," she also recounts to him the loss of one of her "dearest older friends," Miss Katharine Wormeley (Fields, 243–44). The "book friendship" was only one aspect of their alliance. When abroad, Jewett always made it a point to visit Douglas and his wife in Edinburgh. Upon sending him a volume to read, Jewett cautions warmly: "Do not write just to acknowledge the book; those dutiful notes rob us of time to write the letters we care more for!" (187).

In Annie Fields's drawing room in Boston, Jewett was privy to the frequent companionship of a host of women and men artists and friends. In regular attendance were Lowell, Holmes, Aldrich, Whittier, and Whipple (Cary, *Jewett*, 58). Jewett developed close associations with at least three of these men. At Elmwood, Lowell's home, Jewett often engaged in discussions of books and the art of writing (144). Lowell often teased her, mimicking her Maine colloquial speech (144). After his death, upon receiving a poem entitled "Elmwood" from Aldrich, Jewett replied: "To me it speaks of him as his own presence used to speak, and brings him back again as if he came back with the old life and the new life mingled, as indeed they are, and then I feel the loss afresh . . ." (Fields, 87).

Among the great male writers of the day, it was with Whittier that Jewett "felt most at home" (Cary, *Jewett*, 26). She talked to him of everything, including her desire not to marry. For her first trip to Europe, he wrote "Godspeed," and she soon reciprocated with the poem "The Eagle Trees." He praised *Deephaven*, and she dedicated to him her volume *The King of Folly Island* "with grateful affection" (26).

While Thomas Bailey Aldrich published twenty of Jewett's stories in the *Atlantic Monthly*, it was probably with him that

Jewett experienced her deepest and most profound friendship with a man. It was certainly as emotional and as intimate as her friendships with women. She and Aldrich shared nicknames with each other, as Jewett did with her women friends. Aldrich and his wife were labeled the duke and duchess of Ponkapog, after their Boston home, while Jewett was Miss Sadie Martinot to Aldrich (Frost, 71). In one letter, Aldrich playfully addresses Jewett in verse: "Cute little spider down in Maine / (All the time we need her) / Spin some silvery webs again / To catch the flying reader" (Frost, 72). Jewett wrote to Aldrich about the craft of writing; she commiserated with him as another "timid young [author]" (Fields, 78); and according to Matthiessen, she "wrote to Aldrich about everything else besides," "enter[ing] into every side of his life" (93–94). When Aldrich's mother died, she tried to empathize with him by relating her feelings of being un-protected and alone in the world for the first time upon the death of her own mother a few years prior. Jewett goes on to console Aldrich through her own experience: "I never felt so near to my mother or kept such a sense of her love for me and mine for her as I have since she died. There are no bars of shyness or difference or inexpressiveness or carelessness . . ." (95). The letter ends with Jewett's desire to offer Aldrich the physical comfort only a good friend can provide: "But it is no use to try to write these things. If I were with you, I should take hold of your hand and not say anything, and I do that now" (95).

Coupled with the positive male friendships Jewett experi-enced as an adult, her interaction with three early mentors would have to be mentioned as contributing to Jewett's hope for men's emotional development. Discarding the prevalent attitude that destined women to be a subclass of nonachievers, these three men nurtured the young Jewett to do her best. For several years before and after her father's death, Jewett corresponded with Theophilus Parsons, professor of law at Harvard, who in-troduced her to the teachings of Emanuel Swedenborg and so much more. Jewett wrote to him enthusiastically in "letters, endless pages long, telling him everything that came into her head" (Matthiessen, 39–40). The erudite professor gave weighty consideration to the efforts of the young writer:

> You learn easily, think quickly, & write excellently. The time will come when you will even write without knowing that you are going to say something which will make your readers wiser & better,—unless they reject it, which is not your affair. . . . Then you will rejoice when you feel that you have succeeded on clothing a valuable truth with a beauty that is at once attractive and transparent;—that wins reception for the truth and does not obscure or disguise it. (Letter, 18 September 1873, Houghton Library, Harvard University)

In keeping with the Swedenborgian thought to which he had introduced Jewett, Parsons also guided her in the acceptance of her father's death. While Jewett admitted that "in that grave all my ambitions & hopes seem sometimes to be buried," Parsons assured her of her father's continued presence: "never in your life were you *less* without him. He is with you now, not to sense, but if you can resist the falsities which tell you that he is *dead*, you will feel that he cares for you now more than he ever did, & enwraps you in his love" (Letters to Jewett, 4 October 1878, 22 September 1878, Houghton Library, Harvard University).

Within her own family, Jewett's maternal grandfather, Dr. William Perry, and her own father served as her earliest mentors. A stern, authoritative figure, Dr. Perry was himself a man of action. On his own initiative, he left his childhood farm to achieve a degree from Harvard Medical School and at the age of ninety-two was still performing surgery (Cary, *Letters*, 47). In her "Recollections of Dr. William Perry of Exeter," Jewett recalled his charge, "'*Act—act!*' he used to exclaim with peculiar emphasis—'Go and *do it* if you think you are right. Make the best of yourself'" (MS Am 1743.22 [102], Houghton Library,

Harvard University, 2). Perry believed that "his own grand-sons and grand-daughters and young neighbors were able to do things that had never been done before" (2). Perceiving talent in his granddaughter at an early age, he exhorted her to give it "proper attention" (Cary, *Letters*, 47–48). Jewett remembered that "he was always urging me to do the best I could, to believe that I could do what others did; always showing me where good work had been done and insisting upon my recognition of the moral qualities that led to achievement" (MS Am 1743.22 [102], Houghton Library, Harvard University, 2). It was a legacy Perry had received from his mother: "He always said that he owed what was best in him to his mother—and it was indeed she who helped him to take the difficult steps of his career, who urged him, as he always urged others, to make the best of himself" (5). In "Recollections," Jewett acknowledged her ever-increasing gratitude to the grandfather to whom she dedicated her volume *The Story of the Normans*. His advocacy of Jewett's talent combined with "his instinct as a healer"—"he could give you comfort and stay as few men could"—served as a major early influence for the young author (3).

The most significant and the most androgynous of Sarah's youthful male influences was undoubtedly her father, Theodore Herman Jewett. It may be speculated that Dr. Jewett encouraged his daughter to embark on a career simply because she was the replacement for the son he never had; however, it is far more reasonable to conclude that he did so because he himself did not belong to the male role to which he was assigned and similarly preferred not to curtail his daughter's development. As a boy, Theodore deviated from the masculine norm; he had "delicate health, cared little for sports, but much for reading," and did "poor[ly] in arithmetic" (Frost, 21). As Jewett's ill health as a child may have been an excuse that freed her from the obligation to learn the patterned behavior of a young "lady," perhaps she was merely following in her father's footsteps, for his fragility as a child made it possible for him to elude male-patterned behavior. Abandoning his father's career as a sea captain and merchant, Theodore frustrated his father's hopes that he would become a merchant by determining instead to enter the medical profession, a service career that could hardly duplicate his father's profits. Jewett maintained that her father's "great wish was not so much to be called great, as to be useful" ("Dr. Theodore Herman Jewett," MS Am 1743.22 [28], Houghton Library, Harvard University, 6). In addition to spending his life in the service of others, he further aligned himself with women's nurturing by specializing in women's medicine, becoming professor of obstetrics at Bowdoin College. To Dr. Jewett, the field of medicine was not the science of fixing physical ailments. Sarah Orne Jewett attests that her father was interested in the internal, spiritual, emotional side of the person as well: "[Medicine] was never a dull, necessary trade with him. And he ministered to the souls as well as the bodies of his patients" (8–9). He entered into relationships with his patients, and they, in turn, "put their confidence in him so fully as their doctor and their friend. There never was a man in all that region more deeply loved, and a man never died there at whose loss more tears were shed" (5–6).

Aware of the beauty that surrounded him as he traveled to see his patients, Dr. Jewett opened his companion daughter's eyes to an appreciation of the country and its people, which were to become the basis of her writings. In a poem Sarah wrote in memory of her father, she avers:

And in my mind there was no longer room
For any thought but of that dearest friend
Who taught me first the beauty of these days—
To watch the young leaves start, the birds return,
And how the brooks rush down their rocky ways,
The new life everywhere, the stars that burn

Bright in the mild, clear nights. Oh! he has gone,
And I must watch the spring this year, alone.

(*Verses*, 3)

Dr. Jewett introduced Sarah to numerous and varied writings
as well. In her preface to the *Letters*, Annie Fields confirms
Sarah's enthusiasm for her father's concerns: "After her father's
early death she loved to go into his office to consult his diary; she
knew his papers, his books, his medicines,—nothing that belonged to his mind or his work was foreign to her" (5). Fortunately, her father directly addressed and supported Sarah's
career as a writer, providing her with the maxim that she often
repeated and always tried to incorporate in her work: "Don't try
to write *about* people and things, tell them just as they are"
(*U*, 6). Jewett's father's influence could not be measured and
remained as an influence throughout her life: "Out of your sight
I was not left alone. . . . Heaven's peace you bring who ever
brought me earth's" (*Verses*, 1–2). Dr. Jewett encouraged his
daughter to be serene and courageous regarding her perceptions
and her decisions; he enabled her to grow in every direction, as
he himself had done.

The most frequent appearance of the redeemed man in Jewett's fiction is that of the man sketched in the mirror image of
her father. Both Mr. Leicester in *Betty Leicester* and John Hilton
in "The Hiltons' Holiday" and their own respective daughters,
Betty Leicester and Katy Hilton, reflect the spirit of the relationship between Sarah and her father. Jewett uses *Betty
Leicester* as a showcase to speak of her deep affection for her
father. In the story, Jewett omits the mother figure entirely
(Betty's mother is deceased) in a type of oedipal fantasy in which
Betty (alias Jewett) can have her father all to herself as they
roam the country together. When Betty's father is preparing to
go to Alaska to work without Betty, a rare occurrence, she regis-

ters disbelief: "It seemed wrong and unnatural that she and her father should not always be together everywhere" (6). This echoes Jewett's fear that all her "hopes and ambitions" had been buried along with her father after his death, a fear that she could not function without her father's physical presence. Published in 1890, twelve years after her father's death, Jewett's yearning for her father can be detected in Betty's joyous reunion with her father at the end of her summer without him. Mr. Leicester holds Betty's hand "tighter than ever, and looking at her as if he wished to kiss her again. He did kiss her again, it being his own Betty" (219). Betty is practically dancing along the road with excitement "and could not bear to let go her hold of her father's hand. It was even more dear and delightful than she had dreamed to have him back again" (220).

Betty's fondness for her father, like Jewett's, is directly correlated to an appreciation of her father's nurturing and support. There are decided similarities between Jewett and Dr. Jewett and Betty and Mr. Leicester. Though Mr. Leicester is not a doctor, through his career as a naturalist, he is able to show Betty "the country by-ways": "Mr. Leicester insisted that Betty learned more than she would from books in seeing the country and the people, and Betty herself liked it much better than if she had been kept steadily at her lessons" (93–94). Mr. Leicester likewise introduces Betty to his reading preferences. For him she memorizes specific poems by Milton, Lowell, Tennyson, and Arnold. Just as Jewett absorbed her father's interests and ideologies, Betty copies her father's frequently repeated maxims. Just as Mr. Leicester's professor in college "always roused one's enthusiasm as no one else could, and made whatever he was interested in seem the one thing in the world that was of very first importance" (247), so Betty regards her father: "Betty's heart glowed as she listened; she thought the same thing of papa" (247). Most importantly, Betty, like Sarah, wants to become a writer; her father has only encouragement to offer. Mr.

Leicester, who has treated his daughter as an adult companion all along, urges her to persist in doing the things she really wishes (163). Father and daughter are of one mind. Their affinity is reflected in the identical qualities of their eyes, "kind and frank and pleasant, [with] . . . a good fresh color . . ." (2). Katy Hilton is another Jewett prototype. Nine years old, as Jewett was "always nine" on her birthday, Katy is not as strong physically as her sister, and her father notices that "'Katy ain't one that'll be like to get married. . . . She lives right with herself . . .'" (*LN*, 100). Her favorite pastime is "to be rovin' out o' doors" (101), and when her father takes both her and her sister to town, Katy "silently sat apart enjoying herself as she never had done before" (112), absorbing all there was to see of the countryside. Of his two daughters, John Hilton is aligned with Katy. She works with him on the farm, and when it is time to sit on the porch, Katy "seated herself close to her father. . . . He put his arm around her shoulders, and drew her close to his side, where she stayed" (106). When John Hilton repeats the story of his mother and his lonely childhood after her untimely death, daughter Susan Ellen views the "old" story with disinterest, "think[ing] it tiresome to hear about her grandmother, who, being dead, was hardly worth talking about" (116). But Katy continues to view the same story as "new": "There was a tone in her father's voice that drew Katy's heart toward him with new affection" (116). Katy is slated to take her grandmother's place, to become the "new" teacher. Katy listens to her father because of their relational involvement, but also because he is passing down to her the legacy of her grandmother—a legacy of ambition. At the onset of the story, John tells his wife: "'Ambition's somethin' to me'" (103). He hopes one of his daughters will be a teacher like his mother. Katy is the obvious choice. According to Judge Masterson, she physically resembles her grandmother, and she is an excellent speller. Susan Ellen prefers to work with her mother in the house.

The story can be read as an initiation into the wider world of ambition, but it is not a strictly paternal legacy. Going back in time, Judge Masterson and John's mother went to school together, where "they were always called the two best scholars of their time" (115). The judge remembers Catherine Winn in the context of her brilliance as well as in the context of their youthful friendship. Catherine Winn has bequeathed her sense of ambition to her son John, who, in turn, passes it on to Katy. John's father, on the other hand, did not focus on ambition, but rather, succumbed to loneliness and discouragement after Catherine's death. Ambition links the meeting with the venerable Judge Masterson to the grandmother, to John, and, finally, to Katy. Just as maintaining the hearthside is not genetic, neither is the ambition to belong to the wider world of knowledge. Ambition has no sex; Jewett seems to say ambition does not have to be patrilineal or matrilineal. Some day it may not be necessary to discover the sexual identity of the influence. Yet from Jewett's nineteenth-century frame of reference, the world of ambition is generally reserved for the fathers, so their support of their daughters' ambition is crucial, as Jewett's father's support was to her own career.

Jewett's gratitude to her father can be perceived in the multitude of mirror images projected in doctor after doctor in story after story. The most well-known portrait is that of Dr. Leslie in A *Country Doctor*. Of all the books she wrote, this was Jewett's favorite, and the "portrait of [Dr. Jewett] in A *Country Doctor* may be accepted as accurate, quite without exaggeration" (Thorp, 15). Dr. Leslie is a rare mixture of action and "intuition," which his colleague Dr. Ferris acknowledges, "grows to be a wonderful second-sight in such a man as [he]" (108). "Singularly self-reliant and composed," Dr. Leslie's power is in "his mastery of himself" (33). Refusing to go to the city, where he can be heralded as a great theoretician, he remains content to function as "healer" in the small town of Oldfields, where "from his great knowledge of human nature he could understand and help many of his patients whose ailments were not wholly physical" (33).

It is Dr. Leslie's ability to recognize true success, the development of the entire person, which enables him to help Nan Prince realize her vocation. He does not try to form her to his concept but merely allows her to grow in her own direction: "'And if I can help one good child to work with nature and not against it, . . . and she turns out useful and intelligent, . . . I shall be more than glad. I don't care if it's a man's work or a woman's work; if it is hers I'm going to help her the very best way I can.'" (106). Unlike the mass of men, even the men of God, "Dr. Leslie was the only man who looked far ahead or saw much or cared much for true success," for he is like the only man "possessed by the thought that something wonderful is happening" in Titian's great picture of the Presentation of the Virgin (121). Dr. Leslie is the only one who can perceive that he is not witness to an insignificant girl climbing the temple steps, but instead, "a sacred sight" (121). Dr. Leslie will provide "something else than the business of housekeeping and what is called a woman's natural work, for [Nan's] activity and capacity to spend itself upon" (137). In the face of greatness, Dr. Leslie knows that "[dust] isn't the least matter in the world!" (168). Dr. Leslie and Nan Prince become "friend to friend," often "look[ing] upon life from the same standpoint" (162), for they are both "great doctor[s] [who] worked for the body's health, and tried to keep human beings free from the failures that come from neglect and ignorance, and ready to be the soul's instrument of action and service in this world" (185). To conclude the parallelism, it is a fair assumption to liken the comparison to the "vocation" Sarah Orne Jewett apprehended as the basis of her career as a writer.

And so the great doctor marches in profusion across the pages of Jewett's stories, nurturing as he goes along, reappearing even in Jewett's last great work, *Pointed Firs*, as the cooperative partner of Almira Todd, herbalist. Earlier, in *Betty Leicester*, Betty, while driving with the Dr. Prince of that story, discovers "a great lesson of the good doctor's helpfulness" (208). He, in turn, recognizes that "it isn't so much what . . . Betty does as what she is" (201). Polly Finch's champion is also a doctor who tells her to "go ahead" (*WH*, 65) with her plans to run her father's farm. He will back her financially, for he, too, discerns Polly's unusual capabilities: "'We've got the farm; but I'm only a girl. . . . That's what you might have said, and sat down and cried'" (83). The doctor, who "grew as fond of her as if she were his own daughter" (82), wishes there were more like her. "'You take hold of life in the right way'" (84), he concludes.

Two additional doctors proclaim "the right way" of doing things. The doctor in "The Failure of David Berry" upbraids Sam Wescott for failing to stand security for Berry's rent: "'You took away his pride, and you took away his living . . .'" (*NW*, 133). The doctor is perceptive. It is neither age nor sickness that is causing Berry's death but a "broke[n] . . . honest heart" (133). Another physician who devalues the almighty dollar is John Ashurst in Jewett's uncollected story "In a Country Practice." Since Ashurst is needed in the small town of Alton, he opts to stay in the country rather than to become the partner of the "king of the medical school" in a wealthy city practice (*U*, 212).

Redemption, in this instance the ability to develop the relational side of one's nature, is more likely if the male character in Jewett, similar to her strong women, remains close to nature and rural values. These men make the statement that they care for the natural environment as opposed to the industrial patriarchal value of aggregation. Jewett's mirror images of her father possess this quality. John Hilton, a farmer, resembles a "creature of the shady woods and brown earth" (*LN*, 97); Mr. Leicester studies nature as a field biologist. All of the "great" doctors are country doctors.

In several cases where a country/city dichotomy exists in a story, a man will come forth in favor of country values. At times, his choice is even more pronounced, as when there is a woman in the story whose false value system accentuates the man's more womanly oriented choice for nature and home. Israel Owen is given a favorable review by Jewett since he, unlike his wife, who wants the privileges of wealth, is more than satisfied to live on the "high, fruitful" (11) marsh island. As Mrs. Owen continues to place her hope in Doris's ultimate attachment to a wealthy man, Israel finds contentment in a sunset, the beauty of which is lost on his wife. Jerry Jenkins is another farmer whose only aim is to farm and appreciate "the wide outlook over the fields and woodlands" (*MD*, 73), but his daughter Serena swindles him out of his homestead. Jewett compares Jenkins to "a distressed New England Lear" (60). Serena has gone so far as to sell the one-hundred-year-old desk, depository of family memorabilia as well as important papers, for a sewing machine, symbol of her industrial values. Sentimental Jerry Jenkins is far more concerned about the precious, personal aspect of his mementos—"a curl which his wife had cut from the head of their little child who had died, . . . a piece of the Charter Oak at Hartford, and a bit of California gold that his brother had sent home in the early days of the gold-diggings" (65).

At first, Jacob Gaines agrees with his wife that the fifty-thousand-dollar legacy from his cousin should be used to form a partnership in his brother-in-law's lumber business. Yet Jacob, "a born farmer," as the title of this uncollected story stipulates, displays only discontent after his move to Boston. Jacob Gaines does not put much value on the profits he is making, a reaction that could have been foretold. Upon receiving the legacy, Jacob, a "very affectionate" (*U*, 337) man of "deep emotion" (336), avows: "'I wish he was 'live again, and the money might go hang'" (336). Neither Jacob nor his wife is happy until they return "to his native air in all its noble friendship" (343).

The "Native of Winby," the Honorable Joseph K. Laneway, soldier, statesman, and millionaire, is admirable for retaining his love for his rural community. Laneway has traveled all over the world in his exploits, but "[his] thoughts have flown back to the hills and brooks of Winby and to [the] little old schoolhouse" (11) where he was happy as a child. It is his "touch of true sentiment which added much to his really stirring and effective campaign speeches" (17–18). His visit to his old friend Abby Harran is most rewarding, for Senator Laneway realizes that "the delight and kindness of an old friend's welcome was the loveliest thing in the world" (24).

In "Peach-tree Joe," it is Joe's irrepressible love of living nature that keeps him from insanity while he is a member of another offshoot of the patriarchal system—war. A farm boy, Joe admits that he had never been called a coward until he became a soldier, but now he experiences a freezing fear whenever the battle cry is sounded. Joe finds sustenance in watering, preserving, and literally coaxing (as Miss Tempy does her quince tree) a small peach tree into bloom. Through the sensitive description of Joe, set against the details of the ridiculous behavior of the other men, Jewett's satire of war is complete. The narrator is obviously Jewett herself, listening to the story from John, "the master-of-horse," who was in real life in charge of the horses at the Jewett home. John, the friend of Peach-tree Joe, admits: "There were plenty of good, stout, knock-about men, dare-devils and high fellows that didn't think of anything but fighting and fooling" (U, 203). The men are further described as "stray cattle" who do not think of "killing folks" until "old band tunes would begin to rip the air" (205). Then, like so many robots, the men would "all catch hold and sing and step right out along the road—well 'twas like something that got into your head" (205). The ultimate irony ensues each time the Union soldiers take a break to trade with the Confederate troops; then, "after [they] had been chumming and trading an hour or so, [they] would set and go fighting again" (204).

Joe is different because he has developed his nurturing dimension; he cannot participate in the madness. The moment he does, he is killed by a stray bullet. Jewett signifies Joe's affiliation with the woman's realm. Joe is "girl-faced" and "handy as a woman" (204). He uplifts the spirits of the other men: "he had a pretty voice to sing, was real good company, and never seemed to fail us for a joke" (204).

As Peach-tree Joe is likened to a woman, a few of Jewett's male characters are said to resemble their mothers. It is this proximity to a matrilineal heritage that enables these men to identify with their mothers' values rather than their fathers'. While none of the Ashby men in "Miss Debby's Neighbors" are laudable, Joe Ashby is more emotional and less destructive than his argumentative father and brother. John Ashby demolishes his mother's house. Joe's profound desire is to inhabit his mother's space: "Joe had got to be well off, he could have bought most any farm about here, but he wanted the old place 'count of his attachment. He set everything by his mother, spite of her being dead so long" (*MD*, 203).

In "An Only Son," Warren Price is taking a long time to get settled in an occupation, but his saving grace is that his character resembles his mother's. She was Deacon Price's second wife, "a pale and delicate school teacher, who had roused some unsuspected longing for beauty and romance in Deacon Price's otherwise prosaic nature" (*TN*, 96). While "she had seemed like a windflower growing beside a ledge," Deacon Price had been forced to admit that "she was not fit for a farmer's wife" (96). Neither is Warren a farmer's son. When Warren first appears on the scene, his father will not listen to him, though Warren clearly looks "pleased and almost triumphant" (65) because he has failed to mend the gate. Like his mother, Warren is not practical. He has "odd notions" (67) about machines. While his father considers him "more and more helpless and forgitful" (67), Warren is actually a creative inventor. When the image of the fence recurs as a concern of Deacon Price's, it only serves to reinforce the notion of men "boxed-in" a linear pattern, blinded to all but that which produces immediate profit. At first, Deacon Price had felt "respect and reverence" for his son's ideas, but when no practical, marketable product appeared, his demeanor became one of "impatience and suspicion" (79). As the story continues, Deacon Price, who believed his son had stolen the money left in his care by the other selectmen, finds the sum has merely been misplaced. As Eliza, Deacon Price's niece and housekeeper, has maintained: "'[Men] are generally the most helpless creatur's alive'" (99). Deacon Price offers "solemn thanksgiving" (96), not in the church, but in the burying lot by the graves of his two wives. When Warren returns with the news of the success of his "long-toiled-over machine" (97), his father has been somewhat transformed into the emotional realm of women. It is a slow change. First, through his identification with the natural world, he obtains a kind of Ancient Mariner absolution: "He was glad to see a solitary spring of London Pride . . . [which] sent a bright ray of encouragement into the shadow of his thoughts" (72). Later, through his lonely experience reaped from doubting his son's worth, combined with the accompanying shame Deacon Price feels when he realizes his unjust accusations, he has softened. Before Warren arrives, Deacon Price has already reconciled his feelings toward his son, determining to love him no matter what his bent. He reassures Warren with "a shaky laugh" and "struck his son's shoulder by way of a clumsy caress" (98). It is not a total entry into the nurturing world, but it is a good start. As in "The Foreigner," and other Jewett stories involving transformation, "An Only Son" culminates in a salvific thundershower, the end of a long spell of drought.

Roaming the countryside trying to decide his life's course, Parker Jenkins of "A Landless Farmer," like Warren Price, is taking a long time to get settled. Parker also takes after his mother. His father at first believes that Parker is spoiled for that very reason: "'perhaps I indulged him more than was good for him, but he was more like his mother 'n any of 'em'" (*MD*, 78). Unlike Parker, neither of the two daughters has inherited any ability to interact relationally with people. Serena is concerned with monetary success; Mary Lyddy is insipid and ineffectual. Although neither Parker nor his mother exhibits a perfect emotional level, both being "quick temper[ed]" (79), they are able to see beyond their short fuses to the person underneath the petty quarrel. Jerry Jenkins, Parker's father, admits: "'Parker'll knock ye down with one hand, and pick ye right up again with the other'" (79).

Fortunately for Jerry Jenkins, Parker returns from his travels to save the farm for his father from his sister Serena. When Parker discovers that the father he thought was dead has pulled through his illness, he begins "crying like a child" (81) with relief. Hard-hearted, greedy Serena views his breaking down as a "theatrical performance, and a little unnecessary" (81). But Parker has no use for Serena's capitalistic view of living. He refers to her usurpation of the farm as "one more dirty dollar tucked away in the bank" (85). While Parker "'don't take much to farming,'" he has decided to stay and improve the production of the farm by raising cranberries, for the simple reason that "'father he holds on to me'" (87). The Sunday after his decision, it is Parker who has brought salvation to his father, not the minister's sermon. Parker values relationships, and Jerry Jenkins finds it difficult to listen to the sermon instead of "glanc[ing] round proudly at his son," for "it seemed to him a greater proof of the providence of God than had ever before been vouchsafed him, and he appeared to have taken, as everybody said, a new lease on life" (86).

When Jewett places "redeemed" men in the money-making world of business, away from their mothers and their "natural" homes, they generally have to suffer a great deal in order to maintain a proper relational value system. In the country, they seem to have an easier time displaying emotion and caring for people. It is as if they are too close to the patriarchal values in the industrial city, and with the pressure or temptation to be so-called "real men," they must undergo a struggle in order to display their female dimension. Dan, for instance, the agent of the mill in "The Gray Mills of Farley," is "keen and business-like, but quietly kind" (U, 265). Orphaned at three, he has had to rely on the generosity of good neighbors such as Mrs. Kilpatrick in order to survive. Now a man of forty, who looks fifty, he fights for the workers' rights to no avail. The workers, recipients of low pay and poor housing, are deprived of any share in the company's dividends. When the stock falls and the mill closes, they are left with nothing. Dan himself has suffered at the hands of the system. As the only one at the mill who is still employed, he uses all his resources to keep people from starving. Dan offers pieces of his land and free seeds to workers so they can supply themselves with food. With his own salary, he pays people to do odd jobs around the mill. By the time the mill reopens, Dan has helped virtually every family in the town. The cold business world lends Dan the sacrificial opportunity to display his emotive, nurturing side.

David Berry is broken by the system. He has always upheld the antithesis to the tenets of business—"to love one another," the Bible verse he kept by his workbench. Resisting every suggestion to provide his customers with inferior goods or services, David finds it impossible to live in the city's merchant district. Neither his friend Sam Wescott nor the local creditors make allowances for the person of David Berry, a man of integrity who will pay what he owes if he is allowed a grace period. David's only real relationship is with a poor girl whom he befriends. In this "dog eat dog" world of profits, David is as helpless as a small female child. David pays for his value system with his life.

Through exposure to the business world, Andrew Phillips of "Andrew's Fortune" and John Craven of "A Business Man" comes to discern their nurturing dimensions. Andrew has never liked farming and does not have qualities favorable to the occupation. He has remained for the sake of his uncle Stephen Dennett, who could not bear to lose his companionship. Andrew himself acknowledges that his uncle should have put him into some type of business. Yet when his uncle dies and the will is misplaced, Andrew desperately seeks the paper that will entitle him to the farm. Mr Lysander Dennett, Stephen's cousin, will be the rightful heir if the will is permanently lost. In actuality, Lysander needs the farm more than Andrew. Although Lysander is portrayed as a rather pathetic character, he has suffered through illness and hard times in order to keep abreast of poverty, and he wants to provide his two sons with a chance at success. Andrew is extremely principled. While Lysander will give him half the farm, he cannot accept the offer, never having seen the will. It is a good decision, for he is given a job in the city by Stephen Dennett's old friend Mr. Dunning. Andrew's "steady, painstaking ways" (CB, 82) are far more conducive to business than to farming, and Andrew progresses rapidly. When he returns for a sentimental vacation to the old farm, he finds the misplaced will. But Andrew is a kind man, educated by his uncle, who "'would n't want nobody's feelings hurt'" (46) in any circumstances, a well-loved man who was "like father and mother both to [Andrew]" (45). In his generosity and compassion, Andrew burns the will instead of reclaiming the farm. He goes a step further and provides a place in business for Lysander Dennett's grandson. Since Stephen Dennett had nurtured him well, Andrew makes the right choices despite his involvement in the world of business.

While Andrew Phillips remains uncorrupted, John Craven wholeheartedly endorses the acquisition of money as a way of life. Craven's thirst or "craving" has made him unaware that there is anything else worth desiring, that is, until he is forced to retire due to illness. Since he has spent no time cultivating any relationship on a personal level, not even with his wife, who dies before he can rectify his mistake, he finds himself alone and useless. Patronized and pushed aside, he fills his emptiness, and consequently finds redemption, by caring for a young couple who are struggling to accrue enough money so that they can marry. The couple befriends Craven, who they think is a poor and lonely man, and he, in return, forms a partnership with them in their notions shop, giving them capital and advice. Though the story itself is quite saccharine, Jewett's point is clear: "Yet the money-getter may win great wealth, and fail completely of reaching his highest value, and reward, and satisfaction as a human being" (*WH*, 151). John Craven realizes that he is far poorer than the young couple, "whose best capital was their love for each other" (173).

Some men are taught to nurture, while others seem to do so naturally. Though Jewett's ministers are often unflattering portraits of hollow, ineffectual men, they can reach the other extreme of the spectrum—saints. Jewett's Catholic priests are nearly always of this breed. Like the great doctors, many men of God have renounced the world in favor of helping its citizens. In "River Driftwood," Jewett extends her discussion of the good ministers of the last generation for pages. These ministers prefigure those that follow the industrial revolution, those new ministers whose emphasis lies more on the product, a sermon of "abstract generalities" (*CB*, 22) scientifically based on theological studies, rather than on the people to whom the sermon is delivered. The last generation has been "uncommonly practical men" who "preached all the better because much of their time was spent in a way that brought them in close contact with people's every-day lives" (21). When the Jewett persona of "An October Ride" retreats from the rain into the old parsonage, she muses fondly about the former inhabitant: "I was glad to think what a good, faithful man he was, who spoke comfortable words to his people and lived pleasantly with them in this quiet country place so many years," "always kind to the poor" (111). The Catholic priests fit the pattern of the old pastor except that they can be found tending the immigrant poor in the city as well as in the village. Frequently in Jewett's stories of the Irish and the French immigrants, the good priest appears. There is "saintly" (*KF*, 334) Father Henri in "Mère Pochette" and "earnest" (*SW*, 100) Father Miles in "The Luck of the Bogans." Father Daly in "The Gray Mills of Farley" does all he can for the jobless, starving families of the town, and sacrificial Father Ryan tries every method to reform the swindler Danny Nolan. Granted, all these preachers are one-dimensional, but Jewett was impressed with men who could influence people's lives for good rather than use people's lives for their own self-interest.

While psychic ability is almost exclusively reserved for Jewett's women characters, Jewett shows her confidence in men's capacity to become finely tuned and receptive to all the dimensions around them—seen and unseen. In *Deephaven*, Captain Sands introduces Helen and Kate to the possibility of psychic reciprocity as a mode of communicating deep-felt emotional ties. Unlike most men who deal in the abstract, empathic Captain Sands can set aside the male role to control. The most moving portrait of a man with psychic ability, however, is that of Jim Heron in "The Courting of Sister Wisby." Just as Jim is introduced into the story, Mrs. Goodsoe is expounding on the "second sight" (*KF*, 260) of her grandmother. Jim Heron, she avers, also has "the gift" (261). Heron has cued in to this matrilineal tradition. Jim can identify with people's deepest sorrows or joys; he can "'break your heart with those tunes of his, or else set your heels flying up the floor in a jig, though you was minister o' the First Parish and all wound up for a funeral prayer'" (260). Heron is so in tune with his emotional female dimension that at times his fiddle "'sounded like a woman's voice tellin' somethin' over and over, as if folks could help her out o' her sorrows if she could only make 'em understand'" (260). Jim does understand. When Mis' Jerry Foss has lost her three fatherless children to scarlet fever, she reacts "'like a piece o' marble'" (261). The neighbors fear she will lose her reason if she remains unable to shed tears. Someone thinks to call Jim Heron to help. As Jim plays his fiddle, he is able to translate to Mis' Foss the sympathy and compassion of the whole neighborhood: "' 'twas what the whole neighborhood felt for that mother all spoke in the notes'" (262). At this point, Mis' Foss climbs into Mrs. Goodsoe's mother's lap and cries. It takes both Mrs. Goodsoe's mother and Jim Heron to touch Mis' Foss. Neither could have accomplished the task alone. Nurturing and strength are tantamount.

11

The Postponed Marriage

Men and women working together is not an alien concept in Jewett. She does not rule out marriage for her characters, but she does see the need to postpone the event. Women past childbearing years are free of the biological doom that would encrust them in a mass of stereotypical roles. Even today many women still assume the total responsibility for child rearing. To avoid women's placement into that sphere, Jewett has them marry at an age beyond their capability to reproduce. Here they have equal leverage with a man. They can work hand-in-hand with a man of similar substance in a chosen environment, emotionally satisfied and supported. Of the nine stories in which the postponed marriage is featured, there are only two instances where the woman appears as a manipulator or opportunist and the man, a milksop. In several cases, the man is as anxious, or more anxious, than the woman to form an alliance based on true affection. In almost all cases, both members of the newly formed couple perceive themselves as benefiting greatly from the association.

The least satisfactory coupling occurs in "A Winter Courtship." While it is written in the comic vein, the irony undermines the humor as the story capitalizes on the ancient stereotypes. Mrs. Tobin plays the part of the manipulating woman who chases the reluctant Mr. Briley until *she* is caught.

As Richard Cary observes: "Women, invariably the wilier, conduct a classic strategy while leaving men the illusion that they are planning the battles in the endless war between the sexes" (*Jewett*, 110). Mr. Briley is the ineffectual Walter Mitty–type dreamer, "meek and tired-looking" (*SW*, 1), who reads lawless, bloody Western tales only to envision himself as a rugged pony express rider of old. He carries underneath the cushion of his two-seated covered wagon a heavy pistol, which he insists on displaying to all his regular passengers. As a boy, Mr. Briley wanted to run off to join the circus; now he desires to go out West to drive a coach filled with newly prospected gold, "'where the driver don't know one minute but he'll be shot dead the next'" (10).

Privy to Mr. Briley's romantic inclinations of himself as hero, Mrs. Tobin feels "a sudden inspiration of opportunity" (6); Mrs. Tobin lives on a poor farm that she cannot maintain by herself in the winter, and Mr. Briley has sizable savings but no home. While both Tobin and Briley initially feel sentimental and awkward at the "unexpected crisis" (8), Mrs. Tobin takes the reins and pushes Mr. Briley into a proposal. She inflates his ego by commenting on his courage in the face of so great a responsibility. "With a trace of coyness," she continues by flattering what she deems are his "real nice features" (9). Mrs. Tobin is also not above pointing out the flaws of her competitors, the women who have taken on Mr. Briley as a boarder. Even though Mr. Briley knows "he was in for something more than he had bargained" (10), he is overpowered by the wily Mrs. Tobin, "taken on the road in spite of his pistol" (17). Mr. Briley is made to feel he is the protector, but to Mrs. Tobin, "he's harmless as a fly" (17). As Mrs. Tobin plans to remake Mr. Briley by cutting his hair to have him look more ambitious, she continues to wonder exactly how much money he has in the bank. Mrs. Tobin does not need protecting, but in order to play the stereotypical role, she discloses her wishes under a mantle of manipulation.

Mr. Briley tries to sooth his inflated image of male strength by desiring to perform some dramatic act of daring-do that will shout his importance to the world. He is uncomfortable with developing satisfying relationships as a goal. Mrs. Tobin and Mr. Briley will be able to give each other a comfortable home and welcome companionship. It is too bad they cannot start their alliance on a more sincere emotional level.

Deacon Brimblecom and Sister Wisby in "The Courting of Sister Wisby" display their feelings very much out in the open; the only trouble is that they have a love/hate relationship. They are also rather malformed as human beings. Deacon Brimblecom is another Walter Mitty persona. His daydreams are of a more supernatural nature, however. During a minor hallucination, Brimblecom thinks he can locate water with a divining rod. Later, the pious deacon comes to believe it is possible to dwell among the angels on earth. Leaving his wife and children, he takes up residence with other believers, "[feeling] sure he was called by the voice of a spirit bride" (*TN*, 267). He eventually returns to his family, but when his wife dies, he has one more "pious fit" (268). It is as a great exhorter for the Christian Baptists that he first meets Sister Wisby. Mrs. Goodsoe remarks that too much use of the herb goldenthread has "puckered" (265) Sister Wisby's disposition. A resident of "Windy Hill," stormy Sister Wisby is extremely tight with others except in cases of severe illness. For one reason or another, all unexplained, Brimblecom and Wisby are attracted to each other. Yet Mrs. Goodsoe confirms: "'The way he come a-courtin' o' Sister Wisby was this: she went a-courtin' o' him'" (268).

Despite the tenuousness of their union, Sister Wisby and Deacon Brimblecom must be given some credit for their forthrightness. In the face of community disapproval, they decide to live together before marriage. Sister Wisby believes "'they was showin' excellent judgment, so much harm come from hasty unions and folks comin' to a realizin' sense of each other's fail-ins' when 't was too late'" (270–71). And faults abound. Each of them is unbelievably stubborn and set in his or her own ways. Arriving at Thanksgiving, Brimblecom is sent home again by April. But "'they made it up agin right away'" (274). It seems the very antagonism between them keeps the relationship going. Brimblecom drinks quite a bit, and Wisby never trusts him with anything, but he does work if she keeps after him. Mrs. Goodsoe makes a rather discomfiting comment: "'they was married off fair an' square, an' I don't know but they got along well as most folks'" (275).

Yet Jewett's assessment of the postponed marriage is generally far more positive. In "The Quest of Mr. Teaby," the tables are turned and the scenario takes on a much warmer hue. Here it is the man who wishes to marry and the woman who is reluctant. Mr. Teaby is most sincere and tender about his affection for Sister Pinkham; she ignores his overtures. Guarded Sister Pinkham is dressed in a "worn winter cloak with a thick plaid shawl over it" (SW, 62). But Mr. Teaby is all exposed, symbolized in turn by his "nearly new greenish linen duster," which he wears "as if it were yet summer" (62). Sister Pinkham, nevertheless, is not coy but cautious. Jewett does not adhere to the false notion that women are desperate to marry, incomplete without the attachment. Sister Pinkham is justifiably concerned. Never married, Mr. Teaby has earned "the name of a rover" (69). He is also rather lame. Sister Pinkham, rheumatic and older than Mr. Teaby, wonders if both of them will be incapacitated at the same time. Then again, Sister Pinkham has more than one choice. Elder Fry is also interested in marrying her, but she is concerned because he has relinquished the ministry in order to start a butter business, which will require her to work a great deal at a time when her life has become quite carefree. Although Mr. Teaby is "'long-winded and harpin'" (76), the scales do seem to be tipped in his favor. Sister Pinkham expounds on his virtues to the narrator: "'most likes him, an' there's nobody would be more missed. . . . he'll take right holt an' help, and there ain't nobody more gentle with the sick'" (76).

This is the healthiest relationship so far. Neither party has a hidden agenda, as Mrs. Tobin does in "A Winter Courtship," and neither wants to settle for a loveless match, such as the one pictured in "The Courting of Sister Wisby." Although the reluctance is reversed, both partners are interested and can come together in a realistic, comfortable love. Both want a home. While Mr. Teaby's choice is transparent, Sister Wisby also needs companionship, since she admits entertaining the possibility of a match with Elder Fry. Her feelings for Mr. Teaby, though veiled, are apparent at the end of the story when she retrieves Teaby's forgotten umbrella to mend. Sister Pinkham could leave the umbrella for him at a couple of different locations she knows he will visit, but she takes it with her so he will have to visit her. Even if Sister Pinkham is unsure of her own feelings, the narrator is not: "Sister Pinkham's affectionate thoughts were evidently following her old friend" (78). The outcome has been intimated all along. In the end, Sister Pinkham gathers her possessions along with the ones left by Mr. Teaby, "ready to make a new start" (78), taking the reader full circle to the beginning of the story where "there was a cheerful bravery of green in sheltered places,—a fine, live green that flattered the eye with its look of permanence . . ." (60). Mr. Teaby and Sister Pinkham will offer each other a "green place" in the midst of their autumnal years.

In "Miss Manning's Minister" and "A Second Spring," excellent matches are actualized. Yet they are both contained within a traditional framework, for the men lag behind, unaware and unable to identify with their sentiments for the women concerned until late in the relationship. When the new minister, Reverend Edward Taylor, is incapacitated by a stroke, Miss Manning deplores the reluctance of the parishioners to support

Taylor and takes him home to nurse him back to health. She is content to care for him indefinitely, but, quite naturally, Reverend Taylor is anxious to shed his invalidism. When the possibility of rehabilitation at a big Boston hospital becomes a reality, Taylor jumps at the chance. Miss Manning feels her chance for happiness has been shattered. After his cure, the minister joyfully accepts a missionary post; it appears that Miss Manning will lose him. Finally, Mr. Taylor declares himself: "'I find that I cannot be happy without you, Narcissa'" (*U*, 89). An "energetic" (89) robin begins to sing in the spring of this year as "the lilacs were in bloom" (81). The finale is not quite satisfactory, however. Miss Manning, too, is quite traditional in the sacrificial sense. Jewett admits Narcissa Manning is a woman who has a "craving for somebody to live for and take care of . . ." (89). But Jewett is equally reluctant to portray her as the total giver, with man as the duly acclaimed receiver. Although Miss Manning will have to move if she is to go with Taylor to the missions, Jewett refuses to allow her to relinquish her home; instead, Jewett arranges for Miss Manning's home to be marked for demolition by the railroad. Jewett also signifies that there is reciprocity between Taylor and Manning, an indispensable element for the survival of the relationship: "There was, however, a real bond of the best sort of friendship between them; for each had been both giver and receiver. There can be no true friendship or true love without this" (89). While Miss Manning has taken care of Taylor, he has encouraged her "capacity for greater things than housekeeping" (83). Reading outloud to this scholar has revitalized Miss Manning. She "became interested in books and literature in a way that opened a wider horizon to her than she had ever dreamed to be in existence" (87). And, most importantly, each is, in Mr. Taylor's words, "happy" together.

The scenario of "A Second Spring" is similar, in that a man's tragic situation brings a woman who cares for him. In this instance, Israel Haydon's wife has died, and he experiences a "dull hunger in his heart" (*LN*, 167). As spring arrives, Israel plants his wife's flower garden as usual. He remembers how she loved this season: "The grim old man leaned on the fence, and tried to keep back the sobs that shook his bent shoulders" (168). He cannot seem to function well without her. This is not necessarily a virtue, for Mrs. Martin, Israel's sister, complains: "'Men is boys. . . . They always want motherin', an' somebody to come to'" (171). Maria Durrant must come to serve as his housekeeper. Like Miss Manning, Maria has a "truly sympathetic, unselfish heart," and she "fairly longed to make the lonely, obstinate old man comfortable" (182). Maria Durrant differs from Narcissa Manning in that she has far more to gain from the alliance, the home she does not have. When she becomes aware that her neighbors are gossiping, insisting that she has overstayed her welcome at Haydon's farm, she is duly upset. Maria has "spent" her life "trying to make other people comfortable" (197), and if she loses this position, she will have to return "to her brother's noisy shiftless house; to work against wind and tide of laziness and improvidence" (189). Since Israel has just as much to lose as Maria if she goes, he proposes marriage. Maria is so overjoyed that she does not realize "the bleakness of his love-making," for she sees in his face "a truly anxious and even affectionate man" (192). Israel will never be effusive, but when he overhears a conversation between Maria and a visiting friend of his first wife's, in which Maria admits she "'marr[ied] for love'" (200), Israel realizes why he has felt young again lately and why "his heart grew very tender" (198). After the guest leaves, Israel enthusiastically avows: "'I've got a good wife *now*'" (202). The couple has been prompted "to new confidence and affection, to speak the affectionate thoughts that were in their hearts . . ." (201).

In "Miss Becky's Pilgrimage," the sentiments of both parties are ignited simultaneously. There is no other need here except the strong desire to be together. Although Miss Becky is looking for a place to settle after her brother's death, she is not destitute. Her brother was a minister, and a new minister is coming to inhabit the parsonage, so she will move. For a long time, Miss Becky has known what she wants from a relationship. Believing it impossible to find that closeness and equality in a marriage, Miss Becky has refused several offers, opting to live with her brother. They have been "capitally suited to each other, having that difference of disposition and similarity of tastes which make it possible for two people to live together without being too often reminded of the fact that we are in this world for the sake of discipline, and not enjoyment" (CB, 219). During a visit to her old hometown, Miss Becky encounters Mr. Beachum, the minister, another man with whom she can experience "the difference of disposition and similarity of tastes." At the tea party where they first meet, Mr. Beachum is shy, and Miss Becky draws him out to everyone's delight (the women of the parish have long since stopped "setting their caps" [239] for the immovable widower). Miss Becky and Mr. Beachum's source of affinity is the church; Miss Becky is bright and "well posted on clerical and religious questions" (239). More than these tangible reasons for a union is their overwhelming attraction for each other. Jewett accentuates their mutual flirtations by recording the community's reaction, which is one of "great fun and astonishment" (248) that two such mature people could act so young and poetic. The language of Mr. Beachum's proposal also differs from the prosaic utterances of Edward Taylor and Israel Haydon. On a garden walk, Beachum's announcement—"'you have already become very dear to me'"—commingled with his assurance "of a most heart-felt and enduring affection" (247), results in a "resounding kiss" (248). Miss Becky and Mr. Beachum will prove to be "made for each other" (249).

A youthful, romantic tone also pervades "The Dunnet Shepherdess" and its sequel, "William's Wedding," stories with the Dunnet Landing setting. Having courted for forty years,

William and Esther are finally to be married amid sunshine and spring. Though well advanced in years, the narrator affirms that "they were going to be young again now . . ." (Cather, 288). The obstacle all this time has been Esther's mother, a "cold," "disapproving," "forbidding" woman reduced to immobility after a stroke (228). Mrs. Todd comments: "'Well, the Lord's seen reason at last an' removed Mis' Cap'n Hight up to the farm, an' I don't know but the weddin's goin' to be this week'" (283).

The implication is that Mrs. Hight has been a hindrance in more ways than one. Mrs. Hight would surely have made William and Esther miserable if they had married while she still lived. Not only ornery but also very traditional, Mrs. Hight probably could not have tolerated a marriage between two people who did not walk the straight line of their respective male/female roles. These two stories chronicle an alliance between a man, silent and intuitive, and a woman, strong and purposeful. Although Esther's career as a shepherd has made it possible for her to save the farm after her father's death and support herself and her mother all these years, Mrs. Hight still complains "she ought to have been a teacher" (237), a proper job for a woman. The fact that Esther has revolutionized sheepherding in the area matters little to her mother. William alone is proud of her achievement; only he knows "the noble and patient heart that beat within her breast" (237). It is doubtful Mrs. Hight could have appreciated William, who is "kind of poetical" (211). His forte is his intuition, generally regarded as a woman's territory. The narrator is impressed with William's way "of answering [Esther's] unspoken thoughts as if they reached him better than words" (215), for "to be with him only for a short time was to live on a different level, where thoughts served best because they were thoughts in common" (222). William is also unafraid of a strong woman. Unlike the depiction of the standard marriage in Jewett, no longer does a man marry a woman who hides fearfully behind windows. Esther has reached new "Hights."

As the wedding approaches, William displays some of Esther's strength of purpose, and she manifests some of William's poetry. Much to his sister's amazement, William uncharacteristically comes to get Esther by "strikin' right in across the open bay like a man" (286) instead of "dodg[ing] round among the islands so he'll be the less observed" (286). With regard to Esther, the narrator remarks: "I never saw a young bride half so touching in her happiness as Esther was that day of her wedding" (297). As the couple is ready to set sail for their new home, a charming scene ensues, with William as nurturer: "then he wrapped her own shawl round her shoulders, and finding a pin in the lapel of his Sunday coat he pinned it for her. She looked at him fondly while he did this, and then glanced up at us, a pretty, girlish color brightening her cheeks" (298–99).

Jewett reinforces the ingenuousness of true affection as the definitive motivation for marriage in "All My Sad Captains." Although the widow Mrs. Lunn is a bit devious in asking three different men advice on shingling her roof (a roof that, incidentally, needs no shingling), in order to perk their personal interest in her into action, she is sincerely searching for the best partner. This plan on her part can only be viewed negatively by those who have a problem with woman as assertive. According to the rules of propriety, Mrs. Lunn is forced to spur the men into active pursuit since she can hardly start to visit and court them. If the rules were different, one feels sure that Mrs. Lunn would be more than happy to outwardly pursue a new mate. Actually, she is quite forthright in her interactions with these men when they come to visit, as well as with her community at large. Her final choice of a spouse will be for the best of heartfelt reasons.

Initially, Mrs. Lunn rejects Captain Witherspoon on practical grounds. While she favors him the most, for "there was nobody who made himself better company" (*LN*, 286) and no one to match his "heart of fire" (282), he is as poor as Mrs. Lunn herself. Captain Shaw is rich, and Captain Crowe has an adequate income but higher social standing than Shaw. But Shaw's drawback is that he is saddled with a band of carping relatives and four unruly children, while Crowe is desperate to marry to rid himself of his two domineering sisters. As Lunn explores her opportunities, the only choice becomes crystalline. In their dealings with Mrs. Lunn, Shaw and Crowe display rage and jealousy toward each other and toward Witherspoon as they wage a competitive male war over property rights. When Mrs. Lunn invites the new minister to be her sole boarder, regardless of the gossip that ensues among the parishioners, the imagined "rivalry" (311) is more than Shaw and Crowe can stand. Shaw's forehead puckers into "angry lines" and Crowe "thumped his cane emphatically" (311) as they go to force Mrs. Lunn to make a decision. "Warm-hearted" (297) Captain Witherspoon, as always, comes because he cares for Mrs. Lunn. He does not fit the male stereotype. "Little" (297) in stature, "thin and eager" (311), he arrives with "a hopeful light [shining] in his eyes: his choice was not from his judgment, but from his heart" (311). Mrs. Lunn, who has coincidentally received an inheritance from her deceased cousin, dismisses Captain Shaw angrily since "'he's always so full o' business'" (315); refuses pathetic Captain Crowe gently, for he is a "good, kind-hearted man" (318); and claims Captain Witherspoon, her "friend" (318).

Although all of the male/female trappings have not disappeared—Mrs. Lunn asks Witherspoon for more needless advice on how to handle her inheritance, and he "assumed the place of protector" (319)—this is only incipient behavior. In the actual workings of the relationship, it is Mrs. Lunn who will be the business-minded protector. Captain Witherspoon, in turn, sets aside his male ego and accepts Mrs. Lunn's sensible plan to maintain the minister as a boarder in their home for the good company and additional revenue he will provide. By allowing the minister to remain, Lunn and Witherspoon assent to the fact that marriage partners cannot fulfill all of each other's needs.

This is not to be the traditional marriage. Neither expects to live all alone in some Edenic garden. When Lunn and Witherspoon step forward to grasp each other's hands, Jewett is clear: "They may not have been young, but they knew all the better how to value happiness" (320). All three captains had a chance, but only to the measure that they could discard what society maintains is important and plunge into real emotion. Bonding is the true measure of success.

Miss Esther Porley of "Miss Esther's Guest" is another woman who is sure of what she does not want. After her mother's death she cannot bear to have a boarder take her mother's place. She conquers her reluctance to participate in her church's Country Week when she volunteers to be the host for a city woman, elderly like her mother, who will come for a country visit. Unfortunately, the committee in Boston overlooks the fact that Miss Esther has requested a woman. Instead, they send her Mr. Rill, an engraver who lives in a garret and has eyes too worn to continue his close work to any great degree. While Miss Esther Porley is shocked when she discovers the sex of her visitor, the reader can be sure of a successful ending to this dilemma. The names of both parties testify to their readiness for this relationship. Esther, who is called "Easter" (NW, 160) by her old friends, is looking for the prospect of a rebirth. Mr. Rill is the regenerative essence of his watery, life-giving surname. And their new life is conceivable, Jewett seems to be saying, because of Mr. Rill's fluidity with gender roles. In this story, there are many references to different familial relationships, male and female, that Miss Porley and Mr. Rill can fill for each other. The fact that Mr. Rill, who has lost his sister, and Miss Porley, who has lost her mother, are uniting, makes the statement that a man can be like a mother and a wife can be like a sister. At one point, Miss Porley also muses: "if she could have her long lost brother come home from sea, she should like to have him look and behave as gentle and kind as Mr. Rill" (173). At another time she describes him as "fatherly" (174). Rill has also taken his sister's place at home. Since his hands are so used "to delicate work he had been less bungling in his simple household affairs than many another man might have been" (168). In addition to performing delicate work, his attachment to his songbird speaks of his love of beauty and his need for companionship. He can tend a woman's garden, keeping the "garden paths . . . clear of weeds and swept" (174). Miss Porley declares: "'he wa'n't like other men,—[but] kind and friendly and fatherly, and never stayed round when I was occupied, but entertained himself down street considerable, an' was as industrious as a bee, always asking me if there wa'n't something he could do about the house. He and a sister some years older used to keep house together . . .'" (174–75). And so Mr. Rill's visit extends from a week "to a fortnight, and then to a month" (173). When he leaves briefly on engraving business in the city, Miss Porley avows to the minister's wife: "'My old lady's just gone. . . . I was so lonesome I could not stay in the house'" (174). This story abounds in allusions to role interchanges, to the many different types of care, both male and female, that can be given in a gratifying relationship.

Sarah Orne Jewett might not have been able to write of passionate, romantic young love, but she could most certainly write of tender, old love—real love—person to person. Jewett did not lose hope that young lovers might one day be able to marry and enter relationships on equal footing and with fluidity in the roles they chose to fill. Polly Finch, who takes over her father's farm, is not exempt from the possibility. Having averted the patronizing Jerry Minton, Polly believes "it will be a much better man than he whom she falls in love with next" (*WH*, 84–85). And in Jewett's last published story in 1904, she gives a gentle vote of confidence for men's and women's lifetime alliances. After sixty-two years of marriage, Alonzo and Mary Ann Hallett make a surprise journey one spring morning to the town where they had spent their early married life. Although they have had "many a day's hard pull" (*U*, 389), their love has remained constant. At the end of their visit they rise "with one consent" and link arms to "go home together" (390).

12

"A White Heron"

Symbolic Possibilities for Androgyny

T he world of "A White Heron" is not a people world, though it is very human. While Jewett remains doubtful in "A White Heron" of the present possibility of men and women joining together, she confirms a symbolic hope for androgynous figures and for cooperative relationships. In this realm, the potentiality is credible for a girl, a cow, a tree, and a bird. It is the fairy-tale forest the reader enters, where the creatures act the parts of people who commune with each other.

It was not unusual for Jewett to personify the natural world; she believed it was alive and communicative. In "A Winter Drive," Jewett averred: "There was an old doctrine called Hylozoism, which appeals to my far from Pagan sympathies, the theory of the soul of the world, of a life residing in nature, and that all matter lives; the doctrine that life and matter are inseparable" (*CB*, 168). To Jewett, each tree displayed human characteristics, and every living thing could be addressed: "how long we shall have to go to school when people are expected to talk to the trees, and birds, and beasts, in their own language" (*CB*, 4).

All this Sylvia can do. After playing hide-and-seek with her friend Mistress Moolly the cow, Sylvia travels homeward through a forest "full of little birds and beasts that seemed to be wide-awake, and going about their world, or else saying good-night to each other in sleepy twitters" (*TN*, 141). Sylvia is part of this natural, Edenic conversation. No other human being in this story has the capacity. Sylvia is privy to a dreamscape of Jewett's, where the best of all possible worlds continues in one fantastic vision. Sylvia is the new Eve and Adam combined. Personal wholeness is the utmost criterion in this pristine world.

Of the other two humans in the story, the grandmother and the hunter, neither is able to enter the text of the fairy-tale forest. The grandmother remains in the cabin on the periphery; the hunter invades but cannot penetrate its secrets. The grandmother is an anomalous figure. While she is the center of Sylvy's people world, the provider of Sylvy's natural realm (she has rescued Sylvy from the "crowded manufacturing town" [140]), she is duped by the values of the patriarchal system. The grandmother responds to the hunter's charm, wealth, and authority. When she appears at the cabin with the hunter, Sylvy is aware of her grandmother's limitations; she "knew by instinct that her grandmother did not comprehend the gravity of the situation" (143). Unaware of the portentousness of the hunter's intrusion, the grandmother's "long slumbering hospitality seemed to be easily awakened" (144). She "graciously" (144) offers him lodging, "smile[s]" (146) as he tells of his ornithological adventures, and, finally, slides into the same comatose emotional state as the hunter. When Sylvia leaves the house in the early morning to find the heron, the narrator is sure to comment that both "the young sportsman and his old hostess were sound asleep" (152). The grandmother's misguided values are evident at the end of the story when Sylvia returns and refuses to trust her with the heron's whereabouts. Again, the grandmother is linked with the hunter—"the grandmother and the sportsman stand in the door together and question her" (157). Whether the grandmother regrets losing the ten-dollar reward or the approbation of the male hunter remains unknown, but the betrayal of Sylvia and the maternal world is clear. Sylvia, thankfully, cannot speak, "though the old grandmother fretfully rebukes her" (157).

Sylvia's decision not to please the hunter presents a far more terrifying prospect for her personally. It is sometimes lonely in the woods, and a human friend would be welcome. The hunter is externally very appealing. He is frequently described favorably as "kindly" (143), "kind and sympathetic" (149), "charming and delightful" (149), and "very cheerful and persuasive" (142). He gives Sylvia his scientific knowledge of the birds she loves, and he promises her a close relationship with him. When he first appears, the hunter presents himself as "lost" and in "need [of] a friend very much" (143). But like the satanic snake in the garden of paradise, his charm is veneer and his intent is destructive. Sylvia is slow to learn and, even in the end, not entirely convinced of his callous corruption, but the signs are all intact. The hunter's arrival is announced by his "determined," "aggressive" (142) whistle, reminiscent of "the great red-faced boy who used to chase and frighten [Sylvia]" (142). The parallel is drawn; the whistle is the manifestation of male behavior in general. Gun in hand, the hunter is ingrained in the process of male conquest, for he has been annihilating birds for his collection since he was a boy. Killing is "his day's pleasure" (157). His "heavy game bag" (143) attests to his prowess, and his offering of a bribe of ten dollars to Sylvia for information on the heron makes it clear that birds are not the only creatures he desires to subdue. Several critical studies have interpreted the hunter's gun as a simulated phallus and his quest of birds as reminiscent of the plight of the Victorian woman at the hands of her husband—killed, stuffed, and put on a pedestal for viewing.

Sylvia is almost convinced; she "could have served him and followed him and loved him as a dog loves!" (158). In actuality, Jewett does not feel that a person who displays a dog's loyalty is necessarily denigrated. Echoes of this phrase occur several times in her works. Jewett is quoted as using the phrase in reference to her own father: "I used to follow him about silently, like an undemanding little dog, content to follow at his heels" (Spofford, "Jewett," 329). Nan Prince observes Dr. Leslie in church, "the child's eyes watching him as a dog's might have done, forcing him to forget the preaching altogether and to attend to this dumb request for sympathy" (*CD*, 45). Men reciprocate this stance with women. Angered by Doris's attention to Dick Dale in *A Marsh Island*, Dan Lester complains: "'I've waited on her year in and year out, and followed her about like a dog,' and the tears filled the poor fellow's eyes" (156). Women assume this posture with other women as well. With Helena Vernon, Martha of "Martha's Lady" finds a supportive friendship. Consequently, "Martha's eyes were as affectionate as a dog's and there was a new look of hopefulness on her face . . ." (*QT*, 143). This comparison to an affectionate dog speaks of a person's longing to find an emotionally supportive relationship. Sylvia also displays this need, but unlike the characters in all of the other relationships mentioned, the hunter is incapable of returning this loyalty, of loving Sylvia for herself. Jewett, Nan Prince, Dan Lester, and Martha are all compensated for their loyalty with sympathy and care. But Sylvia's "dream of love" (*TN*, 149) has no basis in the person of the hunter. She is a more realistic hero in that she must struggle to make the right choice. In truth, she does not need the hunter, for he is an intruder in this sylvan paradise, and Sylvia does not need completion, though she, like everyone else, would profit from being loved.

Sylvia possesses all the necessary components for the hero's quest; she is both female and male in nature. Her eyes are gray. Sylvia is a blend of black and white, male and female. Gray is a color that has no hue and, therefore, no saturation. Sylvia is everything and nothing; she is pristine in her androgynous adventure. As black absorbs all light rays and white reflects all the rays of the color spectrum combined, Sylvia contains all possibility. She is fluid movement, "a part of the gray shadows and the moving leaves" (141–42). Truly the definition of "in the gray," in "an unbleached, undyed, or unfinished state," she will continue to become a combination of the characteristics of both sexes, though she will choose to remain true to her primary orientation of nurturer.

The possibility of a male nurturer presents itself in the character of Sylvia's uncle Dan to whom the grandmother compares Sylvy. Like Dan, Sylvia can claim intimate knowledge with every inch of the forest and every creature who lives therein. She can tame the squirrels and all different varieties of birds to feed right out of her hands. Before he leaves, Dan tames a crow. Like the hunter, Dan is also good at gunning, but there is no mention of his killing animals for any reason other than survival. He is not culpable in providing food to alleviate his family's poverty. Yet Dan, unable to get along with his father, abandons his family to journey to the West. Perhaps Dan's polarity with his father has resulted from his father's incapacity to accept the more emotional, sensitive dimension of his son Dan's female side. But Dan is at best a primitive androgynous reference. In embracing Western conquest, he has failed to maintain any emotional connection with his mother. She suffers, not knowing whether her son is alive or dead.

Just as Dan wields his gun for the purpose of survival, Sylvia, in turn, does not mind owning a useful weapon of aggression. She accepts the hunter's present of a jackknife, "which she thought as great a treasure as if she were a desert-islander" (149). Being a desert islander is a positive reference in Jewett. Adventurous, spunky Polly in Jewett's children's story "The Desert Islanders" rereads *The Swiss Family Robinson*; Nan Prince of *A Country Doctor* peruses *Robinson Crusoe* before embarking on her quest to become a woman doctor. Women can go on adventures and can fend for themselves. It is not deplorable to use aggressive materials, external or internal, to carve out an existence, while it is to conquer for the lecherousness of the experience. Aggression is part of Sylvia's nature. The knife is not a male weapon to be discarded but a tool to be used with care.

And so Sylvia begins her journey with "a spirit of adventure" and "wild ambition" (151). In a scene involving Sylvia and a tree, the sexual identities of the participants are underscored. The characteristics usually attributed to either male or female are malleable, exchangeable. The pine, the oldest tree in the forest, offers a larger view to Sylvia. His utmost branches are constantly moving, stirred by the wind "no matter how hot and still the air might be below" (151). Sylvia desires to expand her perimeters; she has often stood at the base of the tree, longing to scale its heights and gain the panorama. Now she ascends at "break of day . . . [to] see all the world" (151), as well as the heron and its hidden nest. Sylvia climbs first the oak and then over to the pine; she "pinch[es]," holding on with hands "like bird claws" (152), prefiguring her identification with the heron. At first the pine tree reacts defensively, for his "twigs caught and held her and scratched her like angry talons" (153). As soon as he realizes the girl means him no harm, he becomes "a great main mast," a ship, offering even his "least twigs" "to advantage" (154) Sylvia to her destination. In symbolic intercourse, the tree "lengthens itself out" (154), but it is Sylvia who initiated, Sylvia who "mounted," "tingling, eager blood coursing the channels of her whole frame" (152). Carol Singley describes Sylvia's movement as "a virtual appropriation of the traditional role of the phallus," which results in the pine tree's eventual "surrendering to her power" (79). Yet the tree and Sylvia ultimately achieve a noncombative union. It is intercourse without penetration. There is no sexual imprisonment where active and passive roles can be interchanged. The independence of each gender is secure. The tree known as "the last of its generation" (*TN*, 150–51) on the edge of the woods may be fatherly wise and caring, but he may also be the precursor of a new man capable of womanly compassion. The male tree begins by mauling Sylvia, fighting for the superior stance, but he is the last of the line of men who have to be awakened to their nurturing dimension. For this tree's trunk runs "to the voyaging earth" (154), not to man's commanding pinnacles.

Then Sylvia sights the heron, an uncanny choice of bird on Jewett's part. It would be hard to fasten on a bird with a more androgynous strain. Jewett was an environmentalist who bemoaned any destruction of the natural world, be it the cutting down of a single tree or the polluting of the Piscataqua River. It would be reasonable to conclude that she was aware of the well-known plight of the small white heron, or snowy egret, which was verging on extinction at the turn of the century due to the plumage hunters for the millinery trade (Hancock and Elliott, 216). While Jewett refers to the bird as "he," it must be noted that "he" was the appropriate pronoun at the time to refer to a person or animal whose sex was unknown. With the small white heron or snowy egret, it would be impossible to tell whether it was a male or female bird Sylvia saw that brilliant morning. Outwardly, both sexes develop ornamental plumage in time for mating (219). The snowy egret is "an adaptable species" (219), where both the male and female aid in building the nest, in incubating the eggs, and in feeding the young (219). Whether the "mate on the nest" the heron "cries back to" (*TN*, 156) is male or female is an insuperable question. Sylvia has risen above society's rules, and like the heron, "she too could go flying away among the clouds" (155), part of a vision available to both sexes. For Sylvia and the heron, this is unfamiliar territory, but it is a green land where the heron (and his counterpart, Sylvia) can "[plume] his feathers for the new day" (156).

Yet Sylvia must return to the earth, her matrilineal base, and the first place from which she has been able to sight the heron, "an open place where the sunshine always seemed strangely yellow and hot" (148). James Ellis finds this spot "serves admirably as an ironic symbol of the feminine principle in nature," whose "hidden but soft black mud is as powerful . . . as is the great pine tree that [Sylvia] must eventually climb in order to achieve her epiphany" (6). Sylvia's grandmother, again proffering incorrect, traditional advice, advocates a heterosexual relationship with the hunter rather than an immersion in the maternal world. She warns Sylvia to stay away from the soft, wet earth where "she might sink in . . . and never be heard of more" (*TN*, 148). But Sylvia's choice, as Elizabeth Ammons describes it, signals the reworking of the traditional fairy tale, which demonstrates "the triumph of heterosexuality over matrisexuality," wherein "a sexy young man saves a sexually awakening heroine from an ugly witch" ("The Shape of Violence," 11). For Ammons, the matrisexual world is one where "women would be free to remain woman-identified, emotionally and erotically, throughout life" (9–10). Sylvia elects to maintain her ties with her matrisexual world, "a place defined as free, healthy, and 'natural' in this story, over the world of heterosexual favor and violence represented by the hunter" (10).

When Sylvia returns from her journey, she cannot speak. There is nothing wrong with Sylvia's silence in this situation, for there is no one, neither her grandmother nor the hunter, who would be capable of understanding her decision to save the bird's life and align herself with Mother Nature. But it is quite true that if Sylvia remains solely in the forest, she will never have a voice. Separation from her male dimension would limit Sylvia's existence as well as deprive the patriarchal world of her nurturing centricity. Sylvia is right to resist the male concerns the hunter represents—heterosexuality and industrial acquisitiveness—for this would necessitate death for a woman of Sylvia's historical framework. But having made her choice, she is no longer afraid of humans, of boys' or men's aggressive whistles. She does not have to remain sequestered in the forest for fear of the crowded city if she does not care to. Sylvia deserves a voice in the world at large, and from all indications, she desires it. Sylvia's feeling of being "wholly triumphant, high in the tree-top" (*TN*, 154) at first has nothing to do with the heron or the hunter. Sylvia is amazed, for "truly it was a vast and awesome world" (155). It is "the sea which Sylvia had wondered and dreamed about, but never had looked upon, though its great voice could often be heard above the noise of the woods on stormy nights" (148). Sylvia has wanted to rise with and above the forest for a long time. Like Jewett, Sylvia is ambitious. Sylvia, too, is that magical nine years old that Jewett on her forty-eighth birthday claimed to be her eternal age. On the biological verge of womanhood, Sylvia can envision herself both freed from the bonds of heterosexuality and ready to claim her right to achieve in a man's world.

But unlike Jewett, Sylvia has been tempted by the romantic, illusionary moon. Early in the story, she and the hunter, "the new-made friends," "sat down in the doorway together while the moon came up" (145). In the end, Sylvia climbs the tree while it is "asleep yet in the paling moonlight" (152). She advances to the top of the pine, looking beyond the pale moonlight into the resplendent sun. With her face "like a pale star" (154), Sylvia becomes for Jewett the prophetic "woman adorned with the sun, standing on the moon, and with the twelve stars on her head for a crown" (Revelation 12:1). Sylvia has renounced imprisoning heterosexuality, but she heralds woman's share in the "vast and awesome world," a world in which Jewett herself realized completion.

13

Beyond Gender

The Country of the Pointed Firs

ewett's narrator in *The Country of the Pointed Firs* could easily be Sylvia grown-up, a participator in "the vast and awesome world." But in her final book, Jewett lights on the dilemma of remaining in touch with one's nurturing dimension while becoming a part of patriarchal society. The narrator is a writer who appears to have subsumed more about the world of men than the world of women. It is time for "The Return" (the title of the first chapter) to her true center. Donovan envisions this women's realm as a type of matriarchal Christianity built on the transcending powers of women's friendships; Folsom speaks of a participation in others' lives through the powers of empathic imagination; and Pryse describes a return to mother and mother's powers, as does Sherman in her elucidation of the Demeter/Persephone myth.

Yet Dunnet Landing is more than a place to "return" to female nurturance. Out of society's space and time, Dunnet Landing is a place wherein the allocation of gender roles is called into question. With some characters, in fact, it is sometimes hard to tell who is a man and who is a woman by society's standards for male and female qualities and patterns of behavior. William and Captain Tilley act more like women than men. Joanna in her rigidity mirrors men's method of dealing with per-

sonal conflict by shutting herself off from intimacy. Mari Harris
lacks a nurturing dimension. And for Mrs. Todd, Dunnet Landing, a primarily female realm, is not sufficient for her nature
and talents. Jewett outlines the process of the narrator's struggle
as well as the struggle of the men, in particular, and the women
surrounding her to free themselves from any particular stereotypical molds. Some of these characters, predominantly men,
fail; some settle for less than the ideal; yet even the most misguided, such as Captain Littlepage, is accepted with compassion
in this realm where gender does not mean superior or inferior.
Dunnet Landing is unusually void of polarities between men
and women resulting from rigid gender behavior.

Everything about Dunnet Landing speaks of the person and
relational living. The narrator's return is motivated by the
"simple fact of acquaintance" with that neighborhood, with its
windows "like knowing eyes" (1). Returning to this village is
akin to developing a relationship with "a single person" (2). "The
process of falling in love at first sight is as final as it is swift in
such a case," the narrator admits, "but the growth of true
friendship may be a lifelong affair" (2). All of these relational
references indicate the narrator's hunger for intimacy after a
long sojourn in the male world where she is a writer.

Her tutor, Mrs. Todd, makes her appearance in chapter two.
Almira Todd is a whole person of commanding stature. She is
"very huge" with "*full* skirts" (emphasis mine) (4). Her "height
and massiveness" are suggestive of a "huge sibyl" (10), and later
she will be likened to Antigone on the Theban plain. Mrs. Todd
nurtures "great treasures and rareties" (4) not only in her herbal
garden but in people as well. Streams of people consult Mrs.
Todd, who, the narrator acknowledges, cures more than physical ailments: "it seemed sometimes as if love and hate and jealousy and adverse winds at sea might also find their proper
remedies among the curious wild-looking plants in Mrs. Todd's
garden" (5).

The narrator experiences a "strange fragrance" (10) and "a

dim sense and a remembrance of something in the forgotten past" (4) while she is in the presence of Almira Todd—indications of her removal from her nurturing center. Not yet capable of uniting her goal-oriented self with her relational self, she chooses to absent herself from "seein' folks" (8) and opts for putting words on paper. Avoiding even conversational interruptions, the narrator rents the schoolhouse in order to pursue her literary endeavors. While she feels cruel and selfish for having curtailed Mrs. Todd's harvest of herbs for people's winter ailments, she quickly settles into her former "most businesslike" (13) posture. She is further distanced from the people of Dunnet Landing when she hurries away to the schoolhouse from Mrs. Begg's funeral, instead of participating in the funeral procession. Experiencing "a sort of pain," the narrator acknowledges: "I had now made myself and my friends remember that I did not really belong to Dunnet Landing" (19). Disconnected, she longs for "the outer world" (19), where her inability to live relationally will not be recognized as a deficiency.

The narrator is resisting "the return," but the situation is far from hopeless. Although she sits at the teacher's desk in the schoolhouse, she admits feeling like "a small scholar" (13). She wavers in her determination to remove herself: "Once or twice I feigned excuses for staying at home, while Mrs. Todd made distant excursions . . ." (14). And best of all, Mrs. Todd has not given up on the "small scholar." In true nurturing fashion, rather than withdrawing to match the narrator's withdrawal, Mrs. Todd begins "a deeper intimacy" (9). A number of critics have noted the alternating patterns of solitude and intimacy in *Pointed Firs*. The resisting narrator is about to begin a type of Dickensian journey during which she will encounter three ghosts who will facilitate her reawakening to her relational self. In each instance, Mrs. Todd will serve as the understanding listener, clarifier, and enlightener of the narrator's experiences. Mrs. Todd is the guide to relational living.

After electing to return to the "business" of writing rather than to partake in the funeral procession, the narrator is visited by Captain Littlepage, a rather ghostly figure himself, vaporous in his "loneliness and misapprehension" (22). He is all male in his orientation. At this point, so is the narrator, who feels "like a besieged miser of time" (20), inconvenienced by the arrival of her visitor. Captain Littlepage is also captivated by words (particularly the lofty ones in *Paradise Lost*) and knowledge, rather than by people. He admits reading for company on his sailing ventures, remaining aloof from his crew as a captain should. At present, he is still isolated, generally to be found "sitting pale and old behind a closed window" (17). Didactic Captain Littlepage mocks his ignorant fellow villagers for their insularity and their lack of an active, aggressive quest. "In that handful of houses they fancy that they comprehend the universe," Littlepage jeers. With the loss of shipping, Littlepage continues, it is "low-water mark" (43) in Dunnet Landing: "'There's no large-minded way of thinking now; the worst have got to be best and rule everything; we're all turned upside down and going back year by year'" (29).

Littlepage's male view stipulates the necessity for an authorial, competitive movement alien to the folk of Dunnet Landing. His frustration stems from his inability to convince the villagers of his authority as the only "large-minded" citizen. His claim is his knowledge of the greatest discovery known to "man," the "waiting-place," a ghostly realm between this world and the next. As the story unfolds, it mirrors the monomania in Mary Shelley's account of Victor Frankenstein's pursuit to create his monster. And the scenario Littlepage proffers nearly mimics Frankenstein's counterpart, Captain Walton, in his obsession to get to the North Pole. Enclosed in a myopic vision, Littlepage, and formerly his acquaintance old Gaffett, have pursued this goal, insensible to the welfare of their respective crews. Behind schedule due to foggy weather conditions, Littlepage chooses to forge ahead to deliver his cargo rather than to winter in the

North. This decision results in his loss of his ship, the *Minerva*, and his crew. Gaffett also loses his crew and ship in trying to reach the North Pole as well as in spending days attempting to decipher the meaning of "the waiting-place" he accidentally discovers. Men keep going even when the quest is useless and will result in death. Even though Littlepage and Gaffett have experienced similar tragedies, they cannot communicate to each other the pain of their failures. Part of the problem is that they will acknowledge neither that they have failed nor that they are in any way culpable. The only reason Gaffett, who is usually talking to himself, trusts Littlepage with his knowledge of "the waiting-place," is because he fears he will never get away from the small missionary station where he has found refuge after his shipwreck. Nevertheless, he will not give Littlepage the directions to get there.

The waiting place sounds strangely like a symbolic representation of men and their traditional mode of interacting with others. The inhabitants of this place are illusive, "all blowing grey figures that would pass along alone" (37). They are in "the shapes of folks," but the sailors "never could get near them" (37), for they seemed to recede as the men got closer. These "fog-shaped men" are also combative. Littlepage recounts: "'Those folks, or whatever they were, come about 'em like bats; all at once they raised incessant armies, and come as if to drive 'em back to sea'" (38).

The narrator's encounter with this first ghostly apparition has come to an end, and she has been duly warned of the excesses of a goal-oriented, competitive existence. For she, too, is a Victor Frankenstein in her preoccupation with her writing. And she feels the loss as keenly as Victor when he is left alone after the monster has killed all the people to whom he was connected. The difference is that the narrator is a woman, and she will decide in time to foster the dimension that is her own. Like the swallow who enters the schoolroom during Littlepage's discourse "and beat itself against the walls for a minute, and escaped again to the open air" (25), the narrator's time has come to leave the enclosure. Having seen the narrator with Captain Littlepage, Mrs. Todd approaches her "with an anxious expression" (43). She must counteract the misinformation the narrator has received from Littlepage. The sky has been graying and clouding over, "and a shadow had fallen on the darkening shore" (45). But "suddenly . . . a gleam of golden sunshine struck the outer islands" (45), the place, Mrs. Todd informs the narrator, where her mother lives. After calming the narrator with a mug of spruce beer treated with the herbal sedative chamomile, Mrs. Todd will take the narrator the following morning to absorb the atmosphere of Green Island rather than the sterile, stagnant air of the waiting place up North.

As the narrator and Almira Todd set sail, Todd seems intent on emphasizing the insufficiency of the male point of view epitomized in the story of Captain Littlepage in order to prepare the narrator for the reception of the female perspective encapsulated on Green Island. Todd insists on taking a small boat to avoid the inclusion of men on the journey: "'[We] don't want to carry no men folks havin' to be considered every minute an' takin' up all our time'" (49–50). The only male to join them will be cousin Johnny, who will not function as a controller of the situation, but as a relation who will work with the two women. A typical man, however, Asa, "who was too ready with his criticism and advice on every possible subject" (51), is shouting directions from the shore. With perfect composure, Mrs. Todd ignores Asa's legislation while referring to his country origin. The implication that Asa knows nothing of sailing is not lost on the spectators, who chuckle at Asa's embarrassment and indignation. To finalize her picture of men's inflexibility and egocentricity, Mrs. Todd laughingly tells the narrator of two feuding farmers, living on an island they are passing by, "who had shared the island between them, and declared that for three generations the people had not spoken to each other even in times of sickness or death or birth" (53).

Leaving the world of men far behind, the company arrives on Green Island. Instead of receding shadowy gray forms there is "a quicker signal [that] had made its way from the heart on shore to the heart on the sea" (55). Mrs. Blackett seems almost too good to be true. God has become a woman who teaches nurturance. Like God, Blackett appears eternal. Though eighty-six, she has the "look of youth, . . . as if she promised a great future, and was beginning, not ending" (61). She is all-knowing, possessing tact, which "is after all a kind of mindreading," and sympathy "of the mind as well as of the heart" (73). Mrs. Blackett can discern and cultivate the best qualities in all living creatures. The cat she adopts is the "homeliest" one of the litter, but she takes it because she knows it is also the "smartest" (58). With the narrator, Mrs. Blackett makes a miraculous, instant connection. The narrator recalls: "You felt as if Mrs. Blackett were an old and dear friend before you let go her cordial hand" (56). Walking with the two women "in peace and harmony" (58), the narrator is eager to become "a citizen of such a complete and tiny continent" (59). In this society, there are no men like Captain Littlepage who quest alone. Mrs. Blackett's little island has the dimensions of a continent, for she is "one of those who do not live to themselves" (63). She holds "the gift which so many women lack, of being able to make themselves and their houses belong entirely to a guest's pleasure,—that charming surrender for the moment of themselves and whatever belongs to them, so that they make a part of one's own life that can never be forgotten" (72–73). To the narrator, this quality is "that highest gift of heaven, a perfect self-forgetfulness" (73).

Mrs. Blackett's success as a nurturer can be seen in her children, William and Almira Todd. She has been self-forgetting enough to have fostered a son and a daughter capable of developing their own sense of completeness. Neither William nor Almira fits into the traditional male/female stereotypes. They have become what it was in their respective natures to become. Now the narrator will perceive the ideal. Both William and Almira will each take her on an excursion. In their respective presences, she will experience the flip sides of a gender-free coin.

Though at least one inept, stunted man is present in each major section of *The Country of the Pointed Firs*, Jewett is sure to include a man who does not fit this norm to show that male behavior is not genetic but learned. In the opening sections, the village doctor is present, a man who knows the value of cooperation, a man who exists on "the best of terms" (5) with the herbalist Almira Todd. In this Green Island sequence, William shares the center stage with his mother and sister. It seems Jewett's way of expressing her assurance that men can move beyond their gender-limited stereotypes as well as women can.

William has been "'son an' daughter both'" (62) to his mother since Almira married and moved off the island. He looks like his mother; he even works in the kitchen as she does, cleaning and cutting up the haddock for dinner. And William also has "very deep affections" (64–65). He even infuses objects with sentiment as women do, making sure his mother shows the narrator the tea caddy his grandfather brought as a gift to his grandmother from the island of Tobago. But when he invites the narrator to go for a walk to the "great ledge" (69), he shows her a symbolic male view, a journey to the linear "highest point," where "all the far horizons" (70–71) can be seen. It is reminiscent of Sylvia's view of the "vast and awesome world," where "nothing stopped the eye or hedged one in,—that sense of liberty in space and time which great prospects always give" (71). Yet William's view is tempered by his emotion for his native heath, his home. He does not desire to go out and conquer, but to remain within the intimate circle. He is aware of the expansive view, as is, incidentally, his mother, whose eyes express "a far-off look that sought the horizon" (75). But while people expect his mother to remain at home, they express concern that William "'had been 'most too satisfied to stop at home 'long o' his old mother'" (63). While Mrs. Blackett is comfortable with his decision, replying, "'I always tell 'em I'm the gainer'" (63), others, including Almira, see William as lacking in ambition.

William's shyness is also a bone of contention. His sister is disgruntled that he comes into the kitchen, prepares the fish, and disappears. The general feeling of the populace is that his evasion of people is an oddity. Yet if a woman were shy, no one would consider her strange. To draw attention to the male enculturation process of having to control everything and everybody, Jewett presents a man who does not wish to attract any attention whatsoever. The last thing William wants to do is control. Mrs. Blackett admits: "'William an' I never wish for any other home'" (81). To underscore this point, the Green Island sections end with Mrs. Blackett and William singing "Home Sweet, Home." William lends his "perfectly true and sweet" (82) tenor voice (even William's singing voice has female dimensions) to his mother's when she misses the high notes, seeming to "carry on her very note and air" (83). It is a demonstrable blending of the sexes; it is cooperation rather than male competition.

Perhaps Almira Todd regards her brother as unambitious because she is so assertive by nature. When she and the narrator are out on their walk, she expresses disappointment over William's "excellent judgment" (75), which has never been fully exercised: "'He ought to have made something o' himself, bein' a man an' so like mother'" (75), yet "'he never had mother's snap an' power o' seein' things'" (75). Instead, it seems that Almira has inherited her mother's snap and power along with her father's male vistas. It is her father whom she physically resembles. Even Mrs. Blackett acknowledges that Almira needed "more scope" and that she would have been "very restless if she'd had to continue here on Green Island" (82). Mrs. Todd needs more than a home; she needs her profession as an herbalist. Later the narrator will comment that even the opportunities of Dunnet Landing have been insufficient for a character of Mrs. Todd's stature: "a narrow set of circumstances had caged a fine able character and held it captive" (174). Yet Mrs. Todd's commanding nature does not exist at the expense of her emotional center, and this is the lesson that the narrator, who has become too influenced by the goal-oriented male world, must relearn. Mrs. Todd takes the narrator down into the pennyroyal grove, down to the intimate female center, where she confides her deepest loss; she had loved a man outside her social class whose mother opposed the marriage. Elizabeth Ammons describes this center:

> Lush, secret, and earthily female, the space to which Jewett's women descend at the middle of *The Country of the Pointed Firs* represents the dramatic core of Jewett's narrative, which instead of being climactic might be described as concentric, even vortical. The emotional energy of the book collects most intensely in Chapter 10, "Where Pennyroyal Grew," from which, in every direction, like rings spreading out when a stone is dropped in a pool, emanates Jewett's drama of female love, which is noncombative and nonlinear. ("Going in Circles," 91)

The question arises—how does Jewett view sexuality, female sexuality in particular. If she seems to advocate freedom from heterosexual bondage in "A White Heron," as well as in her negative comment on romance and in her depictions of the standard marriage, where is sexuality for women, a vital aspect of human existence, to be expressed? Foremost, I do not think Jewett denies sexuality in her productive relationships. But perhaps, like Cather, whom she befriended and influenced, she is more interested in "the thing not named." Jewett tends to use the visual image and the emotional climate as a type of objective correlative for the sexual. In her postponed marriages, the positive male/female relationships are filled with genuine warmth and, often, spring—Mr. Teaby's "greenish linen duster" that reflects the season; the singing robins and blooming lilacs in "Miss Manning's Minister"; the youthful, romantic tone of "William's Wedding"; and, explicitly, "the resounding kiss" in "Miss Becky's Pilgrimage." Heterosexuality in these stories is neither crippling nor imprisoning.

In Jewett's depictions of women's friendship, such as the one between Mrs. Todd and the narrator, there is not only the lush pennyroyal grove but also the cherry-picking scene with Martha and Helen of "Martha's Lady," the sensuousness of the sugary peach preserves shared by the women in "The Town Poor," and the hand-holding of Mrs. Todd and the narrator as they climb the hill for home at the conclusion of "William's Wedding." Whether any of the women's relationships are explicitly sexual, we will never know. Assessing from a twentieth-century perspective is a difficult, if not impossible, task. Carroll Smith-Rosenberg points out:

> The essential question is not whether these women had genital contact and can therefore be defined as heterosexual or homosexual. The twentieth-century tendency to view human love and sexuality within a dichotomized universe of deviance and normality, genitality and platonic love, is alien to the emotions and attitudes of the nineteenth century and fundamentally distorts the nature of these women's emotional interaction. (8)

The most important affair, however, is the powerful emotional bonds between these women. My view comes closest to Sarah Way Sherman's:

> Friendship, finally, was greater, more enduring, than love itself; it comprised love and carried it to a higher, spiritual plane— echoes of Plato and Emerson. Those "shining hours," and "golden moments," [of which Jewett speaks,] were at once mo-

ments of emotional intimacy and spiritual communion. In her doctrines of friendship Jewett fused religious redemption and sensuous/emotional satisfaction. (72)

I would add that Jewett does not confuse genital relations, which are a function of the libido, with an all-encompassing sexuality, a functioning of the substance of a person. Mrs. Todd and the narrator possess such an all-encompassing relationship.

The narrator has now completed her journey to the very center of the nurturing world of Green Island. Mrs. Blackett's promise upon the narrator's arrival: "'I shan't make any stranger of you'" (*CPF*, 63) has been completed. From Mrs. Blackett's kitchen to William's panoramic view to Mrs. Todd's pennyroyal grove, the narrator has come full circle to Mrs. Blackett's bedroom, "the heart of the old house on Green Island" (84). Having been receptive to the nurturing message of all three of Green Island's offspring, the narrator is at "peace" (84) with the wholeness the message brings. When she returns to the mainland, even the village of Dunnet Landing "seemed large and noisy and oppressive" (85). Since the narrator has been to the core of intimacy, everything pales by comparison.

Yet learning intimacy and nurturing does not happen overnight, and in the next chapter, "A Strange Sail," the narrator wavers from Mrs. Todd's recent teaching. A sense of competition emerges before the narrator can see the benefits of widening her relationship with Mrs. Todd to contain another friend, Mrs. Fosdick. Comparing herself and Almira Todd to the sole occupants of a "double shell" (86), the narrator "suffered much from apprehension" at the "signs of invasion" (86) of Mrs. Fosdick. It is "a selfish sense of objection" (86) that blossoms into "an unreasonable feeling of being left out" (90) when the two old friends become so caught up in their conversation as to forget her presence. Resentful, she returns to her room, where Mrs. Todd eventually brings Mrs. Fosdick to make her acquaintance.

Alone with the guest, the narrator stops being defensive. As "sincere friends" (92), she and Mrs. Fosdick join Mrs. Todd in the kitchen. Privy to "a borderless sea of reminiscences" (93) and "subjects of an intimate nature" (93), the narrator is able to view a relationship where people of unequal capabilities are able to bond rather than to compete. Mrs. Fosdick possesses the "power of social suggestion," "dignity and elegance" (91, 93), but "Mrs. Todd's wisdom was an intimation of truth itself" (93). While Mrs. Fosdick does not always understand Mrs. Todd, Mrs. Todd always understands Mrs. Fosdick. The narrator begins to extend her jealously guarded "double shell." She learns that visiting, the spreading of intimacy and nurturance, is "the highest of vocations" (90). Finally, she, too, is admitted to this ever-widening sphere. When Mrs. Fosdick asserts that old acquaintances are the best, "'else you've got to explain every remark you make, an' it wears a person out'" (97), Mrs. Todd's agreement contains an important codicil: "'Yes'm, old friends is always best, 'less you can catch a new one that's fit to make an old one out of'" (97). The narrator is rewarded with "an affectionate glance" (97).

Bolstered by her admittance to yet another close circle, the lifetime friendship of Mrs. Todd and Mrs. Fosdick, the narrator is now ready to be confronted by a second ghost living in a waiting place. This next story of isolation moves from men like Captain Littlepage, who do not seem to know any better, to the woman Joanna, who chooses this mode of existence. It serves to warn the narrator that aligning herself with the rules and regulations of men may result in a life without relational living, very little life at all for a woman.

Mrs. Todd and Mrs. Fosdick refer to her as "poor Joanna." Crossed in love, Joanna goes to live alone on Shell-heap Island (representative of the remnants of her own life), where she "'retired from the world for good an' all'" (103). Unfortunately, Joanna has swallowed society's dim view of women, which designates, "Marry or you are nothing." Mrs. Fosdick relates: "'All her hopes were built on marryin' '" (104). It does not matter to Joanna that her fiancé ran off with another woman a month before the wedding, or that he was, according to Mrs. Todd, "'a shifty-eyed coaxin' sort of man, that got what he wanted out o' folks, an' only gave when he wanted to buy, made friends easy and lost 'em without knowin' the difference'" (126). To Joanna, or any woman caught up in the enslaving romantic picture propagated by male society, love is blind.

Joanna is also bound by the either/or male way of looking at problems—life boiled down to a set of abstract concepts, good or bad, legal or illegal, moral or immoral. Carol Gilligan, in her study of women's psychological development, concurs with Piaget's findings that "girls are more tolerant in their attitudes toward rules, more willing to make exceptions . . ." (10). Joanna does not fit into this category. When she is jilted, she commits what she refers to as "the unpardonable sin": "'I was in great wrath and trouble, and my thoughts was so wicked towards God that I can't expect ever to be forgiven'" (121). In keeping with the tenets of her male God with his lack of compassion toward people and their deficiencies, Joanna deduces that she has "'no right to live with folks no more'" (121). She leaves, and despite her brother's tears, "never stepped foot on the mainland again [as] long as she lived" (105). Even when her brother comes to the island to visit and leave her provisions, Joanna remains unbending, refusing to even glance out of her window for a glimpse of him. Mrs. Todd explains: "'She done it for a penance'" (106).

Jewett adds a stupid, ineffectual parson to the story of Joanna to underscore the poverty of Joanna's choice to align herself with male religious views. Reverend Dimmick is inept in all ways. When he and Almira Todd go to visit Joanna, he stands up in the boat to screech, fearful of the upcoming gusts. Mrs. Todd has to knock him down to keep the boat from capsizing. But more essential is his bereft soul. Mrs. Todd describes Reverend Dimmick as "'a vague person, well meanin', but very numb in his feelin's'" (110). Instead of trying to comfort Joanna, he reads to her a grim, accusatory passage from the Bible about hearing the voice of God from out of the whirlwind (119). Provoked, Mrs. Todd just glares at him. "[Having] spent the long, cold winter all alone on Shell-heap Island," Joanna, Mrs. Todd maintains, "knew a good deal more about those things than he did" (119). The reverend's only claim to fame is his verbiage. Mrs. Todd encapsulates: "he seemed to know no remedies, but he had a great use of words" (123). Nevertheless, Mrs. Fosdick admits: "he was pompous enough, but I never could remember a single word he said" (113).

While the reader is aware of the unfeasibility of following a religious code preached by a man such as Dimmick, Joanna misses the message. Rigid to the last, Joanna, who "'was one that loved her friends'" (109), embraces deprivation. The frequency of references to Joanna's wide circle of concerned friends and acquaintances who are continuously dropping off provisions for her on the island shore without trespassing against her enforced solitude serves to accentuate her folly. Finally, Joanna refuses the entreaties and soothing balms of Almira Todd herself. After the pastor has gone sightseeing for Indian remnants on the island, Mrs. Todd takes Joanna in her arms and begs her to return and live with her or her mother, Mrs. Blackett. Joanna insists she cannot be forgiven and returns a coral pin to Mrs. Todd, a gift from her cousin, Mrs. Todd's husband, Nathan, symbolic of her relinquishment of all human feelings. Mrs. Fosdick likens Joanna's decision to "bad eyesight": "'if your eyes don't see right there may be a remedy, but there's no kind of glasses to remedy the mind'" (124). Joanna has adopted a narrow, rigid male vision.

Yet as the narrator listens to this story, her empathic powers are developing; she is fighting against her self-imposed solitude in a man's world. First the narrator merely hears Joanna's story;

in the following chapter, the narrator muses, "My thoughts flew back to the lonely woman on her outer island; what separation from humankind she must have felt, what terror and sadness, even in a summer storm . . ." (115). In the end, the narrator actually identifies with Joanna, hearing with her ears, seeing with her eyes. Out for a sail with Captain Bowden, the narrator requests to be set down on Shell-heap Island, where she follows the "paths trodden to the shrines of solitude" (131). She hears "the gay voices and laughter from a pleasure-boat that was going seaward. The narrator comments: "I knew as if she had told me, that poor Joanna must have heard the like on many and many a summer afternoon, and must have welcomed the good cheer in spite of hopelessness and winter weather, and all the sorrow and disappointment in the world" (132–33). While she regards Joanna as "valiant enough to live alone with her poor insistent human nature and the calms and passions of sea and sky" (131), she can not dismiss the poverty of her choice.

Again, Mrs. Todd will show the narrator an alternative to isolation. She immerses the narrator into the world Joanna could have had but chose to leave. It is time for the Bowden reunion. The intimate circle has enlarged again to include "most families" (157) of Dunnet Landing. The weather signals the narrator's imminent transformation: "The early morning breeze was still blowing, and the warm sunshiny air was of some ethereal northern sort, with a cool freshness as it came over new-fallen snow" (142–43). The arrival of Mrs. Blackett sounds the keynote for the event. As many friends greet Mrs. Blackett on the journey to the reunion, the narrator observes: "a look of delight came to the faces of those who recognized the plain, dear old figure beside me; one revelation after another was made of the constant interest and intercourse that had linked the far island and these scattered farms into a golden chain of love and dependence" (147).

Nearly every detail in this section speaks of connection, from the circularity of the doughnuts baked by the people in the farmhouses "all the way along" (148), to the figure of the Bowden house as "a motherly brown hen waiting for the flock" (159), to the eating of the gingerbread Bowden house, which Marjorie Pryse has noted is a "ritual of communion" (xvii). The reunion includes relatives as well as strangers—the mistress of the farmhouse, whom no one recognizes and who is related only remotely through marriage, as well as the narrator herself. The gathering embraces the living as well as the dead; Mrs. Todd looks across to the distant Back Shore town of Fessenden and remembers her sister, who "seems as if she must still be there, though she's long been gone" (153). Compared several times to an ancient Greek rite, the reunion includes present generations as well as those of the remote past. This linking of the reunion to all people—close or remote, present or past—exemplifies the importance of nurturing to all peoples of all times. It is the life-giving source, primarily associated with women but not with-held from men.

Women are in the forefront of the festivities; Mrs. Blackett is "the queen" (161) who walks at the head of the procession with the ministers. She is "serene and mindful of privilege and re-sponsibility, the mistress by simple fitness of this great day" (173). Mrs. Todd knows, "'Mother'll say just the right thing'" (177). And Mrs. Blackett does offer the best approach when the men are being discussed. "'Live and let live'" (170), she "gently" advises. In this section, Mrs. Todd does not condemn men as she has done on earlier occasions. Instead, she preaches tol-erance and compassion for the misguided. Santin Bowden, for instance, organizes the procession at the reunion, but unfor-tunately, he has spent his life trying to round people up into military maneuvers. He is a disappointed soldier, never sound of mind enough to be accepted into the military. Yet Mrs. Todd does not upbraid him for his warped male value system. She speaks admiringly of his shoemaking abilities and kindly of his drinking habits. She even goes so far as to sympathize with Sant, once remarking to him that "'the country'd lost a great general'" (166). Mrs. Todd also prefers Captain Littlepage to his argumentative housekeeper, Mari' Harris. Mrs. Todd maintains that "'Cap'n Littlepage never'd look so disconsolate if [Mari'] was any sort of a proper person to direct things'" (169). Todd advocates "'divert[ing]'" Littlepage or listening to his stories once in a while (169). Relational living is not reserved for women or for men, but it is only with commiserative acceptance that the two sexes will ever be brought together.

Yet implicit in this message of tolerance is the fact that the majority of men have a long way to go before they become full human beings. There is a strange absence of nurturing men in this section. No new gender-freed man has been introduced, and the ones that have already appeared do not attend the feast. But they are mentioned. Shortly after Mrs. Todd, Mrs. Blackett, and the narrator leave for the reunion, they meet the doctor. His goodness is reconfirmed. He is "the warmest of friends" with Mrs. Blackett and "partners" with Mrs. Todd (145, 146). At the feast, Mrs. Todd speaks of her departed husband. Formerly, in the pennyroyal grove, she told the narrator that Nathan had loved her well and made her "'real happy'" (77). Now she adds that Nathan was not like other men. He had "'very nice feelings'" and "'did not make a habit of always opposin' like some men'" (171). William is also discussed. But Mrs. Todd does not condemn him for not attending the reunion; in fact, she does not seem to expect him to go. Mrs. Blackett wishes William had come, but she, too, accepts his nonappearance. While there are "'such a plenty o' men's voices'" (183) singing the hymn at the feast's end, none come to the foreground as men of substance. Men like the doctor, Nathan, and William would be out of place at the reunion. Jewett seems to confirm that while men are capable of a woman's nurturing dimension, most are still in the learning stage.

The narrator's progression, however, has been complete. Initially, she hesitates to participate in the Bowden reunion. Afraid she has misinterpreted Mrs. Todd's intent, the narrator asks: "'Would you like to have me go too?'" (136). But soon she admits that she "felt like an adopted Bowden" (161). Subsequently, she consumes the part of the pie with Bowden written on it (108) and readily "came near to feeling like a true Bowden" (180), learning that "clannishness is an instinct of the heart" (179). The transformation is complete, at least insofar as being part of a nurturing community is concerned.

Yet a negative note has been sounded during the reunion's proceedings. The narrator realizes that the times Mrs. Todd "had seemed limited and heavily domestic, she had simply grown sluggish for lack of proper surroundings" (173–74). At the reunion, Almira Todd is "expectant" and "alert" (174), challenged by the stimulation. But this chance is occasional and insufficient. The narrator continues to "wonder at the waste of human ability in this world," for "more than one face among the Bowdens showed that only opportunity and stimulus were lacking . . ." (174). It is coming to "The Feast's End," the last chapter in this section, and it is time for the narrator to leave Dunnet Landing. Now that she has rediscovered her woman's center, she must return to the world of men, which is her realm as well. It may be an isolating experience, but the narrator is equal to it. She is the tall ash tree Mrs. Todd "eagerly" reins in the horses to see. The narrator has listened "hopefully" to Mrs. Todd's "wisdom": "'There's sometimes a good hearty tree growin' right out of the bare rock, . . . but that tree'll keep a green top in the driest summer. You lay your ear down to the ground an' you'll hear a little stream runnin'. Every such tree has got its own livin' spring; there's folk made to match 'em'" (150–51).

But the narrator has one more step to complete before she departs. She must try her hand at nurturing. Up until this point, she has been mainly the receiver; the circle has widened

for her benefit. Now she comes to understand Elijah Tilley, another man who is learning. It is also the time for her to meet the
third and last ghost, Sarah Tilley, Elijah's departed wife. Unlike
Captain Littlepage's specters and Joanna Todd, Sarah Tilley did
not spend her life trying to isolate herself from others; instead,
she expended herself in the efforts of nurturance and intimacy.
Like Mrs. Blackett, Sarah Tilley was always available, and her
impact continues. Mrs. Todd, who misses Sarah almost every
day, admits "'there ain't one o' her old friends can ever make up
her loss. . . . She was always right there; yes, you knew just
where to find her like a plain flower'" (206). The narrator does
not need any more warnings of solitary ghosts in waiting places.
Sarah's home was always filled with visitors. Captain Tilley as-
sures the narrator: "'You'd have liked to come and see her; all
the folks did. . . . She had a kind o' gift to make it pleasant for
folks'" (196).

The only waiting Sarah ever did was for her husband. Tilley
loved his wife in his male way while she lived, but he never experienced her depth of feeling. Tilley never understood that relational
living was more important than accomplished tasks. Yet the narrator makes contact almost immediately with Sarah's ghost: "I began to see her myself in her home, —a delicate-looking, faded little
woman, who leaned upon his rough strength and affectionate
heart, who was always watching for his boat out of this very
window, and who always opened the door and welcomed him
when he came home" (197). Tilley, on the other hand, was not
as receptive; he "'used to laugh at her,'" "'to make light of her
timid notions'" (197–98) when she waited fearfully for him to
return late from his work. Tilley now acknowledges: "'I used to
be dreadful thoughtless when I was a young man and the fish
was bitin' well. I'd stay out late some o' them days, an' I expect
she'd watch an' watch an' lose heart a-waitin' '" (198).

Now it is Tilley's turn to watch and wait. In "continual loneliness" he remembers his wife's constant care: "'Lord, how I
think o' all them little things!'" (198). "Stricken and uncon-

soled" (190) at Sarah's death, Captain Tilley has decided to trade places with his wife in order to remain close to her. He knits his own socks, keeps his own house "'looking right, same's poor dear left [it]'" (194), and cooks his own meals. He has even learned women's way of infusing objects with personal sentiment. Tilley announces to the narrator: "'now I'm going to show you her best tea things she thought so much of . . .'" (199). Marjorie Pryse has noted that Captain Tilley's story "illustrates that the inner lives, anxieties, and visions of women can be shared by men. They have only to 'find out' about them in order to share them" (xviii).

The narrator has offered a sympathetic ear to Captain Tilley; she has "kept the afternoon watch with him" (197); she is in touch with her female center. But she realizes, however, that trading places, that an either/or approach to life is an attenuated one. Reluctantly, the narrator must leave her comfortable nest and return to patriarchal society, where she "feared to find [her]self a foreigner" (208). Yet the narrator recognizes that she needs both worlds, and that she has a responsibility to bring what she has learned to a society that hungers for relational living. And so the narrator sets sail with Mrs. Todd's gift of the coral pin meant for Joanna, who would not accept it. It is a fitting gift, a reminder of the narrator's intimate bonds, as she reenters a world where she may find herself as isolated with her gender-freed vision as Joanna has been on Shell-heap Island. But the narrator accepts her task, recognizing "the gifts of peace are not for those who live in the thick of battle" (208). She has come to an understanding, Jewett's understanding: "In the life of each of us . . . there is a place remote and islanded, and given to endless regret or secret happiness; we are each the uncompanioned hermit and recluse of an hour or a day; we understand our fellows of the cell to whatever age of history they may belong" (132). It is time to unearth the fragments of men and women imprisoned by gender roles and make them whole.

Afterword

he *Country of the Pointed Firs* signifies a future where a woman's nuturing dimension is tantamount to survival as a human species. What it does not propose is that this future take place in a female utopian realm. Jewett was not in favor of a world separate and silent. Separation means division; it reinforces binary oppositions. Such an isolated stance would leave women without a voice and, ultimately, without any political power in society at large.

While Jewett's characters are embroiled in a struggle against industrial, patriarchal values and, even at times, crushed and consumed by the sexually divisive system, Jewett shows that they can defy the cultural assignations. It is possible to release oneself from the straightjacket of gender. Jewett challenges the historical polarized gender system, and in her writings, she heralds the present-day view that there are no natural gender characteristics.

Jewett perceives the crippling effects of rigid gender roles, and then she looks beyond this polarization of men and women. Her characters are equipped to share that vision. Jewett would be inclined to agree with Monique Wittig, who proffers that "a new personal and subjective definition for all humankind can be found beyond the categories of sex (man and woman) and that the advent of individual subjects demands first destroying the category of sex, ending the use of them, and rejecting all sciences which still use these categories as their fundamentals" (Butler, 136). Judith Butler equates Wittig's vision with a sexless society where "sex, like class, is a construct that must inevitably be deposed" (136). Within the text, Jewett deflates the dyadic gender system and empowers her characters and readers to live beyond that construction.

List of Abbreviations

The following symbols followed by page numbers are used throughout for identifying quotations.

Select Bibliography

Primary Sources

Betty Leicester: A Story for Girls. Boston and New York: Houghton, Mifflin, 1890.

Betty Leicester's English Xmas: A New Chapter of an Old Story. New York: Dodd, Mead, 1894.

Country By-Ways. 1881. Reprint. Freeport, N.Y.: Books for Libraries Press, 1969.

A Country Doctor. Boston and New York: Houghton, Mifflin, 1884.

The Country of the Pointed Firs. Boston and New York: Houghton, Mifflin, 1896.

Deephaven. Boston: James R. Osgood, 1877.

The King of Folly Island and Other People. Boston and New York: Houghton, Mifflin, 1888.

The Life of Nancy. 1895. Reprint. Freeport, N.Y.: Books for Libraries Press, 1970.

A Marsh Island. Boston and New York: Houghton, Mifflin, 1886.

The Mate of the Daylight, and Friends Ashore. Boston: Houghton, Mifflin, 1884.

A Native of Winby and Other Tales. 1893. Reprint. Freeport, N.Y.: Books for Libraries Press, 1970.

Old Friends and New. 1879. Reprint. Freeport, N.Y.: Books for Libraries Press, 1969.

Play Days: A Book of Stories for Children. Boston: Houghton, Osgood, 1878.

The Queen's Twin and Other Stories. Boston and New York: Houghton, Mifflin, 1899.

The Story of the Normans, Told Chiefly in Relation to Their Conquest of England. New York: G. P. Putnam's Sons, 1887.

Strangers and Wayfarers. Boston and New York: G. P. Putnam's Sons, 1887.

Tales of New England. 1895. Reprint. Freeport, N.Y.: Books for Libraries Press, 1969.

The Tory Lover. Boston and New York: Houghton, Mifflin, 1901.

The Uncollected Stories of Sarah Orne Jewett. Ed. Richard Cary. Waterville, Maine: Colby College Press, 1971.

Verses. Boston: Merrymount Press, 1916.

A White Heron and Other Stories. Boston and New York: Houghton, Mifflin, 1886.

Secondary Sources

Ammons, Elizabeth. "Going in Circles: The Female Geography of Jewett's *Country of the Pointed Firs.*" *Studies in the Literary Imagination* 16, no. 2 (Fall 1983): 83–92.

———. "Jewett's Witches." In *Critical Essays on Sarah Orne Jewett*, ed. Gwen L. Nagel, 165–84. Boston: G. K. Hall, 1984.

———. "The Shape of Violence in Jewett's 'A White Heron.'" *Colby Library Quarterly* 22, no. 1 (1986): 75–82.

Auerbach, Nina. *Communities of Women: An Idea in Fiction.* Cambridge: Harvard University Press, 1978.

Bailey, Jennifer. "Female Nature and the Nature of the Female: A Re-Vision of Sarah Orne Jewett's *The Country of the Pointed Firs.*" *Revue Française d'Études Americaines* 8, no. 17 (1983): 283–94.

Baker, Carlos. "Delineation of Life and Character." In *Literary History of the United States*, ed. Robert E. Spiller, et al., 845–48. New York: Macmillan, 1974.

Barron, Hal S. *Those Who Stayed Behind: Rural Society in Nineteenth-Century New England.* New York: Cambridge University Press, 1984.

Berthoff, Warner. "The Art of Jewett's *Pointed Firs*." In *Appreciation of Sarah Orne Jewett*, ed. Richard Cary, 144–61. Waterville, Maine: Colby College Press, 1973.

———. *The Ferment of Realism: American Literature, 1884–1919*. New York: Free Press, 1965.

Bishop, Ferman. "Henry James Criticizes *The Tory Lover*." *American Literature* 27 (1955): 262–64.

Brenzo, Richard. "Free Heron or Dead Sparrow: Sylvia's Choice in Sarah Orne Jewett's 'A White Heron.'" *Colby Library Quarterly* 14 (1978): 36–41.

Brooks, Van Wyck. *New England: Indian Summer, 1865–1915*. New York: Dutton, 1940.

Butler, Judith. "Variations on Sex and Gender." In *Feminism as Critique*, ed. Seyla Benhabib and Drucilla Cornell, 128–42. Minnesota: University of Minnesota Press, 1987.

Cary, Richard. *Appreciation of Sarah Orne Jewett: 29 Interpretive Essays*. Waterville, Maine: Colby College Press, 1973.

———. Introduction to *Deephaven and Other Stories*. New Haven: College and University Press, 1966.

———. "Jewett to Dresel: 33 Letters." *Colby Library Quarterly* 11 (1975): 13–49.

———. *Sarah Orne Jewett*. Twayne United States Authors Series 19. New York: Twayne, 1962.

———. *Sarah Orne Jewett Letters*. Waterville, Maine: Colby College Press, 1967.

Cather, Willa. Preface to *The Best Short Stories of Sarah Orne Jewett*. 2 vols. Boston: Houghton, Mifflin, 1925.

Chopin, Kate. "The Story of an Hour." In *The Awakening and Selected Stories by Kate Chopin*, ed. Barbara H. Solomon, 198–200. New York: New American Library, 1976.

Crumpacker, Laurie. "The Art of the Healer: Women in the Fiction of Sarah Orne Jewett." *Colby Library Quarterly*, 19, no. 2 (1980): 155–66.

Dague, Elizabeth. "Images of Work, Glimpses of Professionalism in Selected Nineteenth- and Twentieth-Century Novels." *Frontiers* 5, no. 1 (1976): 50–55.

BIBLIOGRAPHY

De Beauvoir, Simone. *The Second Sex.* New York: Alfred A. Knopf, 1952.

Delamont, Sara, and Lorna Duffin, eds. *The Nineteenth-Century Woman: Her Cultural and Physical World.* New York: Barnes and Noble, 1978.

Donovan, Josephine. "Nan Prince and the Golden Apples." *Colby Library Quarterly* 22, no. 1 (1986): 17–27.

———. *New England Local Color Literture: A Woman's Tradition.* New York: Ungar, 1983.

———. *Sarah Orne Jewett.* Modern Literature Series. New York: Ungar, 1980.

———. "Sarah Orne Jewett's Critical Theory: Notes Toward a Feminine Literary Mode." In *Critical Essays on Sarah Orne Jewett,* ed. Gwen L. Nagel, 212–25. Boston: G. K. Hall, 1984.

———. "The Unpublished Love Poems of Sarah Orne Jewett." *Frontiers* 4, no. 4 (1979): 26–31.

———. "A Woman's Vision of Transcendence: A New Interpretation of the Works of Sarah Orne Jewett." *Massachusetts Review* 21 (1980): 365–80.

Eakin, Paul John. "Sarah Orne Jewett and the Meaning of Country Life." In *Appreciation of Sarah Orne Jewett,* ed. Richard Cary, 203–22. Waterville, Maine: Colby College Press, 1973.

Ellis, James. "The World of Dreams: Sexual Symbolism in 'A White Heron.'" *The Nassau Review* 3, no. 3 (1977): 3–9.

Engels, Frederich. *Origin of the Family, Private Property and the State.* 1884. Reprint. New York: International Publishers, 1942.

Eppard, Philip B. "Local Colorists: Sarah Orne Jewett, Mary E. Wilkins Freeman, and Mary N. Murfree." In *American Women Writers: Bibliographic Essays,* eds. Maurice Duke, Jackson R. Bryer, and M. Thomas Inge, 21–46. Westport, Conn.: Greenwood Press, 1983.

Fields, Annie, ed. *Letters of Sarah Orne Jewett.* Boston: Houghton, Mifflin, 1911.

Fike, Francis. "An Interpretation of *Pointed Firs.*" *In Appreciation of Sarah Orne Jewett,* ed. Richard Cary, 170–80. Waterville, Maine: Colby College Press, 1973.

Folsom, Marcia McClintock. "'Tact Is a Kind of Mind-Reading': Empathic Style in Sarah Orne Jewett's *The Country of the Pointed Firs*." *Colby Library Quarterly* 18, no. 1 (1982): 66–78.

Forbes, Esther. "Sarah Orne Jewett, the Apostle of New England." In *Appreciation of Sarah Orne Jewett*, ed. Richard Cary, 70–80. Waterville, Maine: Colby College Press, 1973.

Forrey, Carolyn. "The New Woman Revisited." *Women's Studies* 2 (1974): 42–44.

Frost, John Eldridge. *Sarah Orne Jewett*. Kittery Point, Maine: The Gundalow Club, 1960.

Garnett, Edward. "Miss Sarah Orne Jewett's Tales." In *Appreciation of Sarah Orne Jewett*, ed. Richard Cary, 21–25. Waterville, Maine: Colby College Press, 1973.

Gilbert, Sandra M. "What Do Feminist Critics Want: A Postcard from the Volcano." In *The New Feminist Criticism: Essays on Women, Literature and Theory*, ed. Elaine Showalter, 29–45. New York: Pantheon Books, 1985.

Gilligan, Carol. *In a Different Voice: Psychological Theory and Women's Development*. Cambridge: Harvard University Press, 1982.

Griffith, Kelly, Jr. "Sylvia as Hero in Sarah Orne Jewett's 'A White Heron.'" *Colby Library Quarterly* 19, no. 1 (1980): 22–27.

Hancock, James, and Hugh Elliott. *The Herons of the World*. New York: Harper and Row, 1978.

Held, George. "Heart to Heart with Nature: Ways of Looking at 'A White Heron.'" *Colby Library Quarterly* 18, no. 1 (1982): 55–65.

Hicks, Granville. *The Great Tradition: An Interpretation of American Literature since the Civil War*. New York: Macmillan, 1933.

Hobbs, Glenda. "Pure and Passionate: Female Friendship in Sarah Orne Jewett's 'Martha's Lady.'" *Studies in Short Fiction* 17 (1980): 21–29.

Hollis, C. Carroll. "Letters of Sarah Orne Jewett to Anna Laurens Dawes." *Colby Library Quarterly* 8 (1968): 97–138.

Horn, Robert L. "The Power of Jewett's *Deephaven*." In *Appreciation of Sarah Orne Jewett*, ed. Richard Cary, 284–96. Waterville, Maine: Colby College Press, 1973.

Houghton, Walter E. *The Victorian Frame of Mind, 1830–1870*. New Haven: Yale University Press, 1957.

Hovet, Theodore R. "America's 'Lonely Country Child': The Theme of Separation in Sarah Orne Jewett's 'A White Heron.'" *Colby Library Quarterly* 14 (1978): 166–71.

————. "'Once Upon a Time': Sarah Orne Jewett's 'A White Heron' as Fairy Tale." *Studies in Short Fiction* 15 (1978): 63–68.

Howe, Mark A. De Wolfe. *Memories of a Hostess: A Chronicle of Eminent Friendships Drawn Chiefly from the Diaries of Mrs. James T. Fields.* Boston: Atlantic Monthly Press, 1922.

Humma, John B. "The Art and Meaning of Sarah Orne Jewett's 'The Courting of Sister Wisby.'" *Studies in Short Fiction* 10 (1973): 85–91.

James, Henry. *The Portrait of a Lady.* 1881. Reprint. Garden City, N.Y.: International Collectors Library, 1972.

Johns, Barbara A. "'Mateless and Appealing': Growing into Spinsterhood in Sarah Orne Jewett." In *Critical Essays on Sarah Orne Jewett,* ed. Gwen L. Nagel, 147–65. Boston: G. K. Hall, 1984.

Jones, Howard Mumford. "Fifty Guides to American Civilization." *Saturday Review* 29 (12 October 1946) 16.

Kraus, Mary C. "Sarah Orne Jewett and Temporal Continuity." *Colby Library Quarterly* 15 (1979): 157–74.

Kunitz, Stanley J., and Howard Daycroft, eds. *American Authors 1600–1900.* New York: Wilson, 1938.

Leder, Priscilla. "The Gifts of Peace: Sarah Orne Jewett's Vision of Romance." *Gypsy Scholar* 4 (1977): 27–39.

Lidz, Theodore. *The Person: His and Her Development throughout the Life Cycle.* New York: Basic Books, 1983.

Magowan, Robin. "Fromentin and Jewett: Pastoral Narrative in the Nineteenth Century." *Comparative Literature* 16 (1964): 331–37.

————. "Pastoral and the Art of Landscape in *The Country of the Pointed Firs.*" *New England Quarterly* 36 (1963): 229–40.

Matthiessen, Francis Otto. *Sarah Orne Jewett.* Boston: Houghton, Mifflin, 1929.

Morgan, Ellen. "The Atypical Woman: Nan Prince in the Literary Transition to Feminism." *Kate Chopin Newsletter* 2, no. 2 (1976): 33–37.

Nagel, Gwen L. *Critical Essays on Sarah Orne Jewett.* Critical Essays on American Literature Series. Boston: G. K. Hall, 1984.

BIBLIOGRAPHY

————. "'This prim corner of land where she was queen': Sarah Orne Jewett's New England Gardens." *Colby Library Quarterly* 22, no. 1 (1986): 43–62.

Nagel, Gwen L., and James Nagel. *Sarah Orne Jewett: A Reference Guide*. Boston: G. K. Hall, 1978.

Noyes, Sylvia Gray. "Mrs. Almira Todd, Herbalist-Conjurer." *Colby Library Quarterly* 9 (1972): 643–49.

Pattee, Fred Lewis. *A History of American Literature since 1870*. New York: Century, 1915.

Pool, Eugene Hillhouse. "The Child in Sarah Orne Jewett," *Colby Library Quarterly* 7 (1967): 503–9.

Pratt, Annis. "Women and Nature in Modern Fiction." *Contemporary Literature* 13 (1972): 476–90.

Pryse, Marjorie. Introduction to *The Country of the Pointed Firs and Other Stories*. New York: Norton, 1981.

————. "Women 'at Sea': Feminist Realism in Sarah Orne Jewett's 'The Foreigner.'" *American Literary Realism* 15, no. 2 (1982): 244–52.

Renza, Louis A. *"A White Heron" and The Question of Minor Literature*. Madison: University of Wisconsin Press, 1984.

Roman, Judith. "A Closer Look at the Jewett-Fields Relationship." In *Critical Essays on Sarah Orne Jewett*, ed. Gwen L. Nagel, 119–34. Boston: G. K. Hall, 1984.

Romines, Ann. "In *Deephaven*: Skirmishes near the Swamp." *Colby Library Quarterly* 16 (1980): 205–19.

Ruskin, John. "Of Queens' Gardens." In *Sesame and Lilies*, vol. 6 of *The Complete Works of John Ruskin, LL.D.*, 101–41. Philadelphia: Reuwee, Wattley & Walsh, 1891.

Sherman, Sarah Way. *Sarah Orne Jewett, an American Persephone*. Hanover, N.H.: University Press of New England, 1989.

Singley, Carol J. "Reaching Lonely Heights: Sarah Orne Jewett, Emily Dickinson and Female Initiation." *Colby Library Quarterly* 22, no. 1 (1986): 75–82.

Smith-Rosenberg, Carroll. "The Female World of Love and Ritual: Relations between Women in Nineteenth-Century America." *Signs* 1, no. 1 (1975): 1–29.

BIBLIOGRAPHY

———. "Writing History: Language, Class, and Gender." In *Feminist Studies/Critical Studies*, ed. Teresa de Laurentis, 31–54. Bloomington: Indiana University Press, 1986.

Snow, Malinda. "'That One Talent': The Vocation as a Theme in Sarah Orne Jewett's *A Country Doctor*." *Colby Library Quarterly* 16 (1980): 138–47.

Spofford, Harriet Prescott. *A Little Book of Friends*. Boston: Little, Brown, 1916.

———. "Sarah Orne Jewett." *Book Buyer* 11 (August 1894): 329–30.

Stouck, David. "*The Country of the Pointed Firs*: A Pastoral of Innocence." *Colby Library Quarterly* 9 (1970): 213–20.

Thaxter, Rosamond. *Sandpiper: The Life and Letters of Celia Thaxter*. Francestown: Marshal Jones, 1963.

Thorp, Margaret. *Sarah Orne Jewett*. University of Minnesota Pamphlets on American Writers 61. Minneapolis: University of Minnesota Press, 1966.

Toth, Susan Allen. "Sarah Orne Jewett and Friends: A Community of Interest." *Studies in Short Fiction* 9 (1972): 233–41.

———. "The Value of Age in the Fiction of Sarah Orne Jewett." *Studies in Short Fiction* 8 (1971): 433–41.

Van Doren, Carl. *The American Novel 1789–1939*. New York: Macmillan, 1940.

Vella, Michael W. "Sarah Orne Jewett: A Reading of *The Country of the Pointed Firs*." *Emerson Society Quarterly* 19 (1973): 275–82.

Waggoner, Hyatt H. "The Unity of *The Country of the Pointed Firs*." *Twentieth Century Literature* 5 (1959): 67–73.

Weber, Clara Carter, and Carl J. Weber. *A Bibliography of the Published Writings of Sarah Orne Jewett*. Waterville, Maine: Colby College Press, 1949.

Westbrook, Perry D. *Acres of Flint: Writers of Rural New England 1870–1900*. Washington, D.C.: Scarecrow Press, 1951.

Wood, Ann Douglas. "The Literature of Impoverishment: The Women Local Colorists in America 1865–1914." *Women's Studies* 1 (1972): 3–45.

Index